THE
START-UP
CODE

ADVANCE PRAISE FOR THE BOOK

'Mukesh and I first met during his Myntra journey and our relationship has grown over his Flipkart days and now as founder of CureFit. What stands out in Mukesh is his grit, humility, clarity in building firms as an entrepreneur, resilience, positive attitude and never-say-die resolve to grow businesses. Mukesh is one of the few founders who not only has the strategic vision to build a large company but also the ability to get into the trenches to execute it flawlessly. His ability to lead teams as well as to engage investors and get a buy-in into his vision is unmatched. This book is well timed for new start-up founders to learn how to build large new enterprises and gain from the experiences that Mukesh has had over the past decades. *The Start-Up Code* is also a must-read for VCs [venture capitalists], who will get a deep insight into a founder's mindset'— **Sudhir Sethi, founder and chairman, Chiratae Ventures India**

'As our first investor and mentor, Mukesh has been instrumental in Skyroot's journey from seed to the successful launch of India's first private rocket into space. In *The Start-Up Code*, he distils years of entrepreneurial wisdom into a captivating read'—**Pawan Chandana, co-founder, Skyroot**

'In *The Start-Up Code*, Mukesh prepares the reader for the roller-coaster ride of entrepreneurship, with all its ups and downs. Drawing us into the bigger questions of purpose, leadership and culture, while delving into the nitty-gritty of product–market fit, customer focus, strategies for growth and fundraising, this book is a comprehensive guide for entrepreneurs who are or who aspire to be on this thrilling and terrifying journey'—**Sameer Maheshwari, co-founder, HealthKart**

'Mukesh brings his decades-long experience in building some of India's most loved start-ups and brands to this book. His mantra, "just don't die" is spot on, as is his coverage of the nitty-gritty of the start-up journey. A must-read!'—**Gaurav Agarwal, co-founder, 1mg**

'If you are starting a company, you will avoid a lot of mistakes just by reading this book. Mukesh has put the lessons from his twenty-five years in the world of start-ups into these 400-odd pages. My favourite chapter is "Organization Is Product", which emphasizes the importance of intentionally shaping company culture'—**Lalit Keshre, co-founder and CEO, Groww**

THE
START-UP
CODE

TAKING
YOUR
COMPANY
FROM SEED
TO SCALE

MUKESH
BANSAL

PENGUIN
VIKING

An imprint of Penguin Random House

VIKING

Viking is an imprint of the Penguin Random House group of companies
whose addresses can be found at global.penguinrandomhouse.com

Published by Penguin Random House India Pvt. Ltd
4th Floor, Capital Tower 1, MG Road,
Gurugram 122 002, Haryana, India

Penguin
Random House
India

First published in Viking by Penguin Random House India 2024

10 9 8 7 6 5 4 3 2

ISBN 9780670097142

Typeset in Adobe Caslon Pro by Manipal Technologies Limited, Manipal
Printed at Thomson Press India Ltd, New Delhi

www.penguin.co.in

MIX
Paper | Supporting
responsible forestry
FSC® C010615

This book is for every entrepreneur who has attempted to start a company, fuelled by nothing but passion for an idea and the drive to bring that idea to life. The journey of entrepreneurship is a difficult and often lonely one, and I hope this book can be a companion for those who are on this long and bumpy (but constantly thrilling) road.

I'd also like to dedicate this book to the community that supports every struggling entrepreneur—from venture capitalists and strategic partners to friends and mentors, who make the journey a little less lonely.

Contents

Foreword

I first met Mukesh Bansal in 2005. It was still the early days of his journey, but his clarity of thought, passion for building and his quest to improve himself at almost everything set him apart. Over the years, from Myntra to CureFit and now on to Nurix, I've watched Mukesh navigate the highs and lows of entrepreneurship. In the initial days, I used to be his adviser, but since then, the roles have clearly been reversed; I often get his guidance on things I need outside inputs for. I've seen first-hand the qualities that make him a successful founder—his resilience, his adaptability, his relentless focus on self-improvement and value creation for all stakeholders. His experiences and learnings are captured brilliantly in *The Start-Up Code*.

For much of India's history, starting a company was a privilege reserved for a select few. But over the last decade and a half, significant democratization has happened, making entrepreneurship accessible to anyone who has the drive to pursue it. Today, we're witnessing a wave of entrepreneurial energy that is yet unparalleled in India. This kind of surge requires resources that demystify the complexities of company building. Mukesh's book is a road map for navigating the challenges and triumphs of start-up life.

When I co-founded Erasmic Venture Fund (EVF) in 2005, the entrepreneurial ecosystem in India was very much in its infancy. Being the first investor in Mukesh's Myntra, and soon thereafter in Flipkart in 2008, gave me a front-row seat to the transformation that has taken place in Indian entrepreneurship since. EVF rebranded to Accel in 2008 and has continued to be a very active early-stage investor, giving me the privilege of working with founders who have disrupted entire industries, and some have scaled their businesses globally. While it's been duly glorified in the media, what many don't see is the roller coaster of emotions, setbacks and challenges that founders face on this journey.

Mukesh has experienced all of these first-hand, and in *The Start-Up Code*, he draws on his decades of experience to offer practical advice for building an Indian start-up—from finding product–market fit to scaling with purpose. What makes this book stand out is that it doesn't just focus on the tactical aspects of building a company but dives deeply into the internal journey of an entrepreneur. Many founders get so caught up in the grind that they forget to reflect on who they are, what their customers truly want or need and why they would be most suited to solve these customers' challenges.

One of the core themes of the book is the importance of introspection. As Mukesh points out, it's not enough to just build a company—you need to know why you're building it. This clarity of purpose is what separates great founders from good ones. It allows you to stay grounded when the going gets tough (which often is the larger part of the journey) and provides a North Star to guide your decisions. Personally, this resonated deeply with me, as I tried and failed several times before this EVF/Accel journey took off. Furthermore, some of the most successful founders I've worked with are those who have a deep sense of purpose and vision that drives everything they do.

Mukesh's book also offers actionable insights on building a resilient company culture, understanding your customers and creating products that truly matter. One of the lessons I particularly appreciate is Mukesh's focus on how great products are the best marketing tool a company can have. In a world obsessed with growth hacking and quick wins, he reminds us that building a product that customers truly love is the most sustainable path to a company's long-term success.

This book isn't just for aspiring entrepreneurs; it's essential for anyone in the venture industry. As investors, we often focus on the financials, the market opportunity and the competitive landscape. But we also need to understand the mindset of founders, their motivations and the internal struggles they go through.

India's start-up ecosystem is at a pivotal moment. Every year, more high-growth companies and unicorns are emerging, fuelling innovation and driving economic growth. But as exciting as this landscape is, the path from idea to team to execution remains as challenging. What Mukesh has done with this book is create a blueprint—a guide that not only provides practical strategies but also shares the candid, often overlooked emotional and psychological aspects of entrepreneurship. In my opinion, *The Start-Up Code* will give people in the ecosystem a set of tools and frameworks to improve their odds of success.

Subrata Mitra, founding partner, Accel India

Introduction

Things which matter most must never be at the mercy of things which matter least.

—Johann Wolfgang von Goethe

It had been a long day after a long week at the end of a long month of an incessant daily quest to save Myntra. And there was no respite in sight. Prabhakar Sunder, the then CFO, and I were sitting alone in a conference room at around 9 p.m. We had done everything we could in the last six months; we had knocked on every door, reduced every rupee of cost, driven the company hard to have the best two quarters in our seven-year history and yet here we were in the last week of November, with not enough money to make the next month's payroll which was due in just seven days. We had ideated, brainstormed and exhausted all possible avenues to save the company. We were now staring down the barrel.

I had moved back to India from Silicon Valley in 2007 with the dream of building an Internet company. I had invested everything I had into building the business, been through lots

of ups and downs, and now it seemed that it would all add up
to nothing.

The second half of 2013 had been brutal; six months of hell
that made me realize how unforgiving an entrepreneurial journey
could be. Myntra had pivoted into fashion in early 2011, after
experimenting with many business models since its founding in
2007. We got our first big break with Nike during the 2011
ICC Cricket World Cup, and as we started ramping up our
fashion selection, things began to take off in a big way. We saw
accelerated growth every quarter and despite having a late start
in the category, we were the #1 player in online fashion retailing
within a couple of years of pivoting. Myntra was beginning to
build a reputation of being a high-quality player with premium
experience and was gaining trust among fashion brands as a key
partner in their online strategy. But we faced stiff competition
from Jabong, a company incubated by Rocket Internet, which
came out all guns blazing and literally declared a price war. We
were able to fend them off thanks to our superior selection, a
highly differentiated customer experience and a team that was
deeply committed to the mission of building a great company.
Things were going quite well finally, or so we thought.

The year 2013 turned out to be a pretty bad one from a
global macro point of view. While the global economy was
finally out of the doldrums of the financial crisis of 2008, there
were many questions about the health of the Indian economy
in the last years of the UPA government. The pace of GDP
growth slowed down to the 5–6 per cent range, the balance of
trade was starting to get skewed in favour of more imports, oil
prices shot up to over $100/barrel, putting a huge burden on the
economy, and global investor sentiment towards India began to
turn negative. All this resulted in a hiatus in funding among
Indian start-ups and the period saw few, if any, major deals.
Even Flipkart's much anticipated round with General Atlantic

fell through, but they managed to stitch together another round with Naspers, a lifeline for the company.

During this time, Myntra really struggled to raise money. We talked to every potential investor in India and beyond, touted our phenomenal growth rates, our clear differentiation and the potential to build a very large company, but none of it mattered as the concerns of investors centred on the Indian economy and even the viability of Internet businesses in India. Many of them also thought that horizontal platforms like Flipkart would capture the entire market with not much room left for vertical players. No matter what our pitch was, no term sheet materialized. We started 2013 with less than a year of cash, and as the months went by, our runways started to dwindle. In June that year, we decided to have a round of lay-offs and cut costs across the board to extend our runway. We challenged the whole team to rise to the occasion and sign up for the aggressive goal of driving growth while bringing down the burn—always a difficult task in the early stages of a business—but the team came through and delivered.

By September 2013, it was clear that external funding wasn't going to come through and we had just three months of runway left. To make matters worse, Flipkart closed a massive $360 million deal (the largest in Indian start-ups at that time) and announced that they would get into fashion on a big scale. Many investors began to write off Myntra. With no solution in sight, I started haranguing our existing investors for a bridge round. They were ambivalent, however, since they had supported us for five years with many pivots and couldn't internally justify putting more money into the company. So even this door was about to close. Over the next two months, we spent most of our time making more frantic calls, more pitches, and even engaged in strategic conversations about potentially selling the company, but even these talks didn't go anywhere.

So, after two more months, during which I probably aged five years as I felt that I was staring at the end, Prabhakar and I arrived in the office that Friday, determined to make some clear decisions. One of them was to lay off 80 per cent of the company, figure out a way to survive for another six months and try to find someone to back the company. Having failed to come up with any promising ideas, we found ourselves sitting in silence, staring into nothingness. My mind was filled with thoughts about all that I'd given up for this company—a job in Silicon Valley, half my savings, a stable income. I'd dreamt of being an entrepreneur ever since I'd been a college student, and now it seemed that rather than going big, I was actually going home. My fourteen-year journey of chasing the start-up dream was going to end in public humiliation, the loss of over a thousand jobs and almost nothing to show for it except maybe a few hard-earned lessons.

With nothing left to lose, I decided to make one final call. Lee Fixel of Tiger Global was the largest investor in Myntra. He had accelerated the growth of Indian e-commerce in the previous three years with some major bets. I had spoken to him a few weeks ago about finding a solution, and he had said, 'What doesn't kill you makes you stronger.' He had urged me to figure out a way to survive but, unlike the inspiring adage, it seemed as though the circumstances might in fact kill me. I got Lee on the phone again that evening and launched into a passionate plea. I spoke about why Myntra was poised to be a great company, how we had outperformed our competition the entire year, how we had built a very strong foundation and how, with just a little support, we could turn things around. My voice quivering with emotion, I opened up to Lee about everything and he listened patiently. Something must have struck a chord, because he made the impromptu decision to extend $5 million worth of bridge financing. What's even more incredible is that he decided to go ahead with it even before the bridge terms were agreed upon by our other investors. We had the money in the bank by the following Monday, enough not only to meet payroll but give us a clear runway for the next twelve months, with the possibility of resurrecting Myntra from near death.

As you probably know, Myntra did survive, going on to become the largest fashion company in India, online and offline. In the process, we set new benchmarks for the online shopping experience and for innovation in the mobile-first experience. We pioneered the building of online direct to consumer (D2C/DTC) brands while developing a unique inclusive culture. Myntra continues to do well even today, in the spirit of 'Built to Last'—an idea we will explore throughout this book. But it could very easily have gone another way. In an alternate universe, Lee would have decided not to extend the bridge financing, we would have missed payroll, laid off all our staff, and have had to wind down the business or do a fire sale. I probably would have had to find a 'stable' job, after having toiled in start-ups for fifteen years with nothing to show for the effort except the lessons and scars from the experience. But it didn't go that way. In fact, when I step back and look at today's successful start-ups, I notice that many of them have had near-death experiences. There are very few exceptions or stories of a company that has had a fairy-tale journey without any threats of oblivion. What enables companies to stare death in the face and yet somehow emerge stronger? Is it just sheer luck? Is it the unflinching determination of the founding team? Is it the unique differentiation of the product that these companies have built? Or is it the never-say-die culture of the organization? I wish I knew the answer, but what I do know is that the answer is a lot more complicated, and is probably a combination of all these elements, and more.

In this book, we will look at the journeys of start-ups that have succeeded beyond their founders' wildest imaginations, as well as those that are barely a footnote in a long list of dead companies. As we study these companies and try to tease out what increases the odds of success while identifying the common patterns in failure, we will see that there is some method to this madness. While the role of luck in entrepreneurship may not be as high as it is in poker, I would be remiss if I said it didn't play any role. But there are ways to make luck favour you. Sayings such as, 'Fortune favours the brave,' 'Luck is opportunity meeting preparedness,' or 'The harder I work; the luckier I get,' all capture the magic meeting of luck and hard work. Notice how none of these adages exhort you to wait in stillness for Lady Luck to strike. There is no doubt that luck is critical, but you can make choices that continue to tilt the odds in your favour until you get the perfect break. This is exactly what happened to Myntra in 2011 when, after four years of constant failure, everything suddenly lined up perfectly to launch the company on a winning streak at breakneck pace. But more on that later.

I fell in love with the idea of entrepreneurship in 1996. I was in my third year of college, my grades had started falling precipitously and I was dealing with many existential questions about what I wanted to do with my life. Like a typical twenty-year-old, I believed that my time was running out and that if I didn't figure something out very soon, my career would not amount to anything. If only I had come across the power of long-term thinking and the results of compounding back then. I might have processed things quite differently. Instead, my frenetic search for answers frequently saw me in the campus library, which was an oasis of books, magazines and journals from every possible field of study. I soon discovered for myself the unhurried joys of being lost in the world of words, ideas and the imagination—conversing with authors long dead, contemplating everything from how to write better to what is the meaning of life, and everything in between. Somewhere in the midst of this random browsing through the shelves, I stumbled upon the business books section and discovered two books that completely mesmerized me. The first was Sam Walton's *Made in America*, which recounted his journey of transforming one dusty retail store in rural America to the largest company in the world, by obsessing about customers, processes and innovation. Another equally impressive book was Akio Morita's *Made in Japan: Akio Morita and Sony,* in which he tells the story of taking Sony from a supplier of cheap electronics parts to the hottest consumer electronics brand in the world, with the ubiquitous Sony Walkman becoming the ultimate symbol of teenage freedom and self-expression.

To say that I was inspired by these two books would be a gross understatement. I was transfixed. What struck me most was the fact that these were regular people working with simple ideas. Their immense clarity of thought and incredible self-belief in building something better enabled them to keep at it relentlessly for their entire lives. The fact that they built world-changing companies from scratch in their lifetimes wasn't a miracle but the result of a process—a process that was available to everyone. I was hooked; I couldn't wait to learn and explore more. My fascination with entrepreneurship and business was further amplified when I read Tom Peters's then mega bestselling book *In Search of Excellence: Lessons from America's Best-Run Companies.* In this book, Peters looked at the most successful companies of all time across the world and distilled his observations and insights into key principles. Once again, the principles seemed simple and obvious, available for anyone to practise as long as they had the conviction and resoluteness to deeply imbibe and live these principles. The idea that anyone can build a great company and that there are general principles at play caught my imagination. I had no idea when or how I would be able to start something of my own, but there was no

'if' in the equation—that I would start something was a given.
I just had to wait for the right time. In my case, the right time
ended up being ten years later (or ten years too late) than I
thought it would be. But as we will discover over the course of
these chapters, some lessons take time. They take repetition
and even require one to undergo some hard knocks. Otherwise,
these lessons just sail by you towards someone more prepared.
It is said, 'When the student is ready; the teacher will appear.'
I wasn't ready for a long time.

As it happened, my first job after graduation was with
Deloitte Consulting in Chicago. It was a standard consulting
job that expected us to go to client sites, analyse business
problems and help implement solutions, usually by building
new systems or transforming existing ones. It was clear to me
from day one that I was a misfit there. As often happens with
an entry-level job, one can end up feeling like a small cog in
a giant wheel—you have no idea how this wheel is turning,
where it's going or who is in charge of spinning it. I tried my
best to fit in but found no joy in the work I was doing. At the
same time, the dot-com boom in Silicon Valley had taken off
and how. The rise and rise of Internet companies was starting
to reach a fever pitch, fuelling massive growth in the economy.
It was seen as a once-in-a-century phenomenon which would
end up reshaping the world order for the better. Every day there
was yet another spectacular initial public offering (IPO) and
another pundit pronouncing that stock markets were headed
for stratospheric heights. Renowned author Michael Lewis
got it right in his book *The New New Thing: A Silicon Valley
Story*, the basic premise of which is that the normal rules of
the old-world economy don't apply to a digital economy, which
requires the invention of new rules.

Sitting in Chicago, it seemed that the biggest revolution of
my lifetime was passing me by. It seemed to be the best possible

opportunity to try my hand at entrepreneurship. If I didn't take advantage of it right then, I might never have another chance. After spending just a few weeks deliberating on my options, I started asking anyone within earshot if they would consider being a co-founder with me. As soon as the first person said yes, I quit my job, barely eighteen months into it, and started packing to head to the Bay Area. Today I can only marvel at the risk appetite and chutzpah of youth. Despite having no savings, no idea about what to start, no place to live and not knowing anyone in the Bay Area apart from a few college classmates, it still felt like a great idea, and I couldn't contain my excitement. After a five-day drive, we ended up in the Bay Area and the first order of business was to convince someone to let us camp out in their living room while we plotted the next world-changing idea. Even after earnestly trying for a few months, we had only a few half-decent ideas and no clue about where to begin. We soon found ourselves running only on fumes; our lack of preparedness was all too obvious. I had some choices to make. After struggling for six months and maxing out all my credit cards, I had two choices—to apply for a job at another large firm or do something to prepare for an eventual career in entrepreneurship.

Fortunately, I chose the latter. I realized that the only way I could learn about entrepreneurship was by working for early-stage companies, so I found a job at NexTag as an engineer. I had only a sketchy understanding of programming at that time, but I was able to wing it. More importantly, I was part of a real funded start-up that had a clear pioneering idea, a professional team and the hustle of a fast-growing start-up. I enjoyed the environment immensely and learnt how to collaborate with different stakeholders. Being part of a very small organization meant that I had direct ownership for some problem statements that had a clear, tangible impact on the end consumer. I was hooked and had no doubt whatsoever that I would only work in start-ups until I was ready to start again on my own. The excitement didn't last very long though, as by the time the world was done dealing with the anticipated Y2K catastrophe that ended in barely a whimper, the dot-com boom was beginning to run out of steam. The truth is, a vast majority of dot-com companies had no business model and, in many cases, not even a very clearly defined product. Most investors were outsiders who had no clue about tech investing and a lot of purely speculative retail investment was fuelling the rise of the stock market. In other words, we were close to being the last fools holding the stock when the music stopped. That happened in March 2000, as it almost always does after an insane speculative rally that goes beyond all rational parameters. The crash of 2000 halted the dot-com rally in its tracks, reinforcing the fact that the rules of the economy are timeless and that cold business rationale was as relevant as ever.

In the aftermath of the dot-com crash, Silicon Valley was a ghost town. If you were working for one of the newfangled start-ups, it was a miracle if you did not get laid off. Many start-ups laid off as much as 80–90 per cent of their staff, that is if they hadn't immediately shut down or had a fire sale to salvage what they could. The job market completely dried up and a long clean-up exercise lay ahead for the entire Valley. This was my first direct lesson in the boom-and-bust business cycles which are well studied and remarkably cyclical. I would personally experience these cycles over the next twenty years of my career, the most recent one fuelled by the Covid-19 pandemic that was particularly hard for the business I am now in. One of the most reliable things about markets is that eventually common sense and hard business logic prevail. But sometimes, hype-driven mania can last for years and it is nearly impossible to predict when the party will end.

So, I decided that I would continue to work for start-ups until I had the experience, confidence and some savings to try to build something seriously. I worked for three more start-ups in the Bay Area after NexTag, an experience that was like an eight-year-long MBA in entrepreneurship. Out of the four start-ups that I worked for, one had a massive exit, one a moderate exit and two failed. It so happened that I spent the majority of my time in the two failed start-ups. It wasn't clear back then—but is quite apparent in hindsight—that failure or the prospect of failure dramatically enhances the learning curve.

While working in the companies that failed, I witnessed every possible problem a start-up can face. I saw problematic founder dynamics first-hand and observed how excessive burn led to very short runways. I watched how internal politics could lead to a corrosive culture and learnt about the dangers of ignoring customer and market truths in favour of strongly held internal beliefs not backed by data. In other words, everything that could go wrong did go wrong and I was able to watch it from the frontline, often contributing to the issues as well out of my ignorance and lack of experience. But at the same time, I was also able to objectively gauge what was going on. I began to notice the same patterns repeating themselves often and in different contexts, leading to the same outcomes.

The great thing about being in the Valley is that while you may work for one company, you are part of a larger community which is all about innovation, hustle and a never-ending quest for the Next Big Thing. As a result, one gets exposure to the region's happenings and culture, gaining an almost continuous stream of insights about the companies that make it big as well as those that go bust. During my time there, I gained a deep understanding of the Valley, its history, culture and ethos that make it work as a system of innovation, irrespective of individual companies winning or dying. My learning came through this immense exposure, as well as debate and reading about companies like Google, Facebook and Netflix that built products which changed the world. I was surprised to learn that a big part of what drives the Valley is its focus on meritocracy, transparency, challenging the status quo and the larger-than-life ambition that brings some of the top entrepreneurs from around the world to the region. These companies learn from each other, copy successful models in real time, while constantly iterating to improve upon their model, thus fiercely competing to win the minds and hearts of consumers. Barring some exceptions, the best product usually won and, as I learnt, it is not at all easy to build an amazing product.

During my eight years in Silicon Valley, I grew as a product manager and learnt a lot of things about the entrepreneurial ecosystem—lessons that I could not have learnt anywhere else then. While I was involved in the last two ventures, we built development centres in Bengaluru and thus I started coming to the city frequently to work with the offshore teams. On my visits, I began to see early green shoots of the Internet starting to grow, experiencing the immense excitement and promise in the air and the sense that India was ready to take off in a big way. Over a dozen trips, I was convinced that I wanted to get in at ground zero and try to finally start my entrepreneurial journey in India. Despite the eight years I had spent in the start-up world, I knew nothing about things like TAM (total addressable market) and other essential concepts, and hence I decided to pursue the first strong but niche idea that I could think of. What happens with really boutique ideas is that even if you win, you still build a very small business, and that's exactly what happened at Myntra. After four years and numerous experiments and events, we were the largest personalization company in India with barely $5 million ARR (annual recurring revenue)—not much to write home about. While we struggled for a greater part of those first four years, one thing was clear—that we would not die. We would keep learning and getting better. That is what eventually landed us in retailing fashion online.

After Myntra pivoted into Fashion, things took off for us in a big way. We were finally in the right place at the right time. It had been thirteen years since I had driven to the Bay Area entirely on a whim. After thirteen years of bouncing around, starting, stopping, restarting, pivoting and moving continents, I was finally at a real turning point. I was positioned at the forefront of an incredible opportunity: the entire category of e-commerce was poised for massive growth (a rising tide), we were in a huge category (with a large TAM) with strong unit economics (high CM [contribution margin] in Fashion), had a clear differentiation (inventory model and customer experience) and things just took off in vertical directions. It is said that 'Behind every overnight success, there is ten years of hard work.' In my case, it was exactly thirteen years. When I look back now, I wonder whether I would ever again be able to undertake an assignment that would require such a long wait before seeing even a hint of success. But the truth is, this is probably the most common pattern that emerges when you analyse start-ups. Zomato was founded in 2008, Paytm in 2010, Policybazaar in 2008. While the whole Indian start-up ecosystem was galvanized by their IPOs in 2021, these so-called overnight success stories were in the making for the previous ten to fifteen years! We will encounter this theme again and again in our story. Patience, the ability to play the long-term game and being able to toil away in obscurity without any rewards or recognition are just a few of the many tough costs one pays for a career in entrepreneurship.

The next five-year period in Myntra was mostly a dream run, barring that unexpectedly tough year in 2013 when several factors created the perfect storm of challenges for us—a moment that nearly brought us to the brink despite actually getting most things right. In fact, it was the first time that things were really working for us, and yet we had to deal with the prospect of closing down for a period of over six months. This is another lesson one learns during the start-up journey: that you can only play the cards that you are dealt. You can do everything in your power, but you cannot control all the factors at play. No company could have prepared for the pandemic, for example, which produced its own winners and losers. In these situations, the stoic wisdom of the Greek philosopher Epictetus comes to mind— 'There is only one way to happiness and that is to cease worrying about things which are beyond the power of our will.' It turns out that there are plenty of things which are in your control, from the team you hire, the culture you build and the product features you choose to implement, to how fast you can learn, adapt and grow. Good entrepreneurs figure out what to obsess over and what not to worry about. You also eventually realize that the stronger the foundation you build, the greater is your ability to remain unaffected by the external factors that are beyond your control.

After my Myntra and, post-acquisition, Flipkart journey, I got an opportunity to try entrepreneurship again. By this time, it was clear to me that I loved entrepreneurship and everything that came with the territory. I was also able to choose a category that matched a personal passion in the field of health and fitness. While the TAM for the category we chose was arguably low at the time, I believed that interest in a healthy lifestyle would continue to grow as it is a long-term macro trend, and that's exactly how it has turned out. Today CULT is India's #1 fitness chain, and we have a high growth trajectory ahead of us.

When I look back on the last twenty-five years I've spent in the world of start-ups—the first eight working for very early-stage companies in the heart of Silicon Valley and the next seventeen in India, funding two companies, investing in others and closely partnering or collaborating with many more—I realize that the entire world of entrepreneurship is filled with several misperception and romantic ideas. On the one hand, there are views that reduce start-up success to simplistic cliches of relentless toil, perseverance and burning the midnight oil, while on the other, the focus is on the role of luck, hustle, connections or being in the right place at the right time. While much of this is true, I have come to believe that the reality is a lot more nuanced. There are some deeper principles at play and some heuristics that tend to get repeated over a period of time. While the role of luck cannot be undermined, it is possible to gain a much deeper understanding of what makes an entrepreneur. You can thus shape the journey in a way that not only maximizes your chances of success but also enables you to have a lot of fun in the process, accelerating your personal development and growth, which is often as, or even more, rewarding than the outward success of your efforts.

After working in start-ups for a long period of time, I began to observe patterns that would often repeat themselves. It is said that 'Those who don't learn from history are condemned to repeat it.' In the world of start-ups, it can be said that you can maximize the odds of success only by understanding the common pitfalls and foibles of others and incorporating their best practices. At one point, I believed that the principles involved in entrepreneurship can not only be understood but also practised. When I started Meraki Labs, my incubator for building start-ups, we began to share and imbibe these principles among the start-ups that we were working with. The first two start-ups in our incubator, Groww and Skyroot, have done phenomenally well and we have many more in the pipeline. In 2023, I started a course titled ELD (Entrepreneurship, Leadership, Design) to teach the same principles to aspiring entrepreneurs and high-potential leaders. We have completed four cohorts and received encouraging feedback. We now want to double down and keep raising the bar on ELD, continuing to train the next generation of entrepreneurs, thus doing our bit to accelerate entrepreneurship in India.

It is in the same spirit that I decided to write this book. What took me twenty-five years to understand about entrepreneurship can be understood in a far shorter time, and the knowledge can significantly improve the quality of your first venture. The same principles also apply in any high-growth business, whether you are in mid-management or senior management. By imbibing these ideas, you can play an outsized role in helping your organization achieve its objectives, while accelerating your own learning and growth curve in the process. Entrepreneurship in any context is primarily about mindset; it is about a shift from 'It's not my problem' to 'Everything is my problem if I am part of the project.' Once you start thinking this way, you look at everything differently. You don't think about how to pass the buck, but what you can do to move the agenda forward, irrespective of organizational boundaries or the limits of your role. You may be an engineer at CULT, but if you go to a gym for a workout and notice that the paint on the walls is chipped, you will take the initiative to reach out to the facilities team, file a ticket and follow up until the problem is rectified. You will go one step further and ask why it was chipped in the first place. You will try to figure out a process that can ensure that all centres always look brand new, in a structured and systematic manner. Perhaps you will even volunteer time to design the process and implement the system. No one asked you to do any of this, and it definitely is not part of your job description, but by doing so, you are choosing to practise an entrepreneurial mindset.

Entrepreneurs develop this particular mindset as well as a habit of spotting problems around them, asking, 'How can I make this better?' They don't need anyone's permission to rectify the problem. One of the offices I used to go to during the Covid-19 lockdown had massive issues with the video conferencing system. Every day, everyone would spend the first ten or fifteen minutes of a meeting fiddling with the system, making jokes about it, complaining about it and eventually just watching a good chunk of productive time waste away. While it was merely a source of frustration and even amusement for most, one team member chose to say, 'This is not acceptable. I will fix it.' He researched all available video conference systems, tested them and went ahead and bought the best one he could find for six major conference rooms, paying out of his own pocket (content to be reimbursed later). And he implemented this over a single weekend. From the following week, everyone could stroll into a conference room, click a button and actually start their meeting on time. In my mind, this person is an entrepreneur. He saw the problem and fixed it for good in the best way he could.

The history of entrepreneurship is replete with such examples. Someone encounters a problem in daily life and chooses to do something about it. Spanx founder Sara Blakely didn't like how regular underclothes looked beneath certain outfits, and once ended up cutting the feet off a pair of pantyhose so she could wear them under white pants.[1] She immediately realized that many women like her probably had the same problem and eventually she decided to convert her idea into a full-fledged business, ending up with a multi-billion-dollar company. The founders of Airbnb were struggling to make rent on their San Francisco flat when they noticed all the hotels were booked out due to an industrial design conference in town.[2] So, they bought a few airbeds, created a quick site called 'Air Bed and Breakfast' and offered their first-ever guests a place to sleep and breakfast for $80 per night. The founder of Uber puzzled over why getting a cab was so difficult, when Google Maps was so accurate about trip times, giving rise to the idea of ride hailing. This pattern, of an entrepreneur noticing a problem and choosing to do something about it, is the most promising way to find a starting point for a new business. When you have familiarity with a problem and you earnestly want to do something about it, chances are that you can find a solution that other people will also find relevant, thus kickstarting your entrepreneurial journey.

But just starting up alone is not enough. Nearly 90 per cent of all ventures die.[3] In a majority of the cases, almost everything goes wrong from day one. When I was starting Myntra, my first three potential co-founders decided to back out within the first six months, and I had to start the process all over again each time. Building a product in the early stages of a company is difficult and unpredictable. Naysayers will tell you why something won't work and very often those naysayers are right. If something has never been done before, there is usually a good reason, and you need to understand that reason and identify your plan to overcome it. Sometimes, teasing out customer insights and preferences may seem like black magic. Customers often change their minds, say contradictory things, have very different life contexts from one another and often, what they say and what they do are totally disconnected. Then, there is the matter of finding some financing for an early-stage company which may require first-time entrepreneurs to jump through all kinds of hoops, hearing 'no' repeatedly, which can get quite disheartening. As you transition from the safety and predictability of a stable job to the chaos of an early-stage start-up, life goes into a tailspin, causing you to wonder what you are doing here in the first place. But if you walk into the first few years of your start-up armed with a good understanding of what to expect and how to navigate the journey, this could also be a time of highly accelerated learning and a lot of fun.

Just like a child growing up, all start-ups go through distinctive phases. There are the infancy years in which you are just trying to stay afloat and get to initial product–market fit. Once you have a decent product, you need to worry about building some clearly defensible differentiators and building an organization that can help scale the product meaningfully. These are the toddler years when a lot happens in a day, many things fall apart, learning is exponential, and your unique company culture can be shaped and nurtured so that it will come in handy in later years. If you continue to make your product and organization better, at some point you will hit an inflection point and growth will just happen—not unlike those teenage growth spurts! Eventually things will start to stabilize, and you will begin to think about profitability, long-term sustainability and defensible moats to secure the business for the long run. All stages of business have unique requirements and need to be navigated using different mental models. In this book, we will look at the challenges and the relevant toolkits for each stage so that you are fully equipped to deal with them when you encounter them.

In this book, my aim is to distil everything I have learnt into simple patterns and principles that you can consider adopting in your own entrepreneurial journeys. I will draw from my experience of building companies and from studying the history of business and entrepreneurship, as well as from my learnings as an investor in early-stage companies and working closely with many funds and investors. While I think entrepreneurship is always a mix of art and science with a healthy measure of luck, timing and sheer grit, I also believe that there is a method to the madness. A few clear patterns, tools and best practices can make the path more familiar and prepare you to make the most of the good times and bad. In this book, we will systematically consider everything that one can expect from an entrepreneurial journey, look at numerous case studies, draw out lessons from both spectacular successes and failures and develop a comprehensive model to demystify entrepreneurship and hopefully dramatically improve the odds of your success.

Below is a brief overview of everything we will cover in this book so that you have a road map for what to expect and a bird's-eye view of how the narrative will evolve.

The History of Entrepreneurship

To set the context, let's take a whirlwind tour of the history of modern entrepreneurship. Looking back on the evolution of trade, business and financial institutions—which have shaped the world in profound ways—will give us an insight into where we are today.

Foundation Matters

When is the right time to start up? Who should you start with? Should you even start a company in the first place? How can you make good choices up front to set yourself up well for the long run? This chapter addresses some of the most important questions entrepreneurs must ask themselves before launching a venture, in order to create a strong foundation for a long-lasting, meaningful business.

Start with Why

As important as a solid foundation is a deep sense of purpose, which is a company's guiding light. Finding your 'why' as a company will define everything you do, and so this task requires deep immersion in your domain as well as contemplation about your company's raison d'être. The most long-lasting organizations are very clear about why they exist and what purpose they serve.

Why Start-Ups Fail

Unfortunately, a large majority of start-ups do not live to see their first birthdays. While failure is almost a rite of passage for entrepreneurs—one that teaches many lessons—I believe that it is not inevitable. In this chapter, I look at the many reasons and ways in which start-ups fail, in the hope that readers can avoid the same mistakes and pitfalls on their own journeys.

Everything Starts with Customers

The best companies have their fingers on the pulse of the customer; every insight is worth its weight in gold. But customers often say one thing and do another, behaving in strange and unexpected ways. Understanding users and their needs lies at the heart of any effort towards building extraordinary solutions. In this chapter, we shall understand just how to figure out what a customer wants.

Product Is Marketing

Great products sell themselves. Great products lead to profitable business models. Great products earn customer loyalty. The best marketing tool you will ever build is a great product. But building a great product is hard. It takes an obsessive attention to the smallest detail, the blending of deep insights with technological innovation and craftsmanship to build a product that consumers love.

Growth Engine

A company doesn't grow into a success overnight. In fact, success is often the culmination of years of a daily grind. Choosing the right strategies at each stage will help you to harness the magic of compounding. Growth hacking can be tempting, as we'll see in this chapter, but there are no shortcuts to achieving genuinely accelerated growth in a company.

Organization Is Product

Often, company culture is a by-product of copying standard practices from other organizations. But this approach misses out on the opportunity to deliberately shape a unique organization for the mission at hand. This chapter delves into building a company culture with a product mindset—being thoughtful and meticulous about every feature—to transform a start-up's journey and the outcome of that journey.

Leaders Lead

Leadership is a privilege and an immense responsibility. I don't believe anyone is born a leader, because being a leader requires the cultivation of an array of skills and the development of a deep sense of self-awareness and humility. There are many leadership styles to suit different personalities. Leaders have to adapt to changing times while being generous, inspiring and transparent.

Strategy: Where to Play, How to Win

Strategy is often misunderstood. It isn't about *what* your goals are but *how* you plan to achieve them. Good strategy requires you to frame the options available to you, predict the implications of each, factor in the various constraints and then make deliberate and unequivocal choices. In the risky business of entrepreneurship, strategy can make or break a company.

Funding Games

If entrepreneurship is a rocket ship, it is one fuelled by venture money which is the lifeblood of start-ups in the early stages, propelling hockey stick growth once a company hits an inflection point. There's more to fundraising than achieving valuation milestones that are celebrated in the media. Fundraising is about telling a compelling story, approaching the right investors at the right time and asking for the right amount of capital.

Financials for Dummies

As much as I enjoy discussing the thrill of starting up and the magic of extraordinary products, the fact is, as a founder, the true story of your business is reflected in your financials— something many founders ignore for far too long. Running a successful business requires a deep understanding of finance and the ability to infer trends. A strong grasp of things like cash burn, runway and unit economics can ensure good planning and practices for the long term.

I hope this book will not only equip you with the right insights and tools, but also help you gain a deeper understanding of the world of entrepreneurship, to see whether this is something that is suited to your temperament and aspirations. Equally important, I hope this book will convince you that entrepreneurial skill sets and toolkits are not limited to a classic entrepreneurial venture. You can apply similar methods and principles to your personal goals (getting fitter, learning to fly an aeroplane, travelling around the world) or towards making a larger impact in your current organization (starting a new initiative, solving a long-standing problem, being an agent of change and inspiring your team members to achieve a lot more together) or even making the world around you a better place (serving your community, starting a new non-profit initiative, evangelizing a cause that you care about). As we will see in the very first chapter, the entrepreneurial mindset (with no small dose of daredevilry) has played a pivotal role in moving the world forward and this will only accelerate in the coming century, fuelled by the exponential nature of technological progress.

With that, let's dive in.

1

Lessons from History

Entrepreneurship has become very popular lately—whether as a choice of career or a subject of discussion and study. There are numerous entrepreneurship conferences, self-styled entrepreneurial gurus (hopefully I don't fall into that category!) and even the vaunted entrepreneurial lifestyle with its sixteen-hour workdays, co-working spaces, lattes and Red Bulls. We treat entrepreneurship as if it were a new phenomenon that has just emerged in the last few decades and taken the world by storm, but this doesn't really capture the story. Entrepreneurship is in our DNA and the progress of humankind since ancient times has been driven by the entrepreneurial spirit. It is this spirit that led the first humans to venture out of Africa in search of better lands and resources which eventually took them across seven oceans to the far-flung corners of the world, mostly on foot or on makeshift boats, to colonize pretty much the entire planet within 40,000 years of that first wave of migration. The human story is arguably one of ever more daring entrepreneurial adventures.

One can go back in time and argue that fire, the wheel and stone tools are among the greatest inventions ever. Alas, the entrepreneurs behind these inventions are long lost to the pages of unrecorded history and cannot be felicitated as 'entrepreneurs of the year' in our endless parades and perennial celebrations of entrepreneurs. Every time someone asks, 'What's out there?' or 'Is there a better way?' or 'Let me tinker with this and see what happens,' they are being entrepreneurial. This spirit has continued unabated since the rise of Homo Sapiens some 2,00,000 years ago. In fact, 'sapiens', meaning 'the wise one', is an ode to that entrepreneurial spirit that is continually tinkering with its environment, making better tools, developing a deeper understanding of the world and exerting unprecedented control over the resources available on this planet and, soon, even beyond. It is said, 'To err is human,' but it can also be said that, 'To invent through trial and error is to be a "sapient" human.'

One of the things I have found myself naturally inclined towards is deep curiosity about why something is the way it is or how things work. Approaching a topic or domain from this lens reveals rich and colourful histories, as well as several foundational principles that continue to drive the field. Having this perspective allows you to synthesize information and make decisions from a much more informed vantage point. It is also fun to learn and absorb all this information! When I got into the fashion and, later, the fitness business, I enjoyed learning in great detail about the overall architecture of the domains to understand how the industries worked. This enabled me to make some foundational choices that played a role in the eventual outcome of both businesses. In the same way, whenever I'm curious about why the world of entrepreneurship is the way it is today, I turn to history, immersing myself in stories of the past that continue to inform everything we do today.

Today, as entrepreneurs, we take a lot of things for granted. We can pitch to an angel investor or a venture capitalist (VC). Everyone understands what a term sheet is; there is widespread availability of pure risk capital for high-risk ventures in which you might lose the company, but not the shirt on your back or the house you live in. If you make it work, you have public markets available to provide everyone liquidity and to tap into a much wider pool of capital beyond professional money managers. As Isaac Newton famously said, 'If I have seen further than others, it is by standing upon the shoulders of giants.' Today's entrepreneurs have many a mighty shoulder to thank for the opportunity to start something the moment inspiration strikes and be able to credibly dream of changing the world. In this chapter, we look at some of the fundamental conceptual innovations that have happened across the centuries as well as the emergence of some critical ecosystems. In addition, we'll cover a few role model companies and entrepreneurs who not only provide inspiration but also prove that these critical foundational principles continue to be relevant for all entrepreneurs.

It may seem that entrepreneurship is some newfangled thing that has become cool in recent decades, but the truth is that not only is entrepreneurship as old as the history of humanity, even the concepts that we use today have been many centuries, and even millennia, in the making. Mark Twain is believed to have said, 'History does not repeat itself, but it often rhymes.' Knowing the history of these concepts and tools that we take for granted will help us to develop deeper principles and leverage the best possible tools to shape our journey of entrepreneurship. For example, when you realize that VCs are only trying to maximize returns while minimizing risks, you will not fret too much about their 'preference for IIT–IIM grads' or those who 'chase asset light models'. These are just patterns that VCs have latched on to as they believe that these might improve the risk–reward equation, but if you can show that an alternate model has a better chance, they will happily rewrite their mental models. When you understand that VCs have a limited amount of time to return the capital to their investors, you will appreciate the constant exit pressure that they have to contend with.

We are going to look at four major factors that affect every single start-up one way or another.

Business Models: I will argue that, fundamentally, there are only a few business models that keep getting repeated in physical, and now digital, formats.

Innovation and Risk: Innovators who pioneer new tools and technology have repeatedly moved the world forward. But innovation also requires upfront capital, a healthy appetite for risk, a high dose of failure and the corresponding reward potential to go along with the risk.

Financing: Financing has had a long and tortuous history, even surviving religious bans on many kinds of lending, right up to current times, when zero per cent interest rates can drive a massive market frenzy.

Ecosystems: John Donne said, 'No man is an island, entire of itself.' This is even more relevant for start-ups. A few ecosystems around the world have acted as giant catalysts for an ever-accelerating pace of innovation.

ENTREPRENEURIAL WISDOM

The Mouse Merchant

The oldest story of entrepreneurship can be found in the Jataka Tales. An adviser to the king noticed a dead mouse lying on the side of the road while walking by one day. Turning to those who accompanied him, he remarked, 'Even from such small beginnings as a dead mouse, an energetic young fellow could build a fortune.' A passer-by overheard and, recognizing the wisdom of these words, picked up the dead mouse by its tail. As he pondered how he might turn something seemingly worthless into something of value, a shopkeeper called out to him. 'My cat has been pestering me all morning,' the shopkeeper said. 'I'll give you two copper coins for that mouse.' The man learnt an important lesson: Wherever there is hunger, there is an opportunity.

Business Models and Marketplaces

One of the hottest business model trends of the last few decades has been the rise of digital marketplaces. A marketplace is a platform that brings buyers and sellers together and the owner of the platform makes money as a percentage commission on transactions. There are typically three types of marketplaces. In one, the marketplace operator takes the capital risk, buying goods from the provider, stocking them in the warehouse and finding a buyer. In the second type, the marketplace owner produces her own goods and establishes a storefront to sell the goods to the buyer (known today as direct-to-consumer, or D2C). In the third type of marketplace, the operator creates a platform where buyers and sellers come together, find each other and complete transactions, and the marketplace gets a cut. Humans have been engaging in these models for as long as we have recorded history.

Every ancient account of history or fable from the past inevitably features key scenes unfolding in the bustle of a thriving marketplace at the heart of a city. One of the most famous marketplaces of the ancient world was Agora of Athens. This was the central gathering place where all transactions—commercial or otherwise—would take place. This is also where Socrates[1] would find both willing and unwilling pupils to harangue with his emerging ideas about truth, beauty and ethics.

Some of the most well-known marketplaces of the past include the Grand Bazaar of Turkey, Zanzibar's Stone Town, the entire stretch of the famed Silk Road and Venice during the Renaissance, all of which served as melting pots of goods, ideas and cultures from around the world, and had a profound impact on world history. These marketplaces were driven by traders who were the pioneering entrepreneurs of ancient times, taking inordinate risks to embark on multi-year journeys. They did so in the hope of making some serious money if they managed to come back alive, not unlike entrepreneurs of today, except in the former case, not making it back alive was an actual possibility! Today's marketplaces might look very different, but they still function according to the same principles, even if they are online rather than in bustling city centres. Think about Etsy, the marketplace for handmade goods, Nykaa for beauty products, or Amazon for just about anything.

Some of the earliest recorded examples of entrepreneurship are the traders of prehistoric times who exploited arbitrage across vast geographical distances. Some resources are more common in certain geographies, leading to unique skills and an abundance of products made from the combination of these resources and skills. Trade between Europe, India and China was thriving for 2000 years, culminating in the golden years of the Silk Route, a pan-Asian route enabling the export of silk, fabric and spices from the East in exchange for precious metal from Europe. The Silk Route may very well have been the Silicon Valley of ancient times because this is where daring entrepreneurs of the past headed. Wisdom from different parts of the world came together around the many trading hubs that developed along the way. This is where resources exchanged hands, where ideas collided and evolved into completely novel concepts in an endless mingling of the East and the West, and where alliances formed that would continue to shape and reshape Eurasian continental culture and society.

During the Tang Dynasty,[2] the exchange of resources took on a unique form as trade in tea thrived. Merchants would travel to the tea-growing regions in the Southwest of China to purchase produce and take it to cities where they would sell it to other merchants or exporters who shipped tea to the world. Given how well business was going, the traders began to struggle with the sacks of Chinese currency—then called guan—that they had to carry to buy tea, which would only grow on their return journey after trading. Fortunately, China had invented paper not long before, and traders in the Sichuan region developed better ways of transferring credit or wealth. When they sold their shipments of tea in the city, they would receive paper IOUs, which they could exchange for guan in provincial depositories in the south. So light was this paper money compared to sacks of coins that they named it 'fei-qian' or 'flying money'. From flying money to crypto currencies, we have come a long way and the quest for ever more efficient mechanisms of trade and business keeps driving innovation forward.

One of the most successful but often most exploitative business models of the past was the 'rent-collection' model in which powerful monarchs and feudal lords would acquire large swathes of land, usually through conquest or inheritance, and then collect rent on the property forever. From the Pharaohs of ancient Egypt to landed Roman aristocrats at the peak of the Roman empire, and the feudal lords of Europe, rent collection is how the wealthy made their money. It has taken the world more than one revolution and many legal reforms to break the back of this debilitating business model that tends to emerge again and again. We are witnessing its modern avatar with big tech companies. They have become the portal to the Internet for most consumers, and any business wishing to sell something online has to go through these portals and pay rent—which in some cases is as much as 30 per cent of the revenue generated. This has become an issue in India where small online businesses find it virtually impossible to make this business model work with such exorbitant fees. In fact, there is now a growing backlash against such practices in India and around the world.

Till date, global commerce thrives on the idea of arbitrage. Arbitrage is an economic concept in which you find a price difference between two contexts and then systematically exploit that cost difference to make a profit. In middle Europe for example, the price of spices from India and that of fine silk and porcelain from China was exponentially higher than the actual cost of producing these goods in their respective countries of origin. This motivated numerous adventurers and traders to seek efficient trade routes. Just one successful voyage could leave the merchant wealthy for the rest of his life. Today, India's thriving IT services industry is benefitting labour cost arbitrage for the IT workforce. While the likes of TCS and Infosys can hire a good engineer in India at $10/hour, clients in the US are willing to pay $50/hour for the service, as the same engineers in their own country may cost $75–$100/hour. While these firms are able to save money, Indian companies are able to make a healthy profit due to the arbitrage advantage.

Another business model that can be called a 'factory model' has been around forever. The idea of the factory model is to create a large production set-up that enables economies of scale, employing a large workforce and running organized production to convert raw materials into goods that can be exported around the world, often at significant cost multiples. The Egyptians mastered the art of running large-scale construction projects culminating in the creation of the Pyramids. The royal workshops of the Assyrian empire produced textiles, metalworks and armaments, while the silver mines of Laurion near Athens were a huge source of revenue for the Athenian state. The Han dynasty in China monopolized iron and salt production which was then exported along the Silk Route. It takes a considerable amount of capex to build a factory and hence, in the past, only states and wealthy industrial houses could invest in these models. It also takes a lot of time to construct a factory and hence one needs to be very patient in order to finally recoup investment costs.

The modern equivalent is the semiconductor fabrication plant that takes billions of dollars to build but can carry gross margins of up to 80 per cent. There are numerous business models in which whoever controls the means of production has a virtual monopoly in the business. States and large business groups have significant advantages in these models as they can easily marshal up the capital, despite the very long-term ROI horizons, required to build these factories of the future and are then virtually guaranteed to have a secure revenue stream for a long period.

As industrialization grew in the West, most firms recognized that it was difficult to do a great job at every step of the value chain, from manufacturing to brand building and distribution, and hence they slowly started to specialize. If you look at how a mobile phone is manufactured, you realize that a very complex supply chain is required to put the product together. There are a handful of players who make the computer chip which also includes components from many different providers. The factories that assemble the phone are different from the companies that design it. The camera comes from a different vendor and so does the specialized glass cover. Even the software is written by different firms than the ones building the hardware. The retailers that sell the phone to consumers are yet another set of companies. Last century was marked by a drift towards specialization with an ever-greater focus on doing one thing well. But some firms realized that they could opt for vertical integration in which they own everything from production to end consumer distribution. Tesla and Apple are examples of such vertical integration in the tech space while companies such as ITC and Titan Company are examples of vertical integration in the consumer space in India.

Innovation and Risk

It is one thing to take locally produced goods such as spices or mining products and then ship them to a faraway place to sell at a significant price differential, but it is a totally different thing to be able to produce a good that no one else can. In ancient times, Chinese porcelain or silk required specialized production processes that no one could replicate for centuries, and the manufacturing process was guarded very heavily until it was eventually discovered and exported to other parts of the world. Fast-forward to the fifteenth century, when Johannes Gutenberg invented the printing press, a game-changing innovation in communication and the spread of ideas.[3] While this is arguably one of those innovations that had a dramatic impact on the world, there was no concept of patents in those times. Pretty soon many others started copying and creating better models of the printing press that spread throughout Europe. Gutenberg, on the other hand, got into debt, was sued by his investor–partner and lost control of his printing shop. The world wasn't yet ready to be able to reward his incredible invention, and it is no wonder there was barely any innovation in these dark ages, as it was a thankless endeavour. Gutenberg changed the world probably more than anyone else in history and yet had nothing to show for the effort.

James Watt, the quintessential inventor–entrepreneur, had a much better experience. He figured out how to improve upon the Newcomen engine to harness the power of steam to drive almost any machine, as long as it could be translated into the back-and-forth movement of a piston. For this he was awarded his first patent, British Patent No. 913, titled 'A New Invented Method of Lessening the Consumption of Steam and Fuel in Fire Engines'. On the back of this patent, he was able to get financing and build a company, 'Boulton & Watt,' which became very successful. It ushered in the era of steam-powered engines that eventually found application virtually everywhere, from mines and factories to steam ships, and the Industrial Age was truly on its way to completely transform the world over the next two centuries. Sometimes inventors and entrepreneurs have that kind of impact. We are seeing this play out with OpenAI/ChatGPT today, but the global impact may only take a few decades instead of a few centuries.

As inventors started making breakthroughs, they realized that others could easily reverse engineer and replicate their inventions, often at an even lower cost. This threatened to cut into the profit potential of their innovations. One of the key motivations for aspiring innovators, even today, is to find a practical application that they can sell to a large number of people at profit, and they need protection against potential copycats. This protection first evolved in mediaeval Europe through a rudimentary system of granting limited and time-bound monopolies to inventors, but these were restricted to the jurisdiction of the king granting these monopolies. The process was formalized in England in 1624 with the English Statute of Monopolies and the creation of the US Patent Act in 1790. The Patent Cooperation Treaty of 1970 has finally enabled the protection of one's patent across the entire planet. IP protection and the relentless infringement on IP is a saga that continues, with even state actors getting involved, and a widespread fear that reverse-engineering in China has soured the US–China relationship.

Industrialization coincided with remarkable breakthroughs in the fundamental sciences, as humans started to map the heavens. Newton uncovered the laws of motion and gravitation, Faraday and others pioneered electric currents and the motor, Maxwell discovered the electromagnetic equation and then, in a flurry of scientific enlightenment in the early twentieth century, Einstein, Bohr and others established modern physics as we now know it, with the laws of relativity and quantum mechanics. This pace of scientific breakthrough was astounding and provided the fundamental underpinnings for numerous practical applications that followed, with each application a potential source of creating wealth, fame and impact.

There evolved a symbiotic relationship between three kinds of actors: scientists who would come up with deep theoretical breakthroughs, engineers and inventors who would translate these concepts into practical applications such as the laser, transistor and GPS, and the entrepreneurs who would figure out how to find a market, make the business model work and reach incredible scale. All these three require different skill sets, time horizons and investment profiles, and the ecosystems have evolved to enable seamless and productive collaboration between them. Sometimes, skills overlap and sometimes people make transitions from one to the other. Google's founders did all three, going from research scientists at Stanford to being the engineers who figured out how to map the entire Internet, to the entrepreneurs who translated the technology into usable consumer products with a highly profitable business model.

However, as the pace of innovation expanded, so did the effort and investments required to make a breakthrough. Charles Babbage, the first scientist to seriously attempt building a mechanical computer, spent nearly all his life and savings on building increasingly better models, but his idea was so far ahead of its time that it never actually worked despite being conceptually correct. His collaborator, Ada Lovelace, invented the programming language, now known as Ada, in the process and became the first programmer in the world. Unlike the multi-million-dollar packages that the AI engineers of today receive, these pioneers only have their names in history books but didn't see any financial rewards or accolades during their lifetimes.

But the idea of the inventor–entrepreneur slowly took off as a precursor to the thriving entrepreneurial ecosystem of today. These early tinkerers were steeped in science and yet unafraid to get their hands dirty, fiddling with instruments and wires to put something useful together. If they did, they could rush to the patent office to get exclusive rights for their invention and profit from it until the end of the patent life cycle. Originally, most patents were for ten or twenty years, thus providing a clear window to commercially exploit the innovation without the fear of copycat competition. The most standard patent duration today is twenty years, reflecting the fact that innovations now require much longer periods and investments, justifying the correspondingly larger windows of commercial exclusivity. From the first Venetian Patent Statute of 1474 to a world that now sees an average of 5,00,000 new patents every year, we have come a long way. The human innovation machine has truly been unleashed.

Thomas Edison is one of the most renowned inventor–entrepreneurs who was granted over one thousand patents in his lifetime. He successfully commercialized many of his patents and became quite wealthy in the process. Alexander Graham Bell, who invented the telephone line, went on to found AT&T, which eventually became the largest company in the world. It also housed AT&T Bell Labs, an innovation hotbed for the whole world in the latter half of the twentieth century. From George Eastman inventing the camera and then founding Eastman Kodak to Steve Wozniak creating the first desktop computer in his garage and then co-founding Apple with Steve Jobs, the inventor–entrepreneur continues to be the leading light of the innovation age. The founders of DeepMind started up in 2010 with the explicit aim of 'Solving Intelligence', going on to do much of the pioneering work to make major breakthroughs and inspiring many other companies in the process to eventually help usher in the age of ChatGPT. Today computer science departments across the globe are being raided by big tech to corner all the top AI talent in the world as they prepare for the coming age of AI. Whoever isn't joining big tech is starting out on their own. The fastest path to securing multi-million-dollar funding is to be a computer science PhD in a top university. The era of the scientist–entrepreneur is alive and kicking.

Finding Money

Every entrepreneurial venture requires money. No one can build a concept or a product entirely on their own; it often takes many years of dedicated effort to build something that customers are willing to pay for. Additionally, you will need people with different skill sets to work with you to help translate your vision into reality. All this requires a significant amount of capital upfront. We now live in an environment where you can crank out a pitch deck in your spare time and try to raise a few million dollars even before you quit your job. But this wasn't always the case. It has taken a very long time for the world to reach a stage where entrepreneurs can knock on the doors of professional investors and get the required capital in exchange for a slice of ownership in the business.

Any worthwhile endeavour has always been dependent on getting access to quality capital. If you were building a ship, you needed massive capital expenditure that may have taken years to pay off. If you were venturing into the trading business, you had to have money for travel expenses, and for the cost of goods or currency to trade with at your intended destination. All this in the hopes of securing profit and paying off the initial start-up capital. The source of this capital back in the day was mostly wealthy moneylenders who would offer loans at interest and for some collateral (not unlike banks), people in your family or extended networks who were willing to take a bet on you (like angels) or people willing to buy into your share of profits (the precursor to shareholders). Entrepreneurs always needed to convince someone to give them the money and couldn't get going until someone was willing to take a bet on them.

Towards the middle of the current millennium, with the rise of the Renaissance, speculation was rife in Europe that the earth might be spherical rather than flat. Europe had established trading routes with Asia that were getting depleted and increasingly dangerous through centuries of religious crusades between Europe and the Middle East. These enterprising adventurers in Europe salivated at the prospect of finding an alternative sea route between Europe and Asia. If the earth was indeed round, one could surely go east by sailing west; a counter-intuitive idea that is typical of the entrepreneurial mindset even today. We may call this an unconventional approach, the path less travelled, or in this case, quite literally, a 'Blue Ocean Strategy!'

It is also no surprise that, like most ambitious business plans of today, these entrepreneurs estimated the perimeter of the earth to be half of what it is—a good way to make a seemingly impossible task more achievable, making it easier for people to bet on you! If entrepreneurs knew how long it would take to make their company work, they would probably never start in the first place. It is no surprise that most VCs double the investment requirement in their pitch evaluation to compensate for this overly optimistic outlook that is apparently timeless among entrepreneurs—even if they are 500 years apart!

Columbus was a daring adventurer who wanted to go on a westward voyage to find a sea route to India and to prove conclusively that the earth was indeed spherical. In an ordeal that all entrepreneurs will relate to, nearly every court in Europe rejected his appeal to get the voyage funded. It was only in 1492, after several years of negotiations, that the Spanish court agreed to partially finance Columbus's dream venture, and he raised the remainder of the funds from investors—most likely from Italy and Genoa. The moon shot that Columbus started clearly paid off in a big way, heralding the new age of globalization that continued to run unabated for 500 years and, in due course, gave rise to mighty global empires, forever altering the course of human history. That's why moon shots are worth it and we need entrepreneurs who are willing to give it everything that they have.

The old world wasn't kind to entrepreneurs who took a loan and then failed to return the money. Debtors' prisons were common. Along with the loss of money, one's reputation and dreams, there was a real danger of spending many years in a prison. Ending up in a debtors' prison made one a cautionary tale for other entrepreneurs, who would need to be very sure about what they intended to use the money for and the probability of success before taking on debt to fund new adventures. In fact, Charles Dickens's father spent time in a debtors' prison and young Charles was so deeply moved by the ordeal that he used it as a plot line in his book *Little Dorrit*. Daniel Defoe, author of *Robinson Crusoe*, also spent some time in a debtors' prison. It took many years and many reforms to streamline the debt process to prevent personal bankruptcy or bodily harm if a proposed venture didn't go well. With a wide panoply of debt options to choose from now, including no collateral venture debts for entrepreneurs, we have indeed come a long way. And no entrepreneur faces the risk of losing their home or ending up in a debtors' prison, at least not unless there is wilful fraud.

Rise of Public Stocks and Financial Markets

Today, companies going public and raising billions of dollars is an everyday affair but until very recently in human history, it was unthinkable. If you were not born into a wealthy family or couldn't secure a loan from a moneylender, you were out of luck. Humanity took a giant leap forward in the sixteenth century with the invention of the joint stock company. The idea was very simple. Can I get many people to invest in my company for fractional ownership and give them the ability to sell their shares (proof of ownership) on a stock exchange? This added rocket fuel to capitalism and industrialization, and there has been no looking back.

Joint stock companies had a humble beginning in 1602 when the Dutch East India Company (VOC) invited, for the very first time, ordinary Dutch citizens to buy shares in the new company. It was being formed for the purpose of waging war against the Portuguese in Asia, ostensibly to get access to the vast riches of the east and make the Dutch shareholders rich in the process. This was the very first time that ordinary people had an equal opportunity to participate in the ownership of a company. Until this point, joint stock ownership was limited to wealthy merchants and noble families with the right connections. At the time of share allocation, VOC didn't have an office and hence the allocation happened at the house of a wealthy merchant, Dirck van Os, co-founder of the VOC. Throughout the day, a total of 1143 investors opted to purchase shares with the initial commitment of twenty-one years. As a harbinger of what was to come, two housemaids who were privy to the proceedings were able to put in small amounts to purchase shares. The fact that two humble maids were able to buy a piece of the action for global wars was a sign of something profound unfolding, which would ultimately culminate in numerous stock market frenzies around the world.

Since all shareholders were locked in for twenty-one years, which was later relaxed to ten years, shareholder capital was stuck, posing a challenge. People started to informally trade shares, selling to interested parties and recording the exchange in the company books to ensure that the transfer was legitimate. But it was difficult to find a seller or buyer unless you knew some of the shareholders directly. As interest in trading shares increased, there was a need for a place that would make this more efficient. This is what led to the creation of the Amsterdam Stock Exchange in 1606, one of the world's first official stock exchanges. Soon, merchants figured out that they could use ordinary citizens as a source of capital, and citizens understood that they could profit from investments in large-scale ventures that would have been beyond their means on an individual basis. This two-sided network of exchange took root and over the next couple of centuries, the world saw the emergence of the London Stock Exchange, the New York Stock Exchange, the Paris Bourse, the Bombay Stock Exchange and the Tokyo Stock Exchange.

Thanks to all these developments, if you build a good company today—one that is able to turn a profit or at least have a credible and believable plan to get there—you have public markets around the world available to offload a portion of your shares to raise money and get your next wave of expansion easily funded. The Indian start-up ecosystem has come a long way with nearly a dozen companies lined up to go public in the next eighteen months and many more that are going to follow suit in subsequent years. But public markets are also very demanding. You need to have a profitable and defensible business model with clear prospects for predictable growth to be able to raise money from them. But at an earlier stage of the business, the risk and unpredictability are a lot higher and therefore you need a different class of investors who are comfortable with the risk–reward equation at an earlier stage of company building.

The Rise of Venture Capital

The biggest unlocking of entrepreneurial energy was the rise of professional venture capital firms. For most of history, the only early-stage capital available to aspiring innovators was either their own capital, debt that came with many stringent provisions or a wealthy patron who was willing to finance the venture. For the most part, finding money was often much harder than building something new.

Among the early pioneers of (what we now call) venture capital was a bunch of brokers who called themselves 'the Group' and met aspiring entrepreneurs over lunch at a couple of restaurants in San Francisco's financial district.[4] Entrepreneurs would pitch them over a meal of fresh fish and sourdough bread, and then go outside to wait on the pavement until a decision was reached. If it was a 'yes', they would be offered $80,000, $100,000 or sometimes more. That same 'Group' went on to become the Western Association of Venture Capitalists. Among its members was Reid Dennis, who had, in 1952, taken a bet on a company named Ampex, one of the first producers of tape recorders. The famous American singer, Bing Crosby, was known to have said that he'd rather play golf on Sunday afternoons than perform live on the radio, so, realizing that the technology had massive potential, Dennis invested his life's savings ($15,000) in the company. He eventually made $1 million on that bet, earning himself a reputation of sorts.

Around the same time, William Shockley, the inventor of the transistor, who had won the Nobel Prize for his discovery, decided to commercialize his technology in Northern California, an area that eventually came to be known as Silicon Valley. His company, Shockley's Semiconductor, was at the forefront of transistor-based chip design in the hope of eventually replacing the cumbersome vacuum tubes that were bulky and faulty, resulting in computers the size of an entire room. While the work was absolutely cutting edge, Shockley was known to be authoritative, running the firm with an iron hand and a very conservative approach to business, which made the engineers feel stifled.

As a result, eight of his employees eventually rebelled and left Shockley en masse. In his fascinating book *The Power Law: Venture Capital and the Making of the New Future*, which traces the rise of venture capital, Sebastian Mallaby argues that the moment the 'traitorous eight' rose up against Shockley's rigid and heavy-handed leadership in 1957 was the moment when the seed for Silicon Valley was sowed. The rebellion of these eight employees marked a shift from traditional ideas of a workplace—questioning hierarchy, authority and the so-called loyalty of working at one single company until retirement. It seems that Silicon Valley has taken this mantra to heart as till date, some of the best start-ups are founded by engineers who cut their teeth at Google, Facebook, Microsoft and the like and, when they are ready, they leave the company to start working on the next big thing.

Eventually, opportunistic investors such as Arthur Rock and others figured out that technology had a unique ability to grow exponentially and that if you bet on the right engineer, you could eventually reap proportionately exponential returns. This idea gave birth to the Venture Capitalist as we now know it today. Rock went on to invest in Intel, Apple and many others and is now widely considered a legend and pioneer in the VC industry. In a fascinating story told about the early days of Apple, a French investor was so keen to buy Apple shares that he decided to camp out in the office lobby until someone said yes. While the company had no need to raise further capital, Steve Wozniak changed his mind over the course of the day. He realized that he would like to offload some shares to be able to buy a home and so he did, much to the delight of the investor who was happy to sleep on the floor for the privilege!

Some of the early VCs in Silicon Valley slowly and painstakingly created the playbook that is all too familiar to venture firms across the world today. These VCs would drive around, walking into a garage that they might have heard about from the grapevine. They would hang out in the office and try to gauge if the technology being built held any promise. Don Valentine, who is considered the 'Grandfather of the venture industry', founded Sequoia Capital in 1972 and led investments in firms such as Apple, Cisco, Oracle and Atari. Atari Games was the ultimate example of a hip company, fully embracing the hippie culture of the California of the Seventies. In fact, Don had to jump into a hot tub for a tête-à-tête with the management team so he could woo them into accepting money from Sequoia. It worked out brilliantly for him.

Pretty soon, the reputation of this new type of financing began to spread beyond Silicon Valley where potential investors were consistently earning 20 per cent plus annual returns— numbers that were unheard of outside the frenzied speculative bubble. Public market investors considered an annual return of 10 per cent to be very healthy and so the prospect of 20–30 per cent annual returns got investors salivating. Soon, money started to flow into upstart venture firms that positioned themselves as the gateway to the next Steve Jobs and the path to untold riches. On the whole, Valley investors have lived up to this reputation, not only fuelling every successive batch of technology innovation but also making their investors and themselves fabulously wealthy in the process. During this process, they also arrived at the business model now commonly known as 'Two and Twenty'. What this means is that they charge a 2 per cent annual fee for the amount invested, as well as 20 per cent of any eventual profits that are generated, which is commonly known as 'carry'. This is the model that almost every firm now uses. But top-end firms can charge as much as 30 per cent carry as they have a much better track record.

Ecosystems as a Massive Force Multiplier

Throughout history, ideas have tended to grow exponentially in very short bursts of time, usually concentrated in very small hubs where certain conditions are met, after an initial catalyst sparks the fire. Ideas feed off each other, when artists, scientists and entrepreneurs find sparring partners, meeting people they can collaborate with and take inspiration from. Often, this spirals into a creative frenzy and, over decades, produces such a massive body of work and progress that the whole world is left to marvel at the creative force unleashed. In his book *How the Scots Invented the Modern World*,[5] Arthur Herman details the contributions of famous Scots such as James Watt, Adam Smith, David Hume and many others whose work in fields like economics, philosophy, engineering and science laid the groundwork for the modern world. What's amazing is that all these intellectuals lived within a few kilometres of each other and produced world-changing ideas within a few decades of each other.

Calcutta, in her prime, was the intellectual hub of India between 1840 and 1920, a period now known as the Bengal Renaissance. As the capital of the British Raj, Calcutta emerged as a promising ground for new, untested ideas. Rabindranath Tagore was at the helm of this cultural movement, but Calcutta had several other thinkers, poets and artists living at the same time and interacting with each other. Over the last 150 years, some of the greatest artists, thinkers, philosophers and scientists, including Nobel Prize winner S.N. Bose, were products of this culture that prized intellectual curiosity and discovery above all else.

Impressionism, the nineteenth-century art movement that changed the world of art forever, was centred on a few French artists like Monet, Renoir, Degas, Pissarro and others, many of whom were close friends. They all worked in the years between 1874 and 1886, often collaborating with one another. They challenged and inspired each other to strive for new heights and to question the conventional dogma in the field of art that had not changed for centuries. These artists created such an extraordinary body of work that they are now considered modern masters. In his book *The Geography of Genius*, Eric Weiner traces the history of creative hotbeds from places such as ancient Athens, which birthed modern philosophy, and Florence, that kick-started the Renaissance, to Vienna of the twentieth century that gave birth to new intellectual ideas across many fields. And finally, it covers Silicon Valley, the hotbed of innovation that has changed the world more than once in the last fifty years. It is very rare for the confluence of historical events, major policy choices and a lot of luck to come together at the same time, creating the perfect situation for an ecosystem to thrive. And when the conditions are right, it often snowballs into unstoppable momentum. We are seeing the new AI ecosystem grow around OpenAI and Google, mostly concentrated in the city of San Francisco.

The rise of entrepreneurial ecosystems in Silicon Valley, Israel, Beijing and Bengaluru has taken place in the last fifty years and it all started with things coming together in Silicon Valley. Until 1950, most skilled engineers worked for large corporations such as GE, IBM, 3M, Kodak and others, companies that had the wherewithal to take innovations outside the lab and into the market, through viable products and distribution. If you were a talented engineer, it would have been difficult for you to take an early-stage insight or hunch and work as an independent operator to build your own equity. If at all you were inclined to take the risk, you would need to have significant collateral to take loans on onerous terms—a big deterrent for many aspiring entrepreneurs. As a result, most engineers worked for large organizations with massive budgets and machinery to be able to translate new breakthroughs into products and distribution. AT&T Bell Labs and Xerox PARC are examples of corporate-funded research centres that contributed to many fundamental breakthroughs, including many Nobel Prize-winning ideas.

The Rise of Silicon Valley

In the aftermath of World War II, many factors favouring Silicon Valley came together at the right time. Stanford University was established in California in the early twentieth century and the administration actively encouraged collaboration between academia and industry, which was not the norm at the time. During World War II, many defence contractors such as HP and Lockheed Martin increased their presence in the Bay Area to be close to the academic excellence of Stanford but also to be as far away as possible from the theatre of war. This significantly increased the density of talented engineers in the Bay Area.

In 1956, Nobel Laureate William Shockley, inventor of the transistor, founded Shockley Semiconductor in Mountain View, thus laying the foundation stone of silicon in what would eventually be known as Silicon Valley. As engineers from Shockley Semiconductor left to start Fairchild Semiconductor, and then many folks from Fairchild left to start Intel, the Valley juggernaut started to move along. The tech prowess of engineers and the ultra-liberal culture of California in the Sixties and Seventies gave rise to the garage culture in which engineers would come together to discuss new ideas and tinker with new gadgets. One such garage encounter brought Steve Jobs and Steve Wozniak together, leading to the founding of Apple and kick-starting unheard-of fortunes at breakneck speed. After this, the flywheel became unstoppable. Each success not only trained the next generation of engineers and entrepreneurs but also brought in more venture firms to build on the momentum;

the successes kept coming, culminating in the dot-com bubble of the late Nineties.

As the prominence of Silicon Valley grew, it attracted talented engineers and entrepreneurs from around the world, thus creating a very dense and colliding network of people who were going to change the world, leading to a flurry of innovation and the creation of massive fortunes in a matter of a decade or less. Many of the folks who found success in the Valley started to carry these ideas and ambitions back to their countries of origin. In the last two decades, Valley-like ecosystems have emerged around the world.

The rise of Silicon Valley is a tale merely sixty years old, but it has created tens of trillions of dollars of value and completely transformed the world in the last half century. I was very fortunate to spend nearly a decade in the Valley, at the height of the dot-com boom, and I got to experience its energy and drive up close. This has shaped many of the ideas and principles that fuel my own approach to entrepreneurship.

Israel Leading the Way in Security and Deep Tech

Another start-up hotspot that has emerged is Israel, which has been called 'Start-Up Nation' due to the extraordinarily high number of ventures that have been founded in the region. Various factors have contributed to this high density of start-ups—other than Silicon Valley, Tel Aviv has more start-ups per capita than any other city in the world, according to a 2019 report.[6] Due to the mandatory military service required in the country, young people are exposed to advanced technology, while learning to think through complex problems in high-risk situations.[7] Many start-up founders are former members of elite military units. In addition, the government of Israel has, since the 1990s, encouraged innovation through various programmes, incubators and funds that support fledgling companies working on unique ideas. Israel also has deep connections with the US due to the very prominent Jewish population in America, making it easy for Israeli start-ups to find relevant networks in the US and to be able to sell their products to the right companies. This led to an increase in companies as well as investments in the region, which in turn led to more government support. These are the kinds of cycles that create thriving entrepreneurial ecosystems.

Israel is now a global leader in cybersecurity, which is driven, in no small way, by the delicate geopolitical balance of the region, forcing the tiny country to be on constant alert and continue to think of ways to outfox any possible adversaries. Now, Israeli firms are leading the pack in many high-tech areas such as biotech, clean energy, robotics and AI.

The Rise of Bengaluru as a Start-Up Hotspot in India

India has seen its own version of a thriving entrepreneurial ecosystem evolve in the last few decades. The foundation stone of new-age entrepreneurship in India was laid by companies like Infosys, whose founders didn't come from traditional industrial backgrounds but who bootstrapped their companies with very modest start-up capital. These companies helped put India on the map and trained the first generation of technology talent that could later consider building more ambitious products and companies. Later on, companies such as Naukri.com, Shaadi.com, Just Dial and MakeMyTrip were founded just as the Internet was starting to have a meaningful presence in India in the late Nineties and early 2000s. The nascent entrepreneurial system in India was jolted heavily and nearly wiped out in the aftermath of the dot-com boom. But the IT services ecosystem continued to thrive and, in fact, got a massive boost in the late Nineties due to the widespread fear of Y2K (the doomsday scenario that many anticipated as the world rolled into 2000 because most early software code used only two digits for the year and hence wouldn't be able to deal with the year 2000 and would malfunction in unpredictable ways). Indian software companies rose to the challenge and in the process created a highly trained pool of software engineers.

The major catalyst for the Indian entrepreneurial ecosystem came in the first decade of 2000 when funds such as Sequoia, Accel (then Erasmic), Kalaari (then NEA-IndoUS), Chirate (then IDG ventures), Helion and Westbridge, among others, started raising funds over $100 million to invest in Indian entrepreneurs for India-specific opportunities. Around the same time, we saw many Indian-origin engineers, entrepreneurs and VCs returning to India after a decade or more of experience in the Valley and, in many cases, with massive success already under their belts. They thus brought back with them not only a highly trained skill set but also elements of Valley culture that have since shaped the Indian entrepreneurial ecosystem.

The digital potential of the Indian economy was fully unleashed with the rise of smartphones from 2010 onwards. This was further boosted by cheap bandwidth with the launch of Jio in 2016. As Indian entrepreneurs figured out how to reach the vast and growing middle class of India through digital channels, they started to see off-the-charts growth that was previously unheard of. Flipkart became a household name within a few years, and I watched the whole story unfold from very close quarters at Myntra. As these companies grew rapidly, they attracted some of the top venture investors from around the globe like Tiger Global, Naspers and Softbank, pumping in billions of dollars to buy a piece of the action.

Simultaneously, companies such as Google, Amazon and Facebook recognized that India is home to nearly 20 per cent of humanity, and as the population grew digitally connected, this was where they could derive a lot of their future growth. With this belief, they have cumulatively invested tens of billions of dollars in the country, helping to grow the talent pool, deepen competencies and train the next generation of entrepreneurs.

The Indian entrepreneurial ecosystem took off in a big way in the second decade of the 2000s and never looked back. Every year, we see thousands of entrepreneurs take on big problems, while we've watched the emergence of over one hundred unicorns, a number that will only grow in the time to come. India continues to attract massive VC and private equity funding, which topped the charts at $60 billion in 2021. While the entire industry went through a much-needed reset in 2023, due to the excesses of pandemic-fuelled euphoria around digital companies, the long-term trends remain very promising. The Indian entrepreneurial ecosystem is coming of age and is poised to play a big role as India emerges as a major global superpower in the next quarter century, topping $30 trillion in its GDP by 2050.

Entrepreneurs have shaped the world in a major way in the last half century and the potential impact of entrepreneurship seems to have no bounds. Elon Musk has single-handedly created the private space sector as well as tipped the world towards the adoption of electric vehicles at a mass scale. Indian entrepreneurs such as Vijay Shekhar Sharma and Sameer Nigam have built world-class payment infrastructure. Sridhar Vembu and Girish Mathrubootham have shown that Indian start-ups can be globally competitive. People like Nithin Kamath and Lalit Keshre have made participation in the broader market as easy as a click of a button and many others continue to challenge the status quo and reinvent entire industries. Bhavish Aggarwal at Ola and Tarun Mehta at Ather are leading the charge in building the electric vehicle future of the country. Today Indian entrepreneurs are super confident, have the necessary skill set and access to resources to be able to take on any major challenge.

India has gone one step ahead of even Silicon Valley by virtue of a very successful private–public entrepreneurship that has created India Stack. This layer of foundational technologies will result in highly valuable public digital goods that can make population-scale innovation a lot easier, cheaper and faster. In the coming decade, India Stack will power a torrent of innovation that will make the past decade look like a warm-up. As we deep dive into the key principles of entrepreneurship in subsequent chapters, I can't be more excited and optimistic about what Indian entrepreneurs will create, not only for India but for the world!

Monopolies and Regulations

As the Industrial Revolution kicked into high gear, it also saw the gradual concentration of capital—both physical and intellectual—in a few hands. Once someone gets a small advantage, it tends to snowball into a progressively bigger advantage. It is a lot easier for anyone with surplus capital or connections to take advantage of a new emerging opportunity. Large companies can throw a lot of capital at a problem to crush emerging new competition. Technology also tends to have network effects play out where the flywheel takes hold and keeps getting better. Amazon, due to its size, can source goods at the cheapest prices which brings in even more customers and the bargaining power for Amazon grows even more. With the dominant share of search, Google collects an incredible amount of data on a daily basis which makes the search algorithms better, then bringing in even more users and search queries, generating even more data and so on. From the early days of industrialization, these patterns have played out again and again and it is important for entrepreneurs to understand and protect themselves from getting crushed or ending up the victim of rent-seeking by large platforms. This is also an area where regulators need to play a more active role.

In the last few centuries, as the size of trade, colonial wars and global empires grew, so did the need for financing on a large scale. The first family to capitalize on this on a global scale was the Rothschilds in Europe who, over three generations, built a massive financial empire and became the financiers for many of Europe's monarchs and large corporations. They were instrumental in financing many wars—sometimes for both sides! The US saw the similar emergence of J.P. Morgan as the pre-eminent financier.[8] He initially played a big role in raising money for the railroads and amassed a major fortune that enabled him to help shape bailouts and significant mergers and eventually help establish the US federal reserve system to steer the currency and the economy. Financiers such as Morgan began playing an outsized role in the global economy, much like George Soros and Warren Buffett do in modern times, albeit not to such an extent. Today the entire financial system of the world is dominated by a few large banks that are commonly seen as 'too big to fail'. When these banks get carried away during bubbles and overexert themselves, governments are forced to bail them out, as we saw during the last financial crisis as well as in the case of quite a few banks in India in the recent past.

As the world embraced industrialization on a global scale, many large industries began to rise across fields such as shipping, trading, railroads, cotton and sugar. The promoters for these companies were able to access global financing systems in order to have massive leverage. Some of them reached incredible heights, exerting a monopoly in their fields, employing all kinds of methods to squash the competition, and raking in unheard of profits, giving rise to billionaires with unchecked power for the first time in history. Governments and regulators were decades behind and were in no position to exert any control over these wealthy and powerful individuals and families. Very soon, tycoons such as Vanderbilt, J.P. Morgan, Rockefeller, Jay Gould and Andrew Carnegie were not only obscenely rich but had deep political influence, often steering government actions in their favour, further boosting their power, privilege and unassailable monopoly. It is not for nothing that many such industrialists and financiers from the late nineteenth centuries are known as robber barons.

As their power and influence grew, so did resentment against the robber barons who had become the new overlords of the world. The growing resentment was not lost on governments, and the Sherman Antitrust Act, enacted in 1890 in the US, took the first definitive steps towards breaking the monopolies. This paved the way for many more legislations against price fixing and anti-competitive mergers and acquisitions (M&As), which eventually led to the break-up of AT&T and a huge government lawsuit against Microsoft in the late 1990s. As the data monopolies and exorbitant fee extortions by large platforms are growing in our times, there is a renewed legislative push in Europe and other parts of the world to limit the predatory tactics of Big Tech.

Platforms such as Google, Apple and Facebook have become the gateway to the Internet. Anyone who wants to sell anything online is compelled to go to these platforms and pay up to 30 per cent of the transaction value to these platforms. This creates a huge Internet tax on fledgling start-ups who are not able to make their business model work. A great example of countering these rent-seeking platforms is the rise of 'Namma Yatri', a free auto-hailing service in Bengaluru that doesn't charge the usual 15–20 per cent that platforms such as Uber and Ola charge, but instead takes a flat fee of just Rs 25 and passes on the entire fare amount to the user directly. This is built on top of the Beckn Protocol, which is an integral part of the India Stack. Now the auto drivers pay barely 1 per cent of their daily fare to the platform, significantly boosting their take-home incomes.

In recent years, regulatory authorities in India are paying more attention to the policies and tactics being employed by large platforms. This is even more important as AI has taken the world by storm. We are looking at a massive wave of automation and productivity boost in the coming years and data will be the largest fuel driving the upcoming AI revolution. Who has access to this data and who gets to control and use it will have a huge bearing on value creation in the future. On the one hand, there is absolutely no dearth of entrepreneurial opportunities in India, but simultaneously it is critical to have a level playing field for new start-ups and a reasonable degree of protection for the entrepreneurial ecosystem to thrive. In India's quest for a $30 trillion economy, strong participation and contribution from entrepreneurs is critical. We have the talent, the right tailwinds and a proactive government that is creating programmes to further boost the ecosystem. We are in for a super exciting time ahead and hopefully the coming chapters will equip potential entrepreneurs with enough tools and inspiration to embark on an audacious journey to make the world a better place.

2

Foundation Matters

The journey of a thousand miles begins with one step.

—Old Chinese proverb

The best way to predict the future is to create it.

—Peter Drucker

The biggest risk is not taking any risk. In a world that's changing quickly, the only strategy that is guaranteed to fail is not taking risks.

—Mark Zuckerberg

To Start or Not to Start!

I'd like to start this chapter by acknowledging that not everyone needs to start a company. Just as everyone doesn't need to scale Mount Everest (which has a 1 per cent fatality rate) or get into politics (damage rate unknown!) or be an IPL star (a club of only 1000 people) or work in Bollywood (unless your parents are in Bollywood, then you have no choice!) and so on. Entrepreneurship is just another profession or way of being that doesn't need to be any more or less glamorous than others.

Every adventure comes with its pros, cons and risk profiles. Skydiving is supposed to be super thrilling, but most people will never attempt it because every now and then, the parachute doesn't open, and then it's not so thrilling after all. For those seeking an even more nerve-racking and goosebump-inducing experience, there is the sport of free solo which is rock climbing without any harness—which means that if you make a mistake, you don't live to tell the tale. And yet, some people are adventurous (or foolhardy) enough to try free soloing. I am no one to judge what's right or wrong for anyone. All you need to do is make an informed choice after truly understanding the risk–reward equation, and then you will be on your way to live out your destiny.

When you're starting a company, it is even more important to understand what risk–reward ratios mean. Here's an example to illustrate this idea. I give you 50:50 odds in a bet in which, if you win, you can double your money, but if you lose, you lose your investment. If you choose to play this game, half the time you will lose. Let's assume you lose the very first time, and that's all the capital you could afford. Then you go home empty-handed, but it's a fair outcome as you chose to play the game knowing fully well what the odds were. Now, let's say, we change the game and the probability is now 10:90, meaning that you have only one in ten chances of winning or that you might lose nine out of ten times. On top of that, we say that the prize for winning is nine times your earnings. Now, let's say, you choose to play this game ten times in a row and you bet Rs 100 every time, and the probabilities play out as per the design, which means you lose nine times and win once. So, you would have bet a total of Rs 1000 over ten bets and the one time that you win, you will get your Rs 1000 back. If you happen to strike the right answer in your first attempt, you would have gotten ten times your initial investment. On the other hand, you might try this four times in a row and lose all four times and that is a very reasonable outcome too, given the odds.

In my opinion, entrepreneurship is quite like playing the betting games I described above. It is a fact that 90 per cent of start-ups will shut down. When you add up the number of people who start up and those who actually walk back with handsome returns after ten years, the risk adjusted rewards just don't seem to make sense. The truth is that there are so many factors at play, many of which are beyond your control, that the probabilities are never fully in your favour. So does that mean that anyone who is able to think reasonably should not try their hand at entrepreneurship? Absolutely not! In fact, I obviously feel that this is the most enriching experience one could ever ask for. But, it's important to know what game you are getting into and what you can expect. Once you accept a bet with certain probabilities, you must accept both outcomes as long as these are in line with the probability you signed up for. There is no shame in losing a bet which has 1:9 odds of working out three times in a row. You may do everything right as an entrepreneur and yet it might not work out, which is an absolutely fair, acceptable and even respectable outcome.

So, why does anyone choose to be an entrepreneur? There are many situations in which the journey itself is the reward and entrepreneurship is one of them. Any entrepreneurial journey ends up teaching you so much about who you are. You will have numerous enriching experiences, your learning curve shoots through the roof and you have adventures (and misadventures!) that you will remember for the rest of your life. In fact, any meaningful entrepreneurial stint ends up making you a much better professional thanks to the accelerated learning curve and ability to problem solve in real-world situations with no safety net, and this is priceless no matter where you work in the future. It is important to get into this with your eyes wide open so that you are able to embrace all outcomes, taking failure in your stride instead of regretting the choices you made.

Why Start in the First Place?

These days, successful entrepreneurs are celebrated on the cover pages of magazines or star in shows such as *Shark Tank* where they are supposed to display instant wisdom about what the next billion-dollar idea is. Entrepreneurs are treated as celebrities and inspire many people to crave the same level of success through the derring-do of building a new company and leading it to a massive, billion-dollar IPO. We all need role models, and there is nothing wrong with taking inspiration from people who have made something out of nothing and are able to share their learning by paying it forward. But that alone cannot be your reason to start.

ENTREPRENEURIAL WISDOM

On Waiting for an Idea

If you really want to start a company, you can't sit around waiting for a good idea to strike. You need to be proactive, finding inspiration everywhere you go. You need to seek ideas out because ideas aren't going to find you. If you truly want to build something, go out there and start building it.

There are many reasons why people start a company, and all of them are valid. Many entrepreneurs start when they find a problem that they feel compelled to solve, or a problem they believe they are most uniquely suited to solve. For example, the idea of Zepto came about during the pandemic when the founders were struggling to get grocery supplies in their rented apartments in Mumbai.[1] The luggage brand Mokobara came to be when the founder himself experienced frustration when his good-looking piece of luggage broke. It led him to the realization that India lacked a brand that offered both quality and affordability. Eric Yuan came up with Zoom as a solution to a long-distance relationship in which he had to travel ten hours just to see his partner. Are there problems you encounter in your daily life that you feel you deeply want to solve?

Another good reason for starting up is if you see yourself as a fairly independent person with stand-alone opinions. Some people want to do things their way. They don't want a boss telling them what to do. This was certainly the case for me when I started my first job with Deloitte Consulting. It was a huge firm, spread over dozens of offices all over the US, and I started at the bottom of the totem pole as a business analyst. The rules of the game were clearly established, and I would be given a task which I was expected to complete without any clarity or big picture understanding of what we as a company were trying to achieve and why. I would feel quite lost and wouldn't get any answers to any meaningful 'why' questions. Despite my best intentions, I was able to last for only eighteen months and my very first attempt at entrepreneurship was borne out of this deep craving for autonomy.

Like me, you too might experience the urge to live and work on your own terms, outside the structures of a traditional company where you feel like a tiny cog in a very large machine.

To some extent, the decision to become an entrepreneur means choosing a life of greater freedom. It is a conscious decision to step away from the safety and comfort of a familiar world in which you can run on autopilot, without having to ask deeper questions or reflect on your true purpose. It can allow you to reconnect with your authentic self, so that you can grow into your full potential. At the same time, not everyone is cut out for entrepreneurship and not everyone gives it a shot for the right reasons. Starting up has become something of a trend, and many people are quitting their full-time jobs for what they think is a better and more glamorous life. They jump into entrepreneurship without really envisioning what it means to be an entrepreneur. And there is often a mismatch between their life goals and their business achievements, resulting in a lack of fulfilment. You might have a great idea and start an incredibly successful business that requires you to work long hours and travel across the world. But if you are the kind of person who values travel for leisure or eating dinner with your family every single night, it doesn't matter how many billions your company makes, you'll never feel truly satisfied.

One motivation for many entrepreneurs is to have a larger impact or make the world a better place. They have this deep conviction that things can be a lot better than they are and that, by creating a new product or service, they will be able to improve the lives of many. Bill Gates wanted to see a desktop in every home. CostCo founder James Sinegal obsessed about helping customers to save every last penny that they could and designed all policies at CostCo to be able to deliver on this. Before Nike was an iconic shoe retailer, Phil Knight was a track runner at the University of Oregon and he, along with his coach Bill Bowerman, tinkered endlessly to create a shoe that would give long-distance runners an edge on the field. Muhammad Yunus, who went on to win a Nobel Prize, pioneered the concept of microcredit and microfinance to help the poor to break the cycle of abject poverty.

It is difficult to decide whether you want to pursue entrepreneurship without knowing what exactly it entails. If you meet a lot of entrepreneurs, including those who might not have had any success for five or even ten years, you will have a much better sense of what the journey will look like. We all suffer from 'survivorship bias'. This bias refers to our tendency to only look at those who have made it to the top, be it sports professionals, film stars or even entrepreneurs. We remain blissfully unaware of all the folk who have taken the same road but whose ideas fizzled out somewhere along the way.

When you speak with entrepreneurs, ask about their journey, the struggles and challenges they faced, what they enjoy about the experience, and how they feel when, despite years of effort and sacrifice, they don't have much to show for it. These stories will help you understand the nature of the game and the likely highs and lows. One of the biggest things most entrepreneurs talk about, irrespective of success or failure, is the accelerated pace of learning and the clearing away of all preconceived notions about how things work. You get to deal with real problems as they are and as you wrestle with these problems, you keep building stronger muscles while also gaining sharper insights about yourself. Often, this alone is worth its weight in gold.

Nvidia founder Jensen Huang puts it succinctly when he says that 'Money is the only singular reason not to start a company because starting a company has a very low probability of success. And so if that is your reason for doing it, you will likely regret the experience.'[2]

After considering what it takes to embark on an entrepreneurial journey and having clarity about why this should matter to you as well as what you hope to get out of the experience, you can make a much more informed decision. And once you decide, you will be mentally prepared for what to expect and ready to enjoy every minute of the roller coaster, where the highs tend to keep getting higher and the lows get lower. But that's why you ride roller coasters.

When to Start

Pixie Curtis is perhaps the youngest entrepreneur, with a brand of fidget toys. She has achieved significant entrepreneurial success already with annual sales of over $100,000. In fact, she retired in 2023, at the age of eleven, so she could focus on school! Michael Dell started Dell computers from his dorm room when he was twenty years old. Mark Zuckerberg was only nineteen when he launched Facebook at his alma mater, Harvard. Colonel Sanders started his restaurant chain KFC at the age of sixty-five. Bernie Marcus started Home Depot at the age of fifty and is now worth six billion dollars. Falguni Nayar was fifty when she started Nykaa in 2012. I was in my early thirties when I started Myntra. We see that entrepreneurs start at almost any age. From teenagers who start companies in high school to college students dropping out to start companies, to every age group thereafter, there doesn't seem to be any one template for when to start a company. In fact, looking at the overall data of entrepreneurs, it has been found that people who start in their forties have the highest record for success. This might be because they have the right combination of experience, drive, energy, wisdom and patience, all critical ingredients for entrepreneurship. We hear a lot more about young entrepreneurs, perhaps because so many people start companies in their younger years, when they have nothing to lose, and the experience is immensely valuable for their future careers, irrespective of the outcome.

At age thirty-nine, Vera Wang was considered older than most brides at the time and found it hard to find a dress she liked.[3] Her father, a businessman, identified this as an opportunity. While he didn't have any experience in the garments industry, he recognized the potential, because people would always want to get married, ensuring a steady stream of customers. Besides, custom bridal wear would not need to have a high inventory. Wang had worked as a stylist for Vogue and as an accessory designer for Ralph Lauren. This experience in fashion prepared her for her journey as a designer.

In an interview with the *Harvard Business Review*, Wang talked about how working for someone else was like getting paid to learn, and that the learning curve at both her jobs was steep.[4] She said, 'You have to learn what came before so that you know (a) you're not really that inventive, and (b) which rules you want to break. Then keep your head down, don't get involved in politics, be respectful, be grateful that you have the job, do your job, and most of all, be available.' In addition, Wang says she draws on her childhood experience as a figure skater—where she learnt discipline and how to pick herself up after falling down—as well as her multicultural heritage and her travels in Europe, in her work. Wang might seem like an 'older entrepreneur', but the problem she faced is a universal one, and she was in the right place at the right time.

More important than thinking about a 'right' age to launch a company is paying attention to one's overall readiness to start. This includes having the relevant skill sets, a healthy appetite for risk, comfort with all the possible outcomes, financial support, social support and a deep belief in the idea which is the seed. These are things one might have at any stage in life and aren't tied to age. If you feel ready and willing to try this out in your twenties, by all means go for it, as long as you understand what you are getting into. Similarly, if you are in your fifties and feel you would like to go through the adventure of building a company, you might have a better shot than most as long as you are also willing to learn new things and demonstrate a beginner's mindset. The bottom line is that no particular age is ideal for a would-be entrepreneur. It is a function of each individual's personal situation and what they hope to get out of an entrepreneurial stint.

What Idea to Start With

Trying to answer the question of what field to start up in can be even harder than figuring out when to start as there is literally no dearth of promising new opportunities. Every year, people start tens of thousands of companies in India alone and perhaps hundreds of thousands around the world. Given that most of these start-ups will fail and that no one is really able to predict which ones will take off, there is a huge degree of uncertainty on day one. When starting out, no one has the clarity required to say that something will work or not with true conviction. But you need to start somewhere, and there are some patterns that will be helpful to follow.

The first and probably the most reliable method is to look for an area that you have already had some meaningful exposure to, giving you some prior context and insight. Sachin and Binny Bansal worked for Amazon before starting Flipkart. No doubt that experience gave them insights into how a large e-commerce giant works. The experience would also have taught them what could be done much better in the Indian context. My friend Dheeraj Pandey, who started Nutanix, chose to focus on the enterprise CRM space once again for his second start-up, DevRev. He knew that he would benefit from his deep understanding of the enterprise tech stack and that he would be able to build a strong enterprise sales engine that could be leveraged. If you work in a large or fast growth company, you can try to zoom out and ask questions such as what are the current gaps in the offering, what are emerging players doing in the space, what you could do to dramatically improve the offering, or what dream projects you would like to work on that the company's current strategy or hierarchy is not enabling. Many people develop deep context and insights from their current work environments and these become the seeds of a start-up idea.

ENTREPRENEURIAL WISDOM

On Sharpening the Axe

You can and should start building the skills and competencies you need for entrepreneurship well before you start a company. The most important of these is learning about yourself: what kind of entrepreneur you want to be, what your strengths and weaknesses are, what purpose drives you and what your ambitions are.

You have to start sharpening the axe hours before chopping down the tree.

Another way to look for new opportunities is to track emerging technology, consumer or business trends. Whenever megatrends such as cloud or AI crop up, they always lead to a reordering of the world, becoming fertile ground for new ideas and companies. Aspiring entrepreneurs would do well to track these trends and study them in great depth. If you feel that generative AI will lead to a lot of new applications, you need to spend a year studying this at a very deep level. Read a number of books on AI, meet a lot of experts, download and play with many apps in this space, enrol for online courses to systematically study the field while continuing to create possibilities in your head and seeing which one is starting to stick.

A third very reliable way to find a good starting point is to be on the lookout for what other people are starting. If there are a lot of really smart people trying to solve the same problem in many different ways, chances are that something real is going to transpire. A gold rush only starts after someone spots gold dust. Let's look back to the period 2008–14 when e-commerce took off in India. There were a large number of people trying all types of e-commerce models in the last few years of the first decade of this century, as everyone could see that the combination of the Internet and a lack of organized retail in the country had the potential to create a market for online shopping. When some of the early companies like Flipkart and Myntra started to get some traction, many start-ups came up in every conceivable consumer category. The same is true of the EdTech companies that started between 2014 and 2018 or the fintech companies of 2016–20. There is obviously a risk in following the herd, and if you are among the last people to join the party without strong clarity about what will give you a unique right-to-win, you might end up being just another copycat company. The right way to look at this is to understand that this area will probably generate some meaningful companies and if you are also able to see an angle that most people are not seeing, you might be able to establish a strong foothold.

Sometimes you happen to have an excellent idea to solve a problem that you encounter on a daily basis. If you can solve the problem for yourself, chances are that millions of other people will also benefit from the same solution and voila, you have a great start-up idea! Reed Hastings, who founded Netflix, was frustrated with the working of Blockbuster film rentals and the enormous late fees they charged.[5] So, he built a service with a no late-fee model. Canva's founders saw how difficult it was to create great graphics with Photoshop,[6] so they came up with their own solution. When I looked at fitness in 2016, I realized that most people found it very difficult to start a fitness journey, as gyms were not of great quality and there was a huge learning curve involved in figuring out the right techniques for various equipment. With this approach, you might not be able to get the timing exactly right or the target market may turn out to be very small. But many meaningful companies have grown because someone cared deeply about a problem and set out to solve it in a unique way, eventually creating a meaningful impact on the lives of millions of people.

Personally, my desire to build something on my own was much stronger than the call of any particular domain or problem that I cared about deeply in my early days as an entrepreneur. I tried my hand at many things over a decade until I finally stumbled upon the idea of selling fashion products online. But in this process, I kept learning about entrepreneurship as well as about myself and it ended up being a very long and practical MBA in entrepreneurship. But this approach can be painful as you may not have anything to show for your efforts for a very long period of time. I have had numerous periods of self-doubt and struggle, bogged down by a sense of being stuck in one place for a long period of time. But as they say, 'You become a painter by painting.' So, spending as much time as possible around entrepreneurial set-ups may be a great way to sharpen your entrepreneurial chops.

Small or Big?

A myth about entrepreneurship is that only people who achieve unicorn status or have a spectacular IPO are truly successful entrepreneurs. Nothing can be farther from the truth. Every time someone opens a *kirana* store or buys an auto to ferry passengers or opens a beauty salon, they are as entrepreneurial as anyone else. The rules of entrepreneurship still apply, albeit at a different scale. You need to have an initial thesis and sense of the market (TAM: total addressable market), you need to decide your initial product or service (GTM: go-to-market), you need to put in the start-up capital through a combination of debt or equity, you need to acquire customers and you need to make the unit economics work so that you start to generate a profit. In fact, most small businesses are really good at generating return-on-capital anywhere between 20–50 per cent which most VCs will be hard pressed to do themselves!

Any level of entrepreneurship can be both meaningful and worthwhile and where you want to play is an independent choice. Someone who builds a small restaurant that is always packed or a law practice that is highly sought after for complicated cases is just as successful as someone with a thousand times the scale. You need to think long and hard about what kind of scale you want to aim for, as this will dramatically change how you prepare for your journey. What future do you see for yourself? What will give you a sense of fulfilment and meaning? Depending on the scale you target, you will be taking proportionately larger risks and will have to let go of ownership to find the capital you need for building the business. If you have larger ambitions, you must pick something with large market potential. You may also be better off building a strong founding team if you want to go after a big opportunity, while for a small business, founders can do very well working solo. Similarly, your own capital or a round of funding from friends and family may be sufficient for a small business, but to build something on a bigger scale, you will have to think deeply about raising capital from professional institutions with significant ownership dilution.

Starting up Without Taking Any Risk

People think that the start-up journey starts with a big bang. You announce to your organization that you are leaving to start a new company, you update your LinkedIn profile with 'stealth entrepreneur', and you start to hang out at cafes and conferences frequented by entrepreneurs. But this is not the only way to be entrepreneurial. I believe entrepreneurship is a skill that can be practised in any domain. Building a company from scratch is just one way to learn and practise these skills, but there are many other avenues that are available to us which come with very little risk.

The organization that you are currently working for may have products that are doing very well; it may also be lagging in areas in which competitors may have better offerings. You might realize that the morale in the company is not great or maybe that people in the company have started losing a first-hand connection with customers. All these gaps offer you the opportunity to develop entrepreneurial skills—so identify a problem and spend some time working on it.

Once you have a deeper understanding of the problem and how you might be able to address it, reach out to your manager or even the CEO of the company, and present your case. If you have done your homework well and you have drafted a crisp, well-articulated note, you may be surprised at the positive reception you might get. Most people fail to get additional responsibilities not because managers deny them but because they never ask. You can start work on your project with meagre resources and try to move the needle forward slowly. That's what entrepreneurs do for a living. The art of making something from nothing can only get better with practice. In my very first job at Deloitte Consulting, I had such an opportunity. Taking the initiative, I suggested a major change in the approach to a project and shared it with the project director after doing my homework. To my surprise, he agreed to make that change.

You can also practise this entrepreneurial approach in your personal life. You could organize a book club or a trekking club or a team for a sport that you love. This will again require you to formulate a plan, recruit members to participate in the activity, organize weekly or monthly sessions, manage logistics and ensure that everyone has a great experience. If you do this well, a few months down the line, you might have something that will acquire a life of its own and might even operate without you. I organized a cricket team from scratch during my Bay Area days. We played regularly for two years, and I made a lot of new friends in the process.

Finding zero-to-one opportunities in your everyday life and then making progress with your own initiative will boost your confidence and make you a better entrepreneur. These initiatives don't require any major risks—you will not lose any capital or even compromise on progress in your current job. In fact, you may see your everyday life get better. You might acquire skills faster and you may even get promoted faster—all of this without ever setting a foot in that cafe where all the cool entrepreneurs hang out!

Preparing to Start Well

Entrepreneurship is hard for everyone, whether you are just starting out or have been at it for a long time. There are so many unknowns. Each area of focus is very different, and you have no idea how many other people are solving similar problems or if there are big companies deploying unlimited resources that you can't match. The only way to get ready for anything difficult is to prepare well. If you want to attempt a trek to Everest Base Camp, you don't just wake up one day and start climbing. You plan meticulously, get yourself in shape, get all the accessories you need, potentially hire a guide and maybe build your stamina with smaller treks first. It should be the same for entrepreneurship. As Abraham Lincoln said, 'Give me six hours to chop down a tree and I will spend the first five sharpening the axe.' Sharpening the entrepreneurial axe starts long before you take your initial plunge.

First comes the journey of figuring out who you are, what your real aspirations are, what you enjoy doing and what your natural strengths and weaknesses are. Having some kind of daily or weekly practice to just reflect on your day or week—what's going well, what's missing and what can be better—can offer you a window into your deeper yearnings. One powerful exercise is to visualize your life five or ten years from now and describe it in detail. I call this 'Ten Pages for Ten Years.' Can you write ten pages about what you think might happen in your life over the next ten years? Your dreams, aspirations, health goals, financial goals, personal development goals, places that you want to visit, skills that you want to learn, new habits that you want to build, bad habits that you want to let go of and so on. There are no rules, and you should write whatever comes to mind, as the act of writing itself helps develop clarity.

You also need to build the mental fortitude to be able to deal with all the ups and downs. To be honest, the initial years consist mostly of downs, with some small wins thrown in every now and then. And even those tiny wins are not guaranteed! Starting up requires a bit of the Navy Seal's mindset of 'embrace the suck' where you learn how to use pain as fuel. Every time you are painted into a corner, just like Captain Kirk from *Star Trek*, you ask, 'How do I win from here?' If you ask that question seriously enough, you will see a ray of hope where earlier there was certain doom. You also need to have a social runway, as a lot of our mental fortitude comes from the people around us. Who are the positive people around you that you can reach out to in your moments of self-doubt when you are ready to throw in the towel? Who will listen to you with an open mind and be a non-judgemental sounding board? Who will just throw a warm, understanding arm around your shoulder with the calm reassurance that you will figure it out?

Next is immersing yourself deeply in your domain. Spending considerable time getting to know the current body of knowledge, the generally accepted rules and principles, the dominant and emerging players, and the new technological shifts will ensure that your initial insights and convictions don't come undone under a cursory scrutiny. There is an advantage to being an outsider, as you can think from first principles, challenge the mainstream dogma and bring in ideas and perspectives from other fields, compared to industry insiders. But still, there is no shortcut to doing the hard work to gain deeper insights into a domain. This takes time, patience and effort and while you do that, you will also need to guard yourself from starting to think like a veteran. If you fall for the accepted dogma, you will not be able to see the new angles or find conviction for something that hasn't yet been tested and tried.

You must also create enough runway for yourself. Start-up journeys are slow, hard and long and if you are going to run out of steam in six to twelve months, you are guaranteed to fail irrespective of how good your ideas are. It may be a long time before you can start to draw a salary or compensation and a big, life-changing cash out may be ten years away if it happens at all. Kunal Shah of CRED, during one of our conversations, mentioned that one of the most important lessons he learnt from his Freecharge days is to never run out of financial runway. This means saving enough from your current income or lining up definitive financial investments from friends and family so that you are not only able to fund the initial operations but also able to manage your personal and family requirements. Nothing is as hard for an entrepreneur as realizing that you can't even take your family out for a dinner or a small holiday as you are stretching your finances very thin. You are better off working for a few more years and tucking away some more money so that you don't have to cut down on the bare necessities. If you are in a double-income family, one person can continue to have a steady income while the other could try their hand at entrepreneurship and maybe eventually you can switch sides if both happen to have entrepreneurial ambitions.

The fifth is deliberately learning some skills. At first glance, an entrepreneur might look like a Jack of all trades, which is true to a large extent. If you run into a problem, you ought to be able to solve it, whether you have the skill set or not. You can think about the hard technical skills you need to know. For example, if you are going to be in the B2C space and customer acquisition is going to be important in the early years, you can do some courses in digital marketing and learn the basics. If you want to build something that will leverage AI deeply, attend a few AI conferences, read books and enrol yourself in some courses to learn as much as you can. You can also deliberately work on soft skills such as communication, the art of storytelling, building strong habits and rituals and even paying attention to your health as all these will play an important role in your entrepreneurial journey.

Entrepreneurship is a very long-term career, often measured in decades. If you truly become successful, you might end up doing this for the rest of your life! Sometimes you may be super excited about an idea and feel that unless you act now, the opportunity will pass you by and hence you must start today. While this may be the case for this opportunity, the truth is that, due to the accelerating nature of the world, the number of opportunities available next year will be more than those available this year, and those available the year after will be even better. A few years here and there will not make a difference, but a few years of strong preparation will give you a very strong foundation to put in your best effort when you do eventually start. This preparation will ensure that you are fortified against all the inevitable setbacks. When someone jumps into a new opportunity believing that they will never get this chance again, without laying the groundwork, it will often end in disappointment.

Who to Start With

When I was getting ready to move to India in October 2006 to start Myntra, I had lined up three potential co-founders with similar desires of returning to India to participate in the upcoming Internet boom. While I was booking my one-way ticket, one of them informed me that he couldn't move back and soon after, another said the same thing. The one remaining candidate and I moved back in November that year, but fundamental differences started emerging between us. Once it became clear that we couldn't work together, we parted ways, and I found myself without a co-founder. That was a pretty hard landing and a harbinger of what was to come. A month later, I had my very first meeting with an investor who told me that I would be better off with a high-paying job at a multinational company. Ouch! Since then, there was never a month without one setback or another. Fortunately, since I had worked for four start-ups in the

Bay Area before, none of this was a major surprise for me and I used every setback to figure out a new way to move forward. Six months into the journey, I had two very strong co-founders as well as our first seed round of $200,000 and we were on our way.

Building a company is a team game. No one, not even Steve Jobs, built a product or company single-handedly. The process of building a well-aligned team starts with choosing your co-founders. There is no template for the right number of co-founders. From Kunal Shah of CRED, who is a single founder, to Jack Ma of Alibaba, who started with fifteen co-founders, there are many possibilities. The most common configuration is two or three co-founders. I personally like this set-up the most. It offers a diversity of opinions and skill sets, and yet the group is small enough to bond tightly and find common alignment in terms of core values.

A common mistake people make is co-founding a company with friends, and while there are some successful examples, this often ends badly—for the company as well as the friendship. Friends might not know how to confront decisions more complex than what restaurant to go out to, and they might find it difficult to have objective debates when they disagree. On the other hand, colleagues you have worked with before might make much better co-founders. You already know their working style and might have had successes under the belt as a team. You'll know how they deal with tough situations—do they rise to the occasion and take responsibility or avoid the problem, hiding behind corporate speak? All of these dynamics are likely to play out in your own company, and with former colleagues, you will know what to expect. The eventual founders I chose for Myntra—Ashutosh and Vineet—were both people I had worked closely with for six months, getting to know their working styles and recognizing similar values and alignments on vision. Similarly, Ankit, who I started CureFit with, had worked closely with me for two years at Flipkart.

One of the things to keep in mind with co-founders is not to rush into making a decision—have several discussions with them in different settings and bring up difficult conversations to see how they respond. It is important that you share certain core values and feel confident about working together. In addition, make sure to have exhaustive discussions about roles and responsibilities, while emphasizing mutual accountability, so there is absolute clarity. The last thing to keep in mind is to ensure that everything is documented in extraordinary detail—from the equity structure, the rationale for different equity if that's the case, initial compensation, exact roles and who is going to be the CEO. Every company needs someone to be the final decision-maker to prevent decisions from dragging on or multiple power centres from emerging which can damage the culture. It is said that a chain is only as strong as its weakest link and a weak or toxic co-founder can destabilize a company. Unhealthy founder dynamics is one of the biggest reasons why start-ups fail in the first few years. On the other hand, when the founders work as a strong unit, they achieve things they could never have achieved individually.

Starting up can be an incredibly lonely journey. But the right co-founder can be the perfect sounding board when you're feeling alone or uncertain. They share your context and might even have their own demons to fight. A culture of frequent and transparent conversation can lead to fresh ideas and creative problem-solving, but, more importantly, can act as a form of therapy to lift your spirits, thus percolating into the broader company culture.

ENTREPRENEURIAL WISDOM

On Making Decisions

Often, single founders are able to make very quick decisions as they do not have to consult with a partner. On the other hand, while the speed of execution might go down when there are co-founders, the quality of decisions might increase. The different perspectives and the ensuing dialogue are likely to lead to decisions that are more well thought through.

So You Have Started ... Now What?

The day you commit to starting something, you will feel at once extraordinarily liberated and terrified. You are finally getting a shot at shaping your vague ambitions into a tangible product. You will be out of your comfort zone every day which will feel daunting but also fulfilling. You will be way out of your depth, but your learning pace will be better than ever before. You will wake up each morning feeling like your own boss, being able to set your own pace and work at your own schedule, and then you will have to find that discipline within yourself to show up at your desk and start laying the bricks with nobody watching over your shoulder or shouting about a deadline that you can't miss.

I like this Sidney Sheldon quote that says, 'A blank piece of paper is God's way of telling us how hard it is to be God.' Every time I confront the blank page to make progress with this book, I realize how challenging it is to fight the inertia to do something else instead. The biggest challenge in the early days of entrepreneurship is that you have no idea what to do. There is no one to guide you, give you tasks for the week or hold you accountable when you are just sitting on your butt all day waiting for inspiration to strike. In the first few months, it is critical that you design a routine that guarantees effort and progress each week. If you have a small team, it will be a good idea to have a team huddle every Monday, setting out clear outcomes that are expected from everyone for the coming week as well as reviewing the progress from the previous week. Make these forums as democratic as possible so that everyone can feel like a founding member, and you benefit from every voice. Create an environment where everyone can hold each other accountable so that even the most junior person on the team can demand quality output from the founders.

It will also help to create a six to twelve-month road map that lays out the journey for the initial product–market fit approach, the initial team that you need to build and your game plan for raising funds. You must set aside time to plan the organization's foundation in terms of key cultural tenets. On most days, you will be better off doing something tangible such as building a product, talking to customers, reaching out to investors or recruiting team members, rather than attending conferences and networking events or talking to other entrepreneurs, as these are unlikely to move you towards your goals.

It may be a great idea to also set aside some time every morning or evening to reflect so that you can process all that you are thinking, feeling and experiencing. In many ways, entrepreneurship is a journey of self-discovery. You have emerged from the protective cocoon of familiarity and found yourself unmoored, out there and completely on your own. Just as in the initial stages of a hero's journey, this is a great time to come to terms with your fears, your deeply held beliefs that may no longer hold water, hidden strengths that you have never explored before and activities and environments that inspire you. The Buddha said, 'The hardest thing to know is to know yourself.' Entrepreneurship opens the doorway to this higher realization, provided you pause every now and then to reflect.

Now that you have taken the first bold step, it is important that you make the most of every single day. Most people will never get the opportunity or have the courage to be on their own in their entire lifetime. Every day is an opportunity to try something new, learn something that you had never thought of before, meet interesting people and try new experiments, and you don't need permission from anyone to embrace it all.

Getting Used to Failing, Again and Again

It is critical to recognize that failing daily is a rite of passage as an entrepreneur. To borrow again from the hero's journey, the protagonist is tested every day. Just when you think it can't get any worse, it does. This is when you must grit your teeth, huddle with your co-founders, and ask, 'How do I win from here?' You might have to make minor adjustments at times or even completely discard the earlier approach for a fresh start. If you accept the failures and setbacks as a very natural and even desirable part of the journey, you can even start to view them as opportunities to grow and find deeper strength within yourself.

Failure is touted as the ultimate teacher in countless quotes. Most of our favourite stories involve a tragically flawed hero who eventually finds her true calling and rises to the occasion when it matters the most. Well, as an early-stage founder, you will find that you encounter your favourite teacher a little too often and, while painful, you will be grateful for this! To make matters worse, you may also start to feel a strain in your relationships or even poor health due to excessive stress and lack of sleep. It is not pretty by any stretch of the imagination and no part of this is glamorous in the least. But you can develop better health habits, make sure you guard your sleep, so you have a well-rested mind and protect your time with those that you care about so that you have some solace away from all the chaos that is part of your everyday life. You can keep chipping away at one problem at a time and you will be shocked at how fast you are able to learn and grow through these adversities.

Light at the End of the Tunnel. Or Maybe Not!

Now if this were a fairy tale, I would tell you that once you have gone through the struggles, figured out who you truly are, paid your dues through accelerated learnings and made all the necessary sacrifices, you will emerge triumphantly and will be feted as the next poster child of entrepreneurship. Alas, that is too simplistic and far from guaranteed. It is likely that you will encounter some wins among various setbacks; there are many possible legitimate outcomes which are all equally heroic in my opinion. Some things in life are truly about the journey, and not the destination, and entrepreneurship is definitely one of them. The line from the Bhagavad Gita, 'Do your duty and don't think about the results,' summarizes the perfect attitude to pursue on the path of entrepreneurship.

FROM PAGE TO ACTION

Now that you have some insight into building a solid foundation for a journey of entrepreneurship, here are a few questions and exercises to help you reflect on your aspirations:

a. **Are you hungry for risk?** Spend fifteen minutes reflecting on how you react to risk and uncertainty. Think about a time that you had to make a decision that involved some risk (financial, physical, emotional) and write a page about how you handled it.

b. Tick the reason why you want to start a company:

    i. The glamour of entrepreneurship
    ii. To make millions (or billions) of dollars
    iii. I want to be my own boss
    iv. I have an idea that keeps me awake at night
    v. I want to make a difference
    vi. I'm the best person to solve a problem that many people face

Fill in the following: After reading this chapter, one thing I would like to change or incorporate in my life and work is _____

_____

_____

_____.

3

Start with Why

I find myself returning often to Viktor Frankl and his extraordinary book *Man's Search for Meaning*.[1] His story is one of resilience, chronicling how he managed to survive the abject conditions of the Nazi prison camp he was sent to. He discovered that his work as a psychologist and a manuscript that he was working on gave him something to hold on to when everything else was stripped away—his family, his dignity, his freedom. He believed that this sense of meaning and purpose kept him alive. In his subsequent writing, Frankl describes humans as being hardwired—not for pleasure-seeking or pain-avoidance, as one might imagine—but for the pursuit of meaning. We think we want to just be happy, but truly, we want a *reason* to be happy, to infuse our lives with meaning.

Towards the end of the Second World War, English novelist Dorothy Sayers wrote an essay titled 'Why Work?'[2] At that time, factories in Europe and America were geared towards manufacturing arms and supplies for the Allied forces, uniting workers with a central sense of purpose. In her essay, Sayers asks what work will mean to people after the war. She writes that work doesn't have to be a means to an end but could be the end itself. We must ask ourselves, 'Is it good?' and not 'Will it pay?' because money cannot be the singular goal in a life of true meaning. Similarly, companies that are solely profit-focused will be unlikely to motivate their people and survive in the long term. People spend as much as 75 per cent of their waking life at the workplace and if their work is devoid of meaning, most people will find it an intolerable drudgery.

Just like people whose lives lack a sense of meaning that drives them forward, start-ups that have not defined their purpose very clearly will also end up floundering. The 'why' of your company articulates why it exists in the first place, acting as both your anchor and your guiding light. Very few companies start with a clear 'why' and hence end up being highly transactional, chasing the next shiny opportunity without any coherent North Star to guide their choices. A purpose binds people behind a single common rallying cry that is worth many years of dedicated commitment and hardship.

Why Should Your Company Exist?

Every year, hundreds of thousands of people start new businesses, from small shops, manufacturing units and trading outposts to venture-funded companies that back people taking massive moon shots to solve huge problems across climate, health care, space and even exotic topics such as quantum computing and gene editing. The entrepreneurial spirit and chutzpah of these people move the world forward. They believe they have something unique to contribute to the world and in their own way, small or big or downright crazy, they think they can make the world a better place.

Yet, these companies don't necessarily need to exist. Most people can find a decent job to earn their living in a predictable manner which provides financial stability, a community of co-workers and a safe environment in which to learn and grow. This could translate into a good life, a life that billions of people around the world enjoy today. Why should you let go of such a comfortable set-up to do your own thing from scratch and deal with all the challenges, including major financial setbacks, potential health risks and maybe even a strain on your relationships? I believe that these risks are only worth taking if there is a deeper reason behind wanting to build a new company from scratch.

The reasons for starting a company vary from person to person and there are many legitimate ones. Some people love the autonomy that comes from being their own boss; others are lured by the potential financial reward and prestige that come with building a successful company. Then there are people who really want to solve a problem and don't see any way of doing so other than building their own company. Whatever your initial motivation is, you need to eventually translate it into a very strong 'Why'. Otherwise, in the end, you will end up being yet another copycat company.

There isn't anything fundamentally wrong with being a copycat company, though, and there are many companies that do well for their customers and shareholders while being very similar to others in their category. We have seen many such examples in India across e-commerce, ride hailing, food delivery and D2C brand platforms. If you know you are very good at execution, then borrowing and improving upon a proven model is a great way to start, as it takes out the product–market fit risk and you are able to leap many steps ahead. But this approach is a bit like an arranged marriage: you better fall in love with the idea after copying it, or else it will be a very long and painful slog—because in entrepreneurship payday can take over a decade or even longer to arrive.

But if you have ambitions for building something that truly stands out, you need to dig deeper into answering why the world needs your company. What is it that you want to solve, that is currently unsolved? In this chapter, we will look into the process of finding that compelling 'Why', which is the hallmark of all truly great companies. When you have a strong 'Why', you end up building a very strong culture around that purpose, you attract talent that truly believes in that mission and your company relentlessly strives to make that purpose happen. As Nietzsche says, 'He who has a "why" to live for can bear almost any "how".'

Purpose Makes the Company Endure

Some of the organizations that have created the most lasting impact on the world were founded with a deep, authentic purpose. Google wanted to organize all the world's information in one place. The founders were doing their PhDs at Stanford when, as part of a project, they ended up downloading the entire Internet on Stanford's servers. Fortunately, the entirety of the Internet's content was still downloadable back then, but it was exponentially increasing. They realized early on that knowledge and information have been growing since the dawn of humanity. Yet most of it is not readily available to most people, who are the rightful inheritors of everything that has been created before us. Their quest to organize the world's information eventually led to projects such as Google Earth, Google Scholar, Google Maps, Google Apps, self-driving cars and more.

Similarly, Facebook realized early on that they could connect all of humanity into a single global village. Twenty years down the line, they have pretty much done that! Today half of humanity logs into various Facebook apps daily—communicating, sharing and collaborating at an unprecedented level. Meta continues to work on taking this to the next level with virtual reality interactions so that people can instantly be wherever they choose to be and see whoever they wish to at any time.

Tesla was founded with the long-term goal of getting rid of the dependence on fossil fuels, which has been responsible for global warming for over a century now. What started as a flex car for the uber-rich in Silicon Valley and Hollywood eventually ended up paving the way for the worldwide electrification of mobility solutions. We are all set to achieve complete electrification by 2040. The power of a deeply meaningful purpose that people wholeheartedly believe in should never be underestimated.

In my own start-up journey, I have thought about purpose deeply in everything I have been involved in. At Myntra, once we started pivoting into fashion, I tried to study the world of fashion and thought about what it means to people. Eventually I realized that 'Looking Good' was a deep human need that everyone cares about at some level. If Myntra could service the purpose of 'Helping people look good' through its offering, it could be an important platform. This idea led to a lot of product innovations and customer experience choices. Myntra continues to be the preferred shopping platform for many people.

Similarly, as we started building CureFit, we studied how people approach health and the challenges that they face. We realized that while everyone wants good health, it is very hard for most people as this pursuit requires enormous amounts of self-discipline, willpower and many healthy habits. With the modern lifestyle and its distractions, everyone struggles with this and, despite their best intentions, most people continue to slide down on the health spectrum. So, we chose 'Making health easy' as the CureFit purpose. This led to the creation of many products over a period of time and we are still at it, finding more and more ways to remove friction and make working out and eating healthy as easy as possible.

If you choose a lofty purpose with deep conviction, it can drive company culture, strategy, the kind of people who join the organization, the strategic bets that you make and the projects that you undertake. Good purpose not only makes the odds of the business working out really high, it also makes the job that much more meaningful for everyone involved. With a credible purpose, people are no longer only working for money but, with their combined effort, they are making the world a better place. Today, Groww is the leading online brokerage firm in the country. But in the early years, the company was completely obsessed with building the best possible product for consumers and hadn't made time to articulate its purpose. A few years into the journey, though, Lalit Keshre and his co-founders decided to write what eventually became the 'Groww Code', clearly outlining the organization's purpose statement and core values, making the company aspire for a longer-term vision, spanning multiple product categories.[3]

ENTREPRENEURIAL WISDOM

Making Purpose Tangible

Purpose can often seem like an abstract concept. One way to make these seemingly lofty ideas more tangible for people at all levels in the company is to organize Purpose Workshops. During these sessions, design exercises for people to understand the purpose and reflect on whether the company is living up to its raison d'etre. These could also take the form of games or projects built around purpose.

Finding True Purpose for an Organization

So, how does one arrive at a meaningful, deep and relevant purpose? Like most things in life, there are no easy answers here. You can't just go into a room, brainstorm, throw a bunch of nice-sounding phrases on the whiteboard and pick the one with the most votes. Such exercises can yield a cute phrase that everyone will forget in a few weeks or at best, someone will put it up on a wall and eventually in the employee handbook. Very often I have seen people do this exercise once or twice, agree on a nice-sounding statement and then carry on with everyday work and the phrase is all but forgotten. This is not a lived purpose that everyone in the company truly believes daily.

An exercise that I find helpful is writing an organizational constitution. We will go over the construct of the constitution in detail in a later chapter ('Organization Is Product'), but the idea is to engage the entire team and debate about key foundational elements like purpose, core values and operating principles. All this should then be documented in the form of the organizational constitution or whatever you would like to call it. We just finished the Organizational Constitution exercise for MerakiLabs and, after many months of deliberation, we have a polished document that reflects the collective vision of the team.

Finding Purpose in the Problem

Purpose often emerges out of the unique problem that you are intending to solve. If you are going to start a company, it must solve a unique problem or make the world a better place. There are problems all around us. They affect our day-to-day life or we read about them in the news or people around us complain about them. Most of us just complain about problems, ruing the fact that no one is doing anything about them and wishing things were better. But there are some among us who look at a problem and see an opportunity waiting to be solved. Every time there is a problem, it is an opportunity to raise your hand and make things better on a small scale or sometimes even on a global scale.

There is a saying that 'A problem is a terrible thing to waste'. So much of the world's great progress is the result of someone encountering a problem and, instead of just lamenting it, deciding to do something about it. Dunzo was born in a similar way. Kabeer Biswas often noticed that when friends were hanging out late at night, it was difficult to get food and alcohol delivered home.[4] He and his co-founders wondered if they could create a late-night,[5] on-demand courier service, giving birth to an entirely new category of service. The act of solving a unique problem of fast late-night delivery eventually made Dunzo a leader in this space. The founders of Rapido realized that during rush hour, cars move at a very slow pace in Bengaluru traffic; they wondered if they could create a taxi service using two-wheelers which could squeeze through the notorious jams. They eventually scaled Rapido to the same scale as Ola and Uber in India. On a side note, I used this hack during my Flipkart days. On days when the traffic was particularly bad, I'd ask my driver to use his scooter instead of the car. I'd ride pillion and we'd breeze through the snarls of traffic to show up on time for yet another action-packed day at work!

You can cultivate a 'Hello, Problem' mindset, so that upon encountering an issue, instead of bemoaning your unlucky stars, you can almost welcome it, spin it around, look at it from different angles and ask, 'What can come out of this?' There is a kind of person who, on seeing a large stone in the middle of the road, stops her vehicle, gets out and moves it aside, thus making the lives of all those who follow much easier—and maybe even saving the life of someone she'll never meet. Similarly, you can also proactively solve a problem, and that might be the seed of what will become your life's work. Mahatma Gandhi was defending the rights of immigrant Indians and the indigenous population in South Africa against the British, and in the process found his life's calling and went on to play an incredible role in India's freedom struggle. The reason this is important is that purpose doesn't just show up one day as a sudden inspiration. You start engaging with a problem and over a period of time you see patterns. As a bigger picture forms in your head, you may realize that this is something you could spend ten or twenty years of your life trying to solve in order to make a larger impact—and there you have your purpose!

Deep Domain Understanding Often Points the Way

To find a worthwhile problem to work on, it is important that you immerse yourself deeply in a domain. This requires spending a lot of time on the ground, meeting lots of players, asking very fundamental questions, reading books and research reports, studying what the current trends are, what new players are trying to do, what the new emerging technology trends are as well as what the most common complaints among users are. Deep domain immersion can take many months or even over a year, but it allows you to see the nuanced patterns and insights that may not be visible to most people. This also makes the process of articulating the purpose very difficult as it is not always obvious unless you understand the nitty-gritty of the field.

As you develop one layer of understanding, you can ask the next set of questions and once you have answered these, you can ask even deeper questions. When Myntra pivoted into fashion, it took me over eighteen months to develop a decent understanding of how the business worked, how art and science seamlessly blend to create magic for a consumer, what a critical role the supply chain played in enabling the entire cycle for a season to run seamlessly over two years and so on. It was only with this understanding that we were able to arrive at the purpose of 'Helping people look good' and also make a crucial strategic choice of going with a full inventory model as we believed that that is what creates the most compelling value proposition for consumers.

As you spend time in the domain, you can start building various hypotheses. For example, in fitness you realize that the trainer is the most important part of the value chain but finding and training good trainers is hard, hence that becomes the core problem to solve. If you study food delivery, you may notice that every time it rains, service levels drop drastically, which can significantly erode consumer trust unless you proactively plan and resolve this issue. You may notice how a new trend is starting to make inroads on the fringes—which is happening with AI now in many industries. You may notice that most people who are part of the industry are complaining about similar issues and if you were to solve them, you might be able to approach the industry in a very different way.

Once you have a hypothesis, you need to stress-test it as much as you can. This is different from looking for validation—which might not come easily, especially if people are very deeply entrenched in the domain's currently accepted wisdom. What you need to look for is whether the facts on which you are building your hypothesis check out. Our hypothesis when we were building eat.fit was that many people want to eat healthy but can't easily find good options. But after we built the product, we realized that while people do want to be healthy, when it comes to ordering food, they end up choosing their favourites, instead of healthier options. It's also important to make sure that the trends really are in line with what you are anticipating. You may assume that the industry is growing by 20 per cent, when the industry might actually grow only by 7–8 per cent, which will dramatically change the projected outlook ten years out. You should also look for all the contrarian views. Ask yourself why people think your hypothesis may not work and what counterarguments can overcome their objections, especially if the objection is echoed by many people.

After immersing yourself in the domain, building multiple hypotheses, thinking through all the objections and potential roadblocks, at some point you need to make a major leap of faith. You need to believe in something. Something that is rooted in the current facts and yet something that most people will not see as obvious or likely to work out or even worth a shot. This is a point where some deep, almost irrational conviction must take hold in your head—what American entrepreneur and venture capitalist Peter Thiel describes in his question, 'What important truth do very few people agree with you on?' This will form the core of the vision, around which you can craft your purpose.

Purpose embodies a lofty vision of the future; it is the unflinching conviction that you are the best person to solve a problem despite the odds and are willing to commit many years of your life to doing so. This is what differentiates entrepreneurs from outstanding managers. Entrepreneurs are willing to take irrational bets and don't feel burdened by having to logically prove to everyone why something will work, while managers are very logical. They extrapolate from available facts and make decisions based on accepted conventional wisdom and hence are not able to take a truly disruptive leap of faith. Entrepreneurs translate this irrational belief into a sharply articulated purpose and evangelize it so much that everyone starts to believe in it.

Your Deeply Held Beliefs Might Hold the Answer

Most people who choose to pursue the path of entrepreneurship are extraordinarily passionate about what they do. They have strong beliefs often borne out of life experiences, major influences and traits that they might have imbibed from role models and mentors in their formative years. One needs to be in tune with this and be able to answer questions such as, 'What do you truly believe in?' or 'What really matters to you?' Entrepreneurs and leaders need to introspect and reflect on these questions to factor them in while making major choices including how to go about choosing the purpose for an organization. In my new organization, MerakiLabs, one of my deeply held beliefs is that in the coming decades, India will be able to create original new technologies that will have a massive impact in India and beyond and hence we are choosing to double down on deep tech in a big way.

Often, these beliefs can be traced to something you've had immense interest in all your life. Both Elon Musk and Jeff Bezos were obsessed with space growing up, immersing themselves in science fiction and daydreaming about alien worlds. No wonder both ended up choosing to build iconic space companies. Yvon Chouinard founded Patagonia because he had a very personal passion for the outdoors and a desire to create environmentally sustainable outdoor gear.[6] Chouinard, an accomplished rock climber, began by designing, manufacturing and selling climbing equipment in the late 1950s. In the early 1970s, he expanded his product line to include clothing for climbers, branding this new line as Patagonia. The company was founded on the principle of making durable, high-quality products while causing the least harm to the environment. If you end up choosing to build a company in an area that you care about deeply, it will automatically translate into an authentic and deep purpose.

Drafting a Purpose That Will Last!

Once you have an inkling of what your purpose is, you should spend some time to find the right words to encapsulate it. Words do make a difference, allowing you to articulate and communicate your purpose to the world. Ideally, this is a collaborative exercise not only including the founders but all the early-stage team members, so that everyone has an opportunity to comment on, critique and suggest alternatives. I am currently in the process of setting up MerakiLabs and have been thinking about our purpose. All the team members, including those who have recently joined, are involved in this process. After nearly a year of effort, we are zeroing in on: 'Incubating the future' as our purpose. We intend to build multiple companies that create massively scaled up impact over a very long period and this phrase seems to capture the intent behind MerakiLabs.

A good purpose statement should be:

1. **Simple and clear:** People should understand it without explanation or elaboration.
2. **Inspiring:** It should inspire anyone working in the organization to do more and feel good about the work that they are doing.
3. **Timeless:** A good purpose statement will last for many decades and will continue to guide and inform every new phase of evolution.

4. **Authentic:** The team must truly believe in the purpose and keep repeating and reinforcing it at every opportunity. That will make the purpose credible.

Once you have zeroed in on a purpose statement that you and the team like, you should stay with it for a period and see if your excitement for it grows or diminishes. A good purpose is something you begin to fall in love with, and it acquires deep meaning in your life. You feel excited about working towards that purpose and it starts to have more significance for you than any milestones you might achieve along the way.

What Does Purpose Do to an Organization?

Organizations with a clearly defined purpose that everyone believes in have a sense of mission. People believe that their work has a greater meaning. As a result, they are more inspired and willing to engage and collaborate at a different level, than in organizations that only care about financial outcomes and winning against the competition at all costs.

Organizations with a deep sense of purpose can take their time solving problems in order to move closer to their purpose. This requires the ability to zoom out and look at the big picture, asking the hard questions about what will truly move the needle. At CureFit, we recognize that to make progress towards our purpose, we need to first make fitness a habit and expand the market in a big way. Both are really tough problems, and it will be a long time before we can make a dent in them.

Purpose also helps filter the right kind of people. A lot of people who work at CureFit care about the mission of an active lifestyle. They work out regularly, participate in sports events and organize activities within the organization. We have even defined one of the core values as 'Nurture your mind and body'. We believe that if everyone in the organization lives this value, we will all have a deeper appreciation for what an active lifestyle can do for us. This will help us understand the challenges and see what kind of solutions are most conducive to making the journey easier.

Purpose also plays a role in shaping strategy. As an organization grows, it needs to keep making strategic choices to improve the odds of winning. There are always many choices available, different acquisitions to pursue, different business lines to start or different geographies to consider expanding into. There is the need to make trade-offs between growth and profitability, business model choices and even choices about organizational structure and key hires. Thinking about whether a given choice is in line with your purpose and is helping you move closer or further from it will be a very important input in making strategy decisions.

Making Purpose Matter—Living It Every Day

Once an organization has defined its purpose, which has been internalized by the early team members, it must make an effort to reiterate its relevance on a regular basis. To begin with, it needs to be a big part of employee orientation so that new employees recognize that they are not only joining an organization, but that they are also signing up to make progress with the purpose that the organization believes in.

Purpose can be translated into core values, policies and rituals that are implemented across the organization. Amazon has defined its purpose as, 'To be earth's most customer-centric organization'. To service that purpose, Amazon instituted the '5 Whys' analysis of any major customer escalation to get the problem addressed at its root. Google makes everything in the organization transparently available to everyone to underscore the fact that access to information leads to empowerment and better decision-making.

ENTREPRENEURIAL WISDOM

On Purpose and Passion

Purpose is not something that can be taught in a classroom. It comes from being in love with a problem and obsessing over it. It comes from understanding your customers and building products that offer unique solutions to their problems. Purpose requires passion and persistence.

Organizations can consider having regular workshops around their purpose. During off-sites and annual strategy meetings, for example, teams can reflect on whether the organization is being true to its purpose or not. They can discuss areas of improvement, new initiatives and how the purpose can reflect more deeply in various goals and project plans.

Many organizations make it a priority to evaluate prospective candidates on whether there is a culture fit or not. Part of culture fit can also focus on whether the candidate is genuinely excited about the company's purpose and if there is anything in the candidate's past background that can imply a potentially stronger fit. For example, anyone with a sports and fitness background tends to be a natural fit at CureFit.

In addition to reinforcing the purpose through employee orientation sessions and workshops, a company's purpose should also be tied to performance indicators. Employees can pick personal goals that align with the larger organizational purpose. Salesforce, for example, has a '1-1-1 model',[7] through which it dedicates 1 per cent of company equity, 1 per cent of its product and 1 per cent of employee time back to the community. In this way, the organizational purpose of creating social impact at the community level is woven into its business model and operations, making it tangible for employees. Taking this a step further, organizations can explore ways of rewarding employees for achieving their purpose-driven goals. Patagonia does this by rewarding employees who embody their 'environmental stewardship' value with internships at nonprofits in the environment sector.

Another powerful way of emphasizing purpose is to host storytelling sessions in which leaders and employees share stories, illustrating how their work has fed into the company's larger purpose. Stories are a universal way of connecting with people and can have a deep emotional impact. Toms Shoes shares stories of their impact on the ground, allowing employees to see the actual difference their work is making. This brings the company's purpose to life and inspires employees to stay true to the mission.

Customer engagement around the organizational purpose can also make it more meaningful. For example, LEGO has a campaign, 'Rebuild the World', in which people use their bricks to visualize a better future. This embodies LEGO's belief in the power of play and creativity to make the world a better place.

Finally, a 'purpose council', comprising people from every department, could ensure that the purpose stays relevant. The council could meet at regular intervals to review the purpose and suggest updates so that it can be adapted to changing times.

Creative ways of weaving purpose into every aspect of a company's life and business practices will bring it to life on a daily basis, forging a deep sense of belonging in the organization. In fact, creating a very different and authentic value proposition for customers and employees alike cultivates deep loyalty.

Purpose Will Eventually Evolve

While a company's purpose should be designed for the long term, it must also be able to adapt to changing times. There are outstanding companies whose purpose has remained the same over many decades, but there are equally great organizations who have been through major pivots or strategy changes. To remain relevant, purpose has to evolve, either incrementally, or be completely reinvented from scratch.

An example of a successful transformation is IBM, which went from being a manufacturer of hardware to being a developer of cloud computing, offering services for digital transformation. The company made deliberate strategic decisions to make this shift, retaining its core values while updating its purpose to stay relevant in times of technological change. Similarly, Ford Motor has evolved from being an automobile manufacturer to being a mobility solutions provider, embracing electric vehicles as a central part of their strategy. This exemplifies how a company's purpose can evolve in response to changing environments and trends.

Redefining a purpose should be a collaborative effort, involving people from every layer of the organization. At CureFit, we have recently redefined our purpose and we saw the immense value of listening to different voices and perspectives from every part of the company. At the same time, however, it is the leader's role to lead by example—modelling and thus reinforcing the new purpose. On becoming the CEO of Microsoft, Satya Nadella infused new life into the company's mission, with an emphasis on empowerment and inclusion. He made it a central part of his role at work to see the evolved purpose implemented throughout the organization.

An important aspect of evolving purpose is communicating it in a way that is compelling and clear, so consumers are a part of the journey too. For years, Johnson & Johnson was known as a company that produced safe surgical products, but the organization has broadened its area of focus to global health. To express this new purpose, they have launched various global health initiatives, and the brand is now synonymous with innovation in health care as well as social impact.

At CureFit, we realized that articulating purpose isn't just about self-reflection but is also an outward expression of our growth and evolution as a company. Recognizing that our old purpose was no longer doing justice to our work, we have redefined it as: 'To enable an active lifestyle for everyone.' Given the changing dynamics of health as well as evolving customer needs—especially since the pandemic—our purpose now embodies a renewed clarity of vision which is reflected in our products and services.

A company's purpose is more than a statement—it is a living, changing concept that is constantly evolving. It is an essential part of a company's identity. If an organization is able to approach purpose as a dynamic process, it will be deeply connected to the essence of why it exists, remaining relevant even as landscapes shift, and leaving behind a legacy that will stand the test of time.

FROM PAGE TO ACTION

I hope you are now convinced about the role that purpose plays in entrepreneurship. Spend a little time thinking about it, and then take a look at these questions and exercises:

a. **A Personal Mission Statement:** Think about your values, the things that inspire you and the big 'why' that drives you forward on your entrepreneurial journey. Now, write a personal mission statement following this format —'My mission is to [action verb] [target audience] by [your unique approach] so that [desired outcome].'

b. Not sure about your purpose? Spend some time contemplating the following questions to help you figure it out:

    i.   What do you consider your core beliefs?
    ii. Is there a field or domain in which you consider yourself an expert?
    iii. Is there a problem you find yourself obsessing over?
    iv. Have you been passionate about an idea or a subject for a long time?
    v.   If you want to start a company, why should that company exist?

4

Why Start-Ups Fail

Start-ups fail. This is an unavoidable truth about entrepreneurship. Start-ups have a very low probability of success, and the statistics confirm this. This high failure rate is taken for granted and attributed to the risk–reward equation, the numerous uncertainties at the beginning of the journey and the vagaries of the market. And yet, there is very little literature on why start-ups actually fail. I have, fortunately, been part of many start-up journeys that survived this valley of death and have also seen, up close, those that didn't last very long. Just as there are common patterns across companies that make it, we can identify common patterns across companies that fail. Aspiring entrepreneurs will benefit immensely from understanding these patterns so that they can significantly improve their probability of success. As American businessman and investor Charlie Munger famously said, 'All I want to know is where I'm going to die, so I'll never go there.' If, as a start-up, you know exactly where the traps are laid, you can avoid them, and drastically improve your chances of making it. Before delving into the nuts and bolts of building a great company, I want to cover the most common reasons why start-ups fail, so readers can look out for the bumps in the road ahead before they hit them.

1. Just Don't Die!

In the early years of Myntra, I used to tell our teams that we would refuse to die, no matter what happened. During the pandemic, when BookMyshow's business had come down to almost nothing, I heard the co-founder Ashish Hemrajani say, 'We are like cockroaches; we will never die no matter the situation.' BookMyshow has certainly bounced back in style since then.

In the *Star Trek* series, there is a training exercise called 'Kobayashi Maru', which tests leadership and ethical decision-making in no-win situations.[1] Most often, the scenario involves a cadet seeing a civilian ship in neutral territory. Entering the territory to help them would be a breach of treaty, putting the cadet's ship at risk of attack. This is quite literally a no-win situation, but Captain Kirk asks himself, 'How do I win from here?' and figures out a way out of the situation every time— even if he must invent the loophole. It is often the same in the real world, where there is an opening in plain sight which we miss because we are too focused on what's not working and lamenting the fact that we have been dealt the wrong cards.

Good start-ups have a knack of staying alive—they just refuse to die. But this can be very tricky as well. There are many situations in which the smarter option is to take a break, reset and come back at a later stage when you are better prepared. How do you make this judgement call? It boils down to who you are working with, how your customers, especially your superfans, see your product, how energized you feel about coming to work and what your personal runway is in terms of your emotional and financial health. If all of these are positive, then finding the grit to stay in the game will eventually reveal many new paths. I recently met an entrepreneur, Samara Mahindra, founder of Carer, who is focusing on curing cancer in India and she has been at it for the last seven years, mostly bootstrapped because she cares deeply about this problem and believes in the solution that she is building. Every happy customer who makes a faster recovery from cancer is her ultimate fulfilment.

What enables a start-up to refuse to die? This can be complicated, but it essentially boils down to a combination of unflinching belief in what you are doing, being super resourceful about the runway that you are able to create and genuinely enjoying the process of building the company despite the ups and downs. Now, this is not to say that shutting shop is not a good idea. If things are truly not working out, if you have run out of runway or are just not enjoying the journey, then closing down and recharging for a better attempt at a later date may be the most prudent thing to do.

2. Founders at Cross Purposes

In his book *Why Start-Ups Fail*, American economist and Harvard Business School professor Tom Eisenmann, chronicles the journey of Quincy Apparel, a company started in 2011 by two of his former students—Alexandra Nelson and Christina Wallace—who were also best friends.[2] They wanted to offer affordable, stylish and well-fitting work wear for young professional women.

When they came to Eisenmann to ask him to invest in Quincy, he thought that, in addition to having done their homework, the two founders complemented each other well. Wallace had worked at the Metropolitan Opera, had big vision and charisma, while Nelson was the more disciplined one, having studied engineering at MIT and then worked at the Boston Consulting Group. Quincy's initial sales and repeat purchases were strong, but, unfortunately, the company soon ran into trouble. A big problem was that the founders did not work as well together as Eisenmann thought they would.

Noam Wasserman, dean of Yeshiva University's Business School, who has done research into founder dynamics, has discovered that co-founders were more likely to break up if they were family members or if they had been close friends prior to starting a company together.[3] While it might appear to make sense to start a company with someone you know well, having a close bond with someone also means that it will be harder to have brutally honest conversations with them. Wallace and Nelson had promised never to let disagreements about work jeopardize their friendship, and they agreed to share strategic decision-making authority equally. This seemed like a good way to avoid tension between founders, when in fact it only exacerbated it. Wallace and Nelson clashed over almost every decision. After barely nine months of running the business, the company was left with just two months of runway. Wallace wanted to quit gracefully, but Nelson wanted to keep searching for investors and reduce operational costs in the interim. The two had a showdown that resulted in Wallace being kicked out of the company. Two months later, Nelson had to give up and the company shut down.

A start-up needs to make decisions from the get-go, even when it isn't clear what the right decision will be. But a decision must be made and the whole company needs to rally behind it— as a decision is often proved right in execution. But sometimes, founders are not clear about who will make the call when there is a difference of opinion. And every time there are opposing viewpoints, this will cause conflict or a delay in decision-making. The early days of Twitter (now X) were marked by

power struggles and disagreements among the founders—
Jack Dorsey, Biz Stone, Noah Glass and Evan Williams.
Disagreements over the roles and visions for Twitter resulted in
Dorsey being ousted as CEO, though he later returned to lead
the company.

When co-founders are unable to make decisions efficiently,
they grow bitter and resentful towards each other and, more
often than not, the whole company witnesses the conflict, and
it affects everyone's morale. Getting your co-founder right
can eliminate one major point of friction. Rather than finding
someone who thinks like you and with whom you know you
can get along, it might be more important to look for things
like deep industry expertise, or complementary skill sets. Try
to find someone who has a proven track record in managing
a company through hardship or who is excellent at problem-
solving. Your co-founder needs to be someone who you can
have tough conversations with, verbally spar with when
required, without feelings being hurt. And of course, it helps
when you and your co-founder are clear about who makes the
final decisions, particularly when it comes to important things
like strategy and finance.

3. **Building a Company on a Fad, Rather Than a Strong
   Problem Statement**

Every few years, something new is touted as the 'next big thing'.
First, it was crypto, then the metaverse and now, generative AI.
While there is usually a genuine technological breakthrough
behind these trends, the hype machine often gets out of hand
and people begin to overestimate the disruption. Bill Gates's
observation about people overestimating what can happen in
the short run plays out, and aspiring entrepreneurs start jumping
in on the trend in droves, hoping to ride the wave. As a result,

people embark on entrepreneurial journeys without much context or with very superficial ideas that are likely to fizzle out. It also takes a few years, or even longer, for the furious evolution of technological trends to play out, making clear what's possible and what's not. With the launch of ChatGPT, for example, many start-ups went after building 'Wrappers-on-ChatGPT' which became obsolete with the next upgrade of ChatGPT.

During the pandemic, many founders believed that the future of fitness was going to be virtual and a large majority of people would work out at home. This led to several digital fitness companies being founded and heavily funded. These companies, however, didn't think about what would happen after the pandemic. Sure enough, people desperately wanted to go out and engage with the real world again, and as soon as restrictions were lifted, they were back at the gym. So, most of these companies are now confined to the forgotten archives of history. Only the hardiest ones have continued to reinvent themselves in the post-pandemic world.

When you start a company driven by the next fad as opposed to starting with extremely sharp clarity about what problem you are trying to solve, you end up groping in the dark and bouncing from one idea to the next. If you are able to develop strong clarity about the problem you are trying to solve, why it can be solved now and why you are the best team to solve it, you will start from a much stronger position than someone who wants to cash in on the bonanza associated with 'real-money-gaming' or some such trend.

4. Not Understanding Your Customers or Markets

This is a cliché but is so common that it defies belief at times. It is easy for founders to get so carried away with their own brilliance and beliefs that they start to believe that they know best what will work in the marketplace. The allure of being the next Steve Jobs is sometimes too hard to resist. I have come across numerous start-ups in the last ten years who seem hell-bent on building 'chai-making' machines. While this may be technically feasible, is there really a customer looking for such a device? Chai is available at every street corner in India for as little as Rs 10 a cup. Some people also enjoy the ritual of making chai at home, taking a ten-minute break from work to do so, while others might have staff to do it for them. People also make chai differently, captured beautifully in the Chaayos slogan, 'Meri wali chai.' Just because something seems possible and appeals to you personally doesn't make it a large, scalable business.

A very public failure of something that was dramatically innovative and perhaps a decade ahead of its time is the Segway Personal Transporter which, despite its innovative self-balancing technology, failed to revolutionize urban mobility as intended. High costs, regulatory hurdles and practicality issues limited its adoption, confining it to niche uses, rather than becoming a mainstream transportation solution. This exemplifies how groundbreaking innovation alone cannot guarantee market success in the absence of affordability and clear utility.

Founders have to obsess about their potential customers and spend as much time as possible observing their lives. Customers are experts in their own lives, as we will discover in greater detail in the next chapter. They may not know the solution they need, but they do know their problems and their aspirations better than anyone else. The more you observe customers, the more grounded in reality your approach is likely to be, and it is less likely that you will build something that nobody needs.

5. No Clear Value Proposition

Your value proposition is what justifies why a customer should part with their money in exchange for your product or service. The perceived value to the customer needs to be dramatically more than the money they are willing to pay for it. Zepto's value proposition on day one was super clear: 'Get your groceries in ten minutes.' And their instinct was right—that customers would value the speed of delivery enough to switch from other providers. This has ended up completely changing the online groceries business. But many start-ups fail to articulate their value proposition simply. When I interact with founders who are unable to articulate their value propositions in one or two sentences, instead launching into elaborate explanations, then I know that the company lacks complete clarity of what their true value proposition is.

When Michal Bohanes launched Dinnr in 2012, he thought he and his team had done their market research right and that they had a clear value proposition.[4] The proposition? An 'at home cooking experience', delivered as a kit containing ingredients and instructions to cook a meal for your loved ones on special occasions. Unfortunately, right from the start, that value proposition did not really convince customers to part with their money. After they shut down, Bohanes wondered whether the problem they thought they were solving even existed! It's likely that if people are ordering something in, they'd rather pay for a delicious meal cooked by someone else in a restaurant rather than have to do the work (and the clean-up) at home.

Artifact, launched by Instagram's founders as a 'TikTok for news', aimed to deliver personalized news using machine learning.[5] Despite a strong start with 1,00,000 downloads, Artifact struggled with feature direction, competition and a small market opportunity, leading to its shutdown in January 2024.

They had initially started as a social news reading app, but their later features were more focused on social networking. From the outside, it appeared that Artifact wasn't delivering any clear value proposition for its users.

Founders need to ask themselves a simple question that they need to contemplate over a long period of time: 'Why should anyone choose my offering over the alternatives?' Only when they have a super simple articulation—something that everyone can understand—can they create a hypothesis about how they will design and deliver that value proposition. Most value propositions boil down to either a cheaper offering (Zudio, LensKart), a significantly better offering at the same price (CULT), a dramatic quality improvement (Urban Company), an improvement upon experience (Nura health check-ups) or offering something entirely new that is not available in the marketplace (ChatGPT).

6. Poor Understanding of TAM

Total addressable market, or TAM, is a very tricky concept to wrap your head around. If you want to build a large business, you obviously need a large TAM, right? Well, not so fast. Yes, you eventually do need a large TAM, but if you start building something which already has a large TAM, that will likely mean competing with very big players. One should look at TAM as how much money is being spent today to service the existing demand. Many start-ups make the mistake of a top-down TAM estimate, making assumptions about the percentage of the population that will eventually use the new product and the amount that they would be willing to pay. This can give a false sense of a large TAM, when it may be really small. When we were starting eat.fit, we looked at the total food delivery market and estimated what portion would be willing to pay for healthy food, but in reality, there was almost no concept of people ordering healthy food—this market needed to be created from scratch. One should strive to find a small sliver of a potentially large TAM and work towards building a dominant niche. For example, Nvidia dominated the market for GPU chips and has now become a major player in the overall chips market.

One way in which a poor understanding of TAM can lead to failure is the danger of thinking that all your customers are going to be exactly like your early adopters—who tend to be the most fanatic followers. One example of this is Fab.com, an online retailer of hand-picked home decor objects.[6] Their early adopters were interior design enthusiasts who bought a lot and bought often, spreading the word among their network and communities of like-minded people. Assuming this following was representative of all their potential customers, Fab.com began expanding, raised funds and spent a huge amount on a marketing campaign. However, later customers who came through these ads were less passionate about interiors, spent less on the website, returned to it less regularly and referred fewer customers. Thus, the cost of bringing customers in went up, while their lifetime value went down, resulting in the eventual demise of the company.

7. Not Able to Raise Adequate Capital

This may sound obvious, but in the early years, if you fail to raise sufficient capital to build the initial product and team or to power growth, you are likely to die early. Capital is the oxygen that start-ups need to breathe. Good founders understand this very well and are proactive about thinking through their fundraising strategy. Funding at an early stage is very much a function of the entrepreneur's credibility, storytelling abilities, as well as the early traction the company has achieved and how many doors the founder is willing to knock on. Even if the first twenty people say no, the twenty-first might say yes. But if you give up after the first fifteen rejections, you will never know if you might have received funding from the sixteenth! It is important not to dwell too much on the fact that someone said no, but instead ask why they said no and what you need to do to address that.

When I was first interacting with Lee Fixel of Tiger Global in 2010, Myntra was starting to transition from personalization to online fashion retailing and in my very first meeting with him, I realized that he was interested in the much larger TAM of fashion, compared to what we had done in personalization. By the time I pitched to him the second time, our entire pitch focused on the potential scale of fashion retailing, and he was in. Investors are ultimately looking at two things. Is there a big opportunity here (i.e., no market risk) and can this team execute on the vision (no team risk)? If you have done your homework and have very deep conviction that the market opportunity is real, have done enough work on the ground to validate your assumptions and have a well-articulated game plan on how you will build a meaningful company, investors will certainly take note and your odds of fundraising go up significantly.

A good fundraising pitch is not just about charisma or telling investors what you think they want to hear. What is most important is to focus on what you truly believe in and whether you think there is real potential for VCs to make money from investing in your company. The VC's job is to deploy capital in a good idea and a team that will eventually help them multiply their investments, and your job is to build a convincing argument to inspire confidence. If your pitch is truly compelling, you should be able to attract many potential investors. We cover the contours and best practices of fundraising in the Funding Games chapter.

8. Failure to Find a Good PMF

Failing to find a good product–market fit (PMF) is probably the second biggest reason why companies fail. PMF is the first validation about whether the company even has the right to exist. We will cover the criteria for PMF later in this book, but at a high level, it means that you have clearly established the fact that there is a need for your offering, that people are willing to pay a sufficient amount for that offering (so you will have viable unit economics) and that customers are willing to come back and be recurring users of your service. Strong word-of-mouth awareness in the initial days is one strong validation of PMF. Founders are often so busy with the hustle and metrics, such as month-over-month growth, that they don't really pay attention to PMF until it is too late. Let's say, you are selling a product like a home treadmill and somehow, through aggressive digital marketing, you are able to make good sales numbers. But your cost of acquiring a customer is too high and not sustainable, or the product is such that customers are just not able to use it. While you may think that good sales numbers are an indication of market demand and you are on a good trajectory, unless the contribution margin is sustainable and the customers truly love your product, it is likely to be a Pyrrhic victory and the music will stop sooner or later. One of the worst mistakes to make is to burn a lot of money only to realize that you are nowhere close to PMF. Housing.com is one such cautionary tale. Due to the founder's charisma and the potential size of the housing market, the company raised a huge amount of capital and built a well-known brand through massive spending while never achieving any real PMF. By the time the investors realized this, it was too late for the company to recover.

In some cases, despite a formidable founding team with domain experience, a product can fail to find market fit.

Quibi was founded by Meg Whitman and Jeffrey Katzenberg, who both had impressive experience—Whitman had worked as a CEO at eBay and HP, while Katzenberg was a former Disney executive and the co-founder of DreamWorks.[7] They launched Quibi in 2018 as a mobile-only streaming service for short-form video, based on the hypothesis that people would consume shorter content on the go. Unfortunately, they didn't realize that the length of the videos was not a significant enough feature to set them apart. By positioning themselves as a paid subscription service, they were competing with Netflix, HBO and other streaming services, but thanks to TikTok and YouTube, consumers didn't really need to pay at all for shorter form content. Quibi was based on various assumptions about what and how people wanted to watch video content, while spending a great deal on marketing, assuming that big Hollywood stars would draw users in. What they didn't do was to actually test product–market fit, create a minimum viable product with different features or invest in high-quality market and customer research. As a result, Quibi, which had officially launched in April 2020 after raising $1.2 billion in funding, had to shut shop by the end of that year.

9. Not Building a Strong Foundation

Start-up founders know from the get-go that they have to build a great product to stand out and get to PMF to be able to survive in an ultra-competitive space. They jump into it headlong and try to make something that customers might like, persevering through long hours despite dwindling resources and faint hope. What they don't know is that they are also building an organization simultaneously which is a whole different ball game but requires equal amounts of the founder's mind space as well as proactive design.

Most start-ups don't think about the organization and culture much and, as a result, the start-up ends up being a heterogeneous group of people who somehow get things done without a coherent identity, purpose or a shared set of values. This morphs into an environment where people often work at cross purposes, focusing more on who gets the credit and the blame than on what's right for the customers and the business.

Building a strong foundation requires thinking deeply about the long-term purpose—why the company needs to exist, what the core beliefs and values are and how all this translates into rituals and policies to create a living, breathing organization. Unless the founders are proactive about this or care about building an organization that will last for a long time, these areas are ignored. Everyone brings their own beliefs and way of doing things to the organization and things may or may not work. All this comes undone when the going gets tough. In difficult times, the organization needs to find deeper resilience, the core team needs to come together and rally around each other instead of focusing on parochial issues or worse, in finding scapegoats and back-stabbing.

Many people who come from well-established organizations are very good at what's known as CYA (cover your ass!) or not signing up for anything that might involve higher chances of failure. Well, nearly everything that a start-up does involves higher chances of failure. Dealing with failure, bouncing back from failure and creative problem-solving in the face of a difficult situation are what test the mettle of a fledgling start-up. Being able to navigate problems skilfully builds character and culture which, in the long run, becomes the most enduring strength of the organization. When Apoorva Mehta was building Instacart, his team realized that places like Trader Joe's did not have an application programming interface (API) or website where they had listed a catalogue with all their items.

To navigate this problem, his team visited the local Trader Joe's, bought one of each item, photographed it and manually entered it into the Instacart system. A good culture ensures that the team members care about winning and doing whatever it takes, rather than being confined to their formal roles or thinking that some work is beneath them.

If founders are not vigilant and committed to investing in a strong foundation, the challenges of an early-stage start-up can quickly devolve into a living hell for everyone involved. This leads to high stress, anxiety about the future, mistrust among the team members and even a significant dent in the self-esteem of the people involved. This is not a high-performance culture and people will soon bolt to a better environment, often when you need them the most. Just as a tall building requires a very strong foundation, so does an organization that is built to last.

10. Chasing Too Many Things Simultaneously

Start-ups very rarely get more than one shot to make something work. Against all odds, you quit your job, get some funding, have a few like-minded people join you to make the vision a reality and you are on your way. The problem is that as soon as you start and spend some time studying the space, you will come across numerous variations of ideas, many possible markets to go after, as well as many other companies that are taking a slightly different approach than yours and getting good traction. It is normal to get tempted and start hedging your bets or feel more ambitious and try to tackle multiple problems simultaneously. But this is going to guarantee that your odds of success will drop exponentially. Most start-ups have very limited resources and often a limited window to make something work. It is critical that you remain fully focused during this period and have all your energy directed towards solving one problem clearly and convincingly. As it is, even that one problem might require many iterations and the longer you stay with the problem, the better your chances are. At CureFit, we tried to tackle everything from fitness to food to mental health and even primary care and as a result our resources stretched too thin and we were not able to do justice to all the projects. Similarly, OYO got into way too many businesses after they saw traction in standardizing budget hotels and they started to suffer across these varied branches of the company.

What makes this worse is that every time you go out and speak with customers, potential partners or investors, everyone will give you different advice and some do so with a lot of confidence. It is difficult to ignore what everyone is saying— and you shouldn't ignore all the advice either. The trick is not to commit to an idea or approach too early until you have done your homework. Keep your options open, study the problem and domain in a lot of detail and only commit once you have a high degree of conviction rooted in a deep consumer or technology insight. Once you commit, stay the course as long as you can unless you encounter something that makes the current path completely unviable. If you still have the runway and energy, you can try a new path, but make sure to completely kill the previous approach and commit wholeheartedly to the new path. Early-stage start-ups have to be laser focused on solving one problem and this is what will give you the best possible odds of pulling something off.

11. Building the Company for What Investors May Want to See

In the investing world, there is always a buzzword going around or a focus on particular metrics, and every time you interact with potential investors, they are sure to bring up these trends.

Over the last two decades, I have seen this range from eyeballs (seriously!) to conversion to customer lifetime value (CTV) or customer acquisition cost (CAC), to social media fan base, growth rates and profitability when the funding markets get tighter. These days it is impossible to find a company that is not doing something with AI even if there is not an iota of real AI in how the problem is being solved. Investors will hear your story, steer you towards whatever happens to be hot and happening and you will feel incredible pressure to be 'on trend'. There is not a single start-up today which is not working on generative AI, in one way or another!

The thing about the trends that investors are interested in is that they are going to change. A few years ago, software as a service (SaaS) was the hottest thing and companies in India were chasing it until they all ran into issues of scaling while sitting in India, and the valuations corrected massively. Every time you interact with a VC, there is a massive lack of information symmetry. You have a great deal of depth of knowledge about what you are building as you spend 100 per cent of your time learning about this domain. The VCs, on the other hand, are meeting with hundreds of companies and they have a bird's-eye view of the macro trends and hence their world view will be coloured with recency bias. Start-ups need to be operating from deeper insights and convictions with or without the current trends on their side. By definition, you have a very narrow focus on what you are trying to solve and it may not fit the popular narrative of the day. Most start-ups create massive value not because they follow the herd, but because they buck the trends and have the courage of their convictions. If your choices are rooted in deeper insights, they will turn out to be true and you will be leading in an emerging field without too many contenders.

Despite their tendency to follow trends, VCs are actually great at betting on good founders with conviction and original ideas. Your job is to be able to convince VCs about why your start-up is worth investing in and not telling VCs what they might want to hear as that will keep changing. But if you keep changing your course every now and then, it will be a journey to nowhere in the end.

ENTREPRENEURIAL WISDOM

On Knowing When to Cut Your Losses

Despite all of us knowing that the chances of failure in entrepreneurship are very high, it is still heartbreaking to watch your venture fail. This makes it difficult to let go. Many founders end up pouring energy and money into a company that is very obviously not going to make it. As hard as it might be, you have to develop objectivity and pragmatism to determine when it's time to cut your losses and move on.

12. Scaling a CM Negative Business

Once you have built your product, you will find your first few customers, and you will be filled with exhilaration. If the early customer feedback is good and the product begins to spread by word of mouth, you will be positively giddy with excitement. If VCs hear about this early traction, they might want you to press the pedal. Now, you think you have arrived and the sky's the limit. But not so fast! There is one small catch, and that is how your contribution margin (CM) is stacking up. Most early-stage start-ups tend to have a negative CM, which means they are losing money on every transaction. This is not bad in and of itself. But this is not the point where you should start rapidly scaling. Focusing on growth while your CM is negative will mean that the burn will continue to grow proportionately and will become untenable at some stage. There are times when companies feel that they are in the capture-as-much-territory-as-possible zone, and they can worry about making the unit economics work later or even that the unit economics will automatically work out with scale. This may sound good in theory but is never really the case in practice. Just think of all the major Indian e-commerce companies that have achieved massive scale but continue to burn money well into their second decade. Things do occasionally work out if there is a large strategic player willing to fund the burn over the long haul, but most start-ups will not live to tell the tale. There are countless e-commerce start-ups that have come and gone and no one even remembers their names.

If you see that you are getting strong traction and that metrics such as retention, engagement and word of mouth are looking solid, it's a good time to pay more attention to your unit economics. Now, you may realize that it will take a certain scale to be able to get your unit economics to work and that's absolutely fine as long as you define the road map clearly, analyse your assumptions critically and have the money in the bank to be able to afford the burn until the target scale with some buffer. Just keep in mind that as long as you are in the negative CM zone, you will be at the mercy of the vagaries of the market and the shifting winds in market sentiment can completely wipe you out. Scaling a CM negative business is like riding a tiger—the moment you step off, you will be gone!

13. Poor Management of Runway

When start-ups run out of runway, they have no choice but to shut shop. It is very rare that start-ups will fold while there is still money in the bank, which goes to show the resilience and fighting spirit most entrepreneurs possess—literally fighting till the last breath. Unfortunately, the last breath comes too soon for most companies and sometimes quite unexpectedly. While start-ups are fuelled by dreams of changing the world and of disruptive innovations, the real fuel is the cash runway. No runway, no start-up. Period.

Unless starting with your own capital, you're unlikely to have any runway on day one of the journey. But if a business idea and team have potential and the stars align, the initial funding should translate into twelve to eighteen months of runway. Once you have this runway, you have a shot at accelerating and hopefully achieving lift-off! The trick is to be really conscious of the runway you have at any given time and be very clear about what you want to use it for, as it is very easy to fritter away the cash on many miscellaneous ideas. Simultaneously, you need to plan the next fundraiser, which will typically take six to nine months and require many iterations of your pitch. Founders have to constantly think about fundraising as money is not necessarily available when you need it. If you have less than twelve months of runway, you have to engage in all possible leads as a lot of fundraising is quite serendipitous.

ENTREPRENEURIAL WISDOM

On the Importance of Runway

As a general rule of thumb, make sure to have a minimum runway of two years. This is especially important if you do not want to compromise on your lifestyle as you build your company.

In the end, all fundraising processes are about whether the start-up is on the right path and whether investors will make money or not. So, you need to be able to paint both the big picture vision as well as the detailed journey from what's working today to the game plan that you foresee. Fundraising is a skill that may take a long time to learn, but early-stage founders ought to understand this in as much detail as possible as soon as possible. Try to be one step ahead of the game so that you give yourself adequate runway to solve the problem that you set out to solve.

14. Raising Too Much Capital and Unmanaged Burn

This is the flip side of running out of runway. I am inclined to say that a great many start-ups also suffer and even die because they end up raising too much capital. This is a bit counter-intuitive because when you announce a $100 million round, you feel on top of the world, as if you have already accomplished the mission. But that's not the mission. All you have done is sell a promise for massive returns to the investors, but the real job of building the business lies ahead of you. Unless there is a substantial return for investors on the horizon, the victory will turn sour very soon.

You might have heard about trees born during periods of low rainfall that end up becoming very sturdy. These trees have to grow much deeper roots to find water and they take much longer to develop since not enough raw material is available for growth. When the good times return, though, these trees are in a much stronger position to take advantage of the conditions due to their solid foundations. Trees that are born in times of excess rainfall initially grow very fast, but have shallow roots and thinner trunks. They become very unsteady as they grow and are easily uprooted in storms. It seems that the same is true for many companies. Companies that develop in resource-constrained environments tend to develop way more resourcefulness, capital efficiency and very high-quality prioritization to ensure that only the most promising projects are funded. These companies don't have the luxury of incubating many parallel ideas which are often wasteful.

Very well-funded companies tend to go in the opposite direction. Because there is a lot of cash, people (including investors), start asking, 'If capital was not a constraint, how fast can you grow?' Unfortunately, this is a silly question that is behind the downfall of too many companies. As you start to press the growth pedal beyond what's realistic, capital efficiency starts to go down, teams take shortcuts; they start throwing money and people at the problem and for a while, the growth rate inches upwards, but the cash burn grows even faster. Sooner or later, the music stops as there is obviously no such thing as a completely unconstrained capital environment and these companies are forced to cut costs. They end up flatlining or even landing in a degrowth stage, laying off staff and shutting down many fancy projects, leading to huge losses in morale, momentum and investor confidence. Some will go through the 'what doesn't kill you makes you stronger' journey but many others will just become a cautionary tale which entrepreneurs will ignore anyway as they will believe that they are different. Alas, if this were only true more often!

As you can see, there are many things that can and do go wrong in a start-up journey. When you study start-ups that have failed, you will see patterns that repeat themselves, making failure seem predictable—at least to some extent. Companies that succeed face very similar challenges but have either built internal capabilities to counter them ahead of time or as soon as first signs of trouble arrive. Some companies react late but recognize that unless they dramatically change their approach, they will not survive. Hence, they go through significant transformations in course, people, strategy and even culture to reinvent themselves to become a much better company. While surviving the crisis builds character and resilience, it can be nerve-racking to navigate and not many companies will survive such deep existential crises. As a budding entrepreneur, it may be prudent to study what the common patterns are and do whatever you need to make choices in a way that minimizes the chances of these kinds of failure. The company building journey will be significantly more fun and rewarding in the process!

FROM PAGE TO ACTION

The painful truth about start-ups is that, more often than not, they fail. Being comfortable with failure and being able to learn from every mistake is, therefore, crucial.

a. **How does failure make you feel?** Spend an hour thinking about how you have responded to a big rejection or failure in the past. Perhaps you didn't get into your dream college or you didn't get the promotion you hoped for or you started a company that didn't survive. Write a page about how you initially reacted to and felt about the failure. Looking back now, what would you say the experience taught you? What would you do differently?

b. Which of the following best describes your approach to failure:

i. I see failure as a stumbling block and am raring to get back up again.

ii. I feel very stressed when I fail, as if all my hard work has been for nothing.

iii. I pause to think about what went wrong so that I can do things differently the next time around.

iv. I decide not to take a risk again and give up on trying.

v. I think failure means that I didn't try hard enough or that I'm not good enough.

vi. I consider failure an inevitable part of any journey of learning.

5

Everything Starts with Customers

It's too easy to think we know our customers from all the meetings, phone calls, and reports we've read about them. To deeply understand how people actually use our products, we need to go to where they work, where they play and where they live.

—Braden Kowitz, lead designer at Google Venture

Who Is Your Customer?

Darshan Patel was travelling through Churchgate station on a Mumbai local train when he noticed something—many of his fellow travellers had what looked like painfully cracked heels.[1] He went on to launch Krack, a cream to soothe dry and cracked feet, which proved successful within just three months. Patel developed a whole range of iconic products based on similarly unique consumer insights, including Dermicool, Itch Guard , Livon and Set Wet. These insights came from constant observation as well as tireless research; asking customers numerous questions about their pain points, the existing solutions they used and why they liked or disliked them. In 2006, he left the family business, Paras Pharmaceuticals, which went on to sell for a whopping Rs 3260 crore. But he was far from done. In the next decade, he created the deodorant brand Fogg. The one thing that came up repeatedly in his consumer research was the fact that people believed their deodorant cans didn't last long enough. Staying true to his motto, 'Differentiate or die,' Patel came up with the idea of a deodorant can that worked without gas, guaranteeing 800 sprays. The marketing focused on this USP, and within a few years, Fogg had achieved #1 market share in its category. What makes Patel and his brands stand out? He probably understands his customers better than anyone else and, as a result, has an enviable record of creating one successful brand after another.

Set this in contrast to the digital start-up ecosystem in India. Entrepreneurs latch on to the newest megatrend or to a company that is getting massive valuations in the West or in China, and start building a 'Copy of X' in India. VCs are only too happy to fund these companies because the entrepreneur claims that the venture will hit a revenue of $100 million in five years and $1 billion in ten years. That sounds great! But who is the customer? Beyond vague definitions such as 'the vast middle class who aspires for a better lifestyle and status', it's likely that most of these start-ups will struggle to clearly define their target customer.

The truth is that most start-ups don't really know who their customer is. They want to claim that anyone and everyone is a potential customer. As a result, they keep going from pivot to pivot, leaking contribution margin money. At the same time, they keep trying to raise money to scale, given the supposedly vast market waiting to lap up the new product. Trust me, I know this because I have been in the same spot, more than once!

It is hard to know your customers, but start-ups can't afford not to. A start-up trying to bring a new product to the market must have a sharp understanding of exactly who the initial set of customers is going to be. When we were building Eatfit, our health food offering, our core customers were very specifically start-up employees in Bengaluru, looking for lunch options. When Dunzo launched in Bengaluru, their customers were single tech employees, living in shared flats, looking for cigarettes or alcohol in the late-night hours.

The process of finding your customer is largely one of elimination. You begin by removing everyone you can think of, until you are left with only a very specific persona of the customer who truly needs what you are building or whose life will be dramatically improved by your product or service. As you do this, you get closer to identifying your real customer. A customer is someone who really believes in you and is willing to sign an unwritten contract of preference for your offering.

As different companies conduct this process of elimination, it is interesting to see how, in some cases, the customer isn't necessarily the end user. For example, pharmaceutical giant Merck doesn't consider patients (who actually buy their medicines) or physicians (who recommend their medicines) their main customers but rather focuses on the research scientists who help them come up with new molecules and drugs. Drug discovery is a labour of love, requiring a collision of ideas, freewheeling collaboration and the autonomy to pursue many promising leads. It requires patience, though, as many leads will turn out to be duds, and finding a new drug can often take a decade or more, costing billions of dollars. Merck wants to make sure that their true customers, the research scientists, are really taken care of so that they can do their best work and help uncover the next miracle molecule. As long as this engine works, the rest of the business machinery is fairly straightforward. After all, who wouldn't willingly part with their life savings for a drug that could actually save their life!

ENTREPRENEURIAL WISDOM

On Knowing Who Your Customer Is

You have to be very clear about who your customer is and everyone on your team must have a shared understanding of the customer's unique profile, needs and problems. If there is even the slightest doubt, you might end up building a product for an entirely different customer. No matter how good this product is, your entire framework will have to change to adapt to the new customer profile.

Finding Your Niche

While entrepreneurs often dream of world domination (and, by all means, should!), a start-up cannot start out by serving everyone who might be a potential customer in the distant future. In a resource-constrained environment and with barely one or two years of runway, a start-up has to make something work in a short order and that requires as few resources as possible. At CureFit, we had the vision of building an integrated health platform to make a healthy lifestyle easy. This is a combination of fitness, food, mental health, sleep and more. Yet, we started with just four gyms in the HSR Layout area of Bengaluru. It was only when we had a very strong product–market fit validation, that we started expanding into other markets and considering new product offerings. In his book *Zero to One*, Peter Thiel calls this going after a 'Dominant Niche'. Can you identify a small niche which is currently unoccupied and figure out a way to become a dominant player in that niche? You can do this knowing that eventually there are many adjacent markets that you can go after.

Uber started out as a very fancy black-car service in San Francisco and New York. It was quite an experience to click on a few buttons and see a black limousine pull up within minutes. The experience became an instant 'wow' factor among its affluent user base and before long, thanks to word of mouth, Uber launched in other cities. The same thing happened with Facebook in its early days. It started out as a platform specifically for students in Ivy League colleges, and it soon became such a rage that many other colleges started joining the long wait-list to get Facebook to their institutions. The resulting word-of-mouth effect created a huge list of potential users long before the service was available to everyone, thus all but ensuring a huge success at launch.

There are numerous examples of companies starting out very small, finding a unique problem to solve for a small group of people, and developing a small but fanatic following. This resulted in a deeply loyal customer base that formed the foundation of a much larger business down the line. As you start out, finding a niche that you can aim to dominate and then wholeheartedly committing to winning that niche can put you on a very strong footing.

Fitness app Strava has a massive fan following among hardcore amateur athletes. The founders were college rowing athletes who later missed the camaraderie that comes from the sense of belonging to a team, training together, challenging each other for better performance and celebrating each other's success.[2] They wanted to recreate that locker room atmosphere for everyday athletes in their own communities. To kick-start this, they focused on serious cyclists, betting on the insight that cycling is usually a team sport, involving a small group getting together early in the morning to go on long rides. It is a technical sport with lots of metrics, training protocols and, of course, motivating group members to show up and push for sustained improvements. Strava became a hit among various cycling groups around the world and armed with this success, it eventually diversified into all kinds of sports, becoming the most preferred app for facilitating the social aspects of any group or team sport.

Nick Woodman, founder of GoPro, was an avid surfer. While on a surfing trip through Australia and Indonesia, he cobbled together a device using an old surfboard leash and a disposable camera that he could wear on his wrist to capture the moment he caught a wave.[3] He returned to California obsessed with the idea of developing a wrist camera that surfers could wear even as they were being tossed around by the ocean. The GoPro went on to become the go-to product for adventure sports enthusiasts of all kinds, mounted on hats, boats, cycles and other equipment to take the most thrilling high-quality action videos.

So how do you go about finding that dominant niche? You have to put yourself in the shoes of the customers, literally. My friend Sameer Maheshwari, who founded HealthKart, told me about how sales of their whey protein brand, MuscleBlaze, completely stalled after early-stage growth and no one inside the company had any idea why. Sameer decided that, for one year, the company would obsess about getting to know their customers really well and would visit them wherever they were. They were shocked to find that many of their customers were at considerably lower-income groups, compared to what they had imagined, and had no idea how to mix the whey and water properly or how to store the product, among other things. These insights led to numerous product improvements over the next few years which eventually made MuscleBlaze the #1 whey protein brand in the country, even beating a reputed international brand.

I recently had a conversation with Atul Satija, who left his corporate job in 2016 and started The/Nudge Institute with the aim of eliminating poverty in India. He spent a considerable amount of time living in some of the poorest places in the country to observe the lifestyles of people who live below subsistence levels of poverty. He narrated the story of families from tribal communities in Jharkhand who work as labourers in brick factories for six months of the year. They, along with their children, stay in shanties provided by the employer, receiving three meals a day as payment, apart from a sum of approximately Rs 10,000 that they receive at the end of the six months. They then have to live on these ten thousand rupees for the next several months until there is more work at the factory. Most days, the families eat nothing more than rice with wild leaves or berries, but despite the frugality, the money is just not enough. They are forced to keep looking for odd jobs and support from the government MGNREGA, scheme to get through this period. Living in close quarters with these communities and observing the everyday problems on the ground eventually enabled Nudge to come up with many pioneering interventions to break the cycle of poverty and help many communities escape the poverty trap permanently.

Customers Are the Only Experts in Their Lives

On the other end of the spectrum are founders who, after some success, start believing that they know what the customer needs. This is what led Steve Jobs to build the Power Mac G4 and

Jeff Bezos to build Amazon's Fire Phone. These products fell flat in the marketplace because customers had no need for them in their lives. Both are among the most successful founders and leaders of all time, and yet they also fell into the trap of thinking that they know the customers' lives better than the customers themselves did. A very simple rule to keep in mind is that you may be a product or business expert, but the customers are experts on their own lives. Customers live their lives one day at a time, in their homes and offices, in the company of their friends and families, experiencing the joys and challenges of life, with their own unique social and cultural backgrounds, and no one knows more than they do what their life's joys, challenges and aspirations are. What's more, these aspirations change from day to day and year to year, so don't be in a hurry to proclaim that you know exactly what the customer wants.

One common mistake I see people make is that they extrapolate from their own lives and assume that's what the customer wants. I often have people come up to me to inform me that CULT should have an offering for at-home trainers. Most people who give me this advice live in gated communities in Bengaluru, where they see personal trainers come into their community every day. What they don't realize is that Bengaluru has only about a dozen such luxury apartment complexes where residents can afford a trainer at Rs 2000 or more per session. Most people in Bengaluru would find even a gym subscription at Rs 2000 a month too expensive. The best and the only way to get to know about the lives of your customers is to spend considerable time watching them in their own contexts. You have to ask their permission to be able to do so and be very patient. You can't just ask, 'So what's the current problem that you are facing that we can solve for you?' A customer is likely to think that it is you who has the problem for being so creepy, and not them! The trick is to observe and process your observations without intruding too much or being in a hurry to jump to any conclusions.

Many consumer brand companies understand this approach to customers very well and institutionalize it in their culture. Sudhir Sitapati, the CEO of Godrej Consumer Products, who has led many iconic brands at Unilever India, narrates in his book *The CEO Factory* how spending one day a week in the field, irrespective of how senior you are at the company, is part of cultural training at Unilever. When people spend time on the ground observing customers in their day-to-day lives, they start to see unique new insights that would never have been available to them during a typical conference room discussion. During my time at Flipkart, I remember going out for a delivery with a member of the delivery staff one day. As we were handing over the package to the customer, he said he didn't have any cash handy and asked if we could take him to the nearest ATM. So, there we were—the three of us riding on a bike to withdraw cash from an ATM! This reminded me how cumbersome cash-on-delivery can be, at a time when nearly 70 per cent of all e-commerce orders worked on this payment mode.

A good product manager should let customers talk about their lives and struggles, and then filter out what is the most relevant problem in the company's context. It is often unhelpful to ask customers what the right solution is or how much they would be willing to pay for some future service that they have never even heard of. Customers might not be able to articulate the kind of solution they need or even imagine a world where that solution exists. If you insist, you will likely hear something similar to what Henry Ford said his prospective customers would have said if he'd asked them what they wanted: Faster horses who don't poop! The product manager or start-up founder is the expert who should be able to take all the available customer context and translate it into a possible hypothesis with products or solutions that might alleviate a problem or improve the quality of a customer's life significantly.

Very early on in my entrepreneurial career, I was given some advice by a maverick entrepreneur: 'Don't trust a 23-degree person but trust a 40-degree person.' What he meant was that people who sit in air-conditioned offices all day where the temperature is maintained at a comfortable 23 degrees have only a superficial understanding of the customers. On the other hand, field executives who are out in the 40-degree heat, seeing what's happening on the street and inside people's homes, have much better insights about real problems and therefore will be able to come up with much better solutions.

Soon after launching, the Airbnb team realized that the photographs taken by hosts were not doing justice to the spaces listed on the site. Photographs were such an essential part of the booking process—it was on their basis that guests would decide whether to stay at a home or not. A lot of the listings had really blurry or poor-quality images. Finally, founders Brian Chesky and Joe Gebbia borrowed DSLR cameras and went out themselves to take better photos of their hosts' homes. Going from door to door, they briefly became their company's official photographers, until they were finally able to streamline the process. In this way, they were willing to get their hands dirty to improve their product. This also enabled Chesky and Gebbia to spend a lot of time in people's homes, having coffee with them and understanding their perspective as hosts, including things they would like to have for a seamless experience.[4] Eventually, these insights translated into numerous product features at Airbnb, undoubtedly contributing significantly to making it one of the most loved consumer apps of the last decade.

ENTREPRENEURIAL WISDOM

On Creating a Customer Persona

In order to develop a detailed picture of who you are building products for, try to imagine your ideal customer. Now, describe everything you can about this person—their age, background, occupation, likes and dislikes, personality, family. Write down everything you can think of; it might even help to give them a name! These specific and personal details will help you and your team feel better acquainted with your customer, inspiring you to create even better solutions.

Seeking Customer Insights

All product or business innovation is rooted in 'insights'. I learnt this much later in my entrepreneurial journey, but now I have come to believe that insights are worth their weight in gold and, just as anyone searching for gold will tell you, good insights are very difficult to find! It may take an incredible amount of effort to arrive at one good insight. A good way to come upon these insights is to spend a huge amount of time on the ground, observing customers, immersing yourself in their contexts, sometimes studying other players in different geographies, taking lots of notes and then zooming out and asking what it all means. There was a time in Myntra's journey when I used to visit various malls around the country to look for space for our offline retail kiosks for the personalization business. I would usually end up at a mall on a weekday afternoon when it was completely empty. Initially, I didn't question why the malls were so quiet and enjoyed the fact that I could go about my business in peace. After some time, though, I noticed that all the shops were selling apparel and footwear and almost nothing else. On top of that, each store was full, with huge amounts of inventory and not a customer in sight. That led to the insight about making all the inventory available online so customers would be able to shop from their homes at any time of the day, finally resulting in the initial pivot towards fashion at Myntra.

Have you ever wondered about the audio notifications you hear after making a purchase at your local grocery store? This is Paytm's Soundbox in action, the result of a valuable insight. Paytm's founder and CEO, Vijay Shekhar Sharma, had just bought milk from his neighbourhood store, but the shopkeeper wouldn't let him leave as he hadn't yet received a payment alert.[5] Sharma asked to look at the shopkeeper's phone and noticed that his message inbox was full, preventing new messages— including the SMS alert from Paytm—from coming in. In the company's first attempt to solve this problem, they introduced a call feature for the merchant, but that wasn't feasible. Soundbox became the 'arbitration device between the merchant and the customer' that was needed, offering instant audio alerts in the preferred regional language. As you might have heard—quite literally—Paytm Soundbox has been adopted rapidly by small businesses around the country.

Insights can come from completely unexpected quarters and may even sound quite counter-intuitive at first. When IKEA founder Ingvar Kamprad started the company, one of the biggest challenges he faced was the logistics of delivering the furniture to customers' homes. It was cumbersome, costly and likely to result in some damage to the products en route. He started experimenting with the idea of flat-packed furniture that would require minimal assembly at home while reducing costs significantly. While this was a cost-driven initiative, very soon Kamprad realized that customer reviews of products were going up and publicity through word of mouth was increasing. This came as a surprise but, as he tried to understand this better, he realized that since customers were investing effort in putting the furniture together, they developed a deeper sense of pride and ownership. They felt as though they were the 'creators' of the furniture and they loved this feeling. This has come to be known as the 'IKEA effect'[6] and today many brands use this to their advantage in cultivating customer love. If you are a fan of Maggi noodles, you know the feeling that just a few minutes of boiling water can produce!

Generating good insights requires asking why repeatedly—five times, in fact—whenever you observe something interesting. This 'five whys' framework was developed by Toyota in its quest for the best possible quality in its processes while nearly eliminating errors from the manufacturing process. The idea of the five whys is that whenever anything goes wrong, you ask 'why'. When you get the first answer, you ask 'why' again, and again until you arrive at the root cause that you can act upon. By incorporating the five whys in your personal and professional lives, you can become a learning machine with a much deeper understanding about the world and the problems that you encounter on a daily basis.

A surprising insight we had at Myntra eventually led us to figure out the problem of returns. It is well known that the bane of online fashion retailing is the massive number of returns that result from size and fit issues or from the customer simply changing their mind. Each year, Myntra came up with various projects to reduce returns and thus improve overall unit economics. While trying to understand the issue, the data science team noticed that customers with the highest number of annual orders also had the highest number of returns—a correlation they couldn't understand. On further analysis, we realized that we had the causation the other way around. The reality was that there was a huge trust deficit in shopping for fashion online. But when customers have a successful return experience, they start believing in the platform and the order volumes shoot up. We completely pivoted and started working on the 'first successful return' as a key activity to build platform trust and loyalty, eventually leading to many variations of 'try and buy' features that drove the bulk of Myntra's growth for many years.

Zomato used an insight into app notifications to change the company strategy entirely. Most online players have realized that push notifications (those annoying pop-ups on your phone) can result in small incremental sales. As brands get more and more desperate for sales, the number of push notifications keeps going up. At some point, Zomato's founder Deepinder Goyal started asking what impact notifications were really having. Were they having any meaningful impact on sales or were they just unwanted interruptions that users largely ignore? He asked if Zomato could send some interesting messages to engage with users, instead of just trying to make them order more food. He wondered if this would lead to better engagement. Sure enough, the engagement on notifications went up four times and eventually became a very powerful brand-building tool for Zomato, unlike most brands that continue to harass customers with pesky notifications.

Insights are one of the most difficult things for a start-up founder or product builder to unearth. Most insights are hiding under many layers of confusing data and masked by widely accepted beliefs that people take for granted. In search of insights, we often stumble upon superficial observations, and think that they are insights, but these do not lead to any fundamental choices. A good framework for coming up with high-quality insights can be:

a. A continuous immersion in the customer or market context to collect a lot of facts.

b. Ongoing debate and deliberation about what something means. Is there any core truth that can be gleaned from all the observations?

c. If you have a semblance of a hypothesis about an insight, ask yourself, does it matter? Is this insight relevant to many users or restricted to some very special cases?

d. Is this insight actionable in terms of a specific solution that can add measurable and meaningful value to customers?

Following these steps repeatedly and filtering out most of the insights that you glean, except for a few genuinely original ones, can be a game changer in business. At CULT, we have always struggled with the problem of retention. Of all the customers that we acquire, nearly two-thirds do not renew their subscriptions, leading to the classic leaky bucket problem. We have thrown in all kinds of product features, as well as incentives to move this metric up, but it never really budged. It seems that for many people, fitness continues to be about short-term inspiration, rather than a long-term lifestyle change. Our product head, Santhosh Kumar, took on the challenge of investigating this problem, conducting numerous studies on the ground and speaking with experts from around the world. Eventually, he came across this insight from gyms in the West—ensuring that someone from the gym speaks to customers warmly, one-on-one, at least twice a month, results in a 50 per cent improvement in retention. Voila! We had our answer, and we are now implementing some form of this across all our gyms.

Value Propositions: Convincing the Customer

Once you know who your customer is, the next job is to convince your potential customers to buy your product, to see if they are willing to pay some value for your offering.

This is where the rubber meets the road. Irrespective of what customers might have told you in surveys and what your business plan might have assumed, the actual act of facing a customer is very different and the choices that customers make will often surprise you. By the time you launch your product in the market, being clear about your customer value proposition helps immensely.

What is a value proposition? It is that aspect of your product that is unique, different or better that will make the lives of the customers better—so much better, that they will be willing to part with their money to be able to add that value to their lives. Really good value propositions are simple to articulate and can be understood by anyone without a complex sales pitch or explanation. At their core, most value propositions boil down to either getting a cheaper price, getting more for the same price, getting a new feature that is not available in the marketplace or getting much better service. When Zepto launched their ten-minute grocery delivery service, it was the only such service in India, and it improved the delivery time considerably compared to the alternatives. The value proposition was so clear and sharp that no one could misunderstand it. Of course, it was not easy to make the business model for this.

In the world of photo editing, Photoshop has been the go-to tool for designers for many decades. But Photoshop also has a huge learning curve and you can make great designs only after achieving a certain degree of proficiency. As a result, the field of creative design has been largely restricted to people who have formally trained as designers. Canva wanted to challenge this and decided to create an extremely simple interface that enabled almost anyone to create professional quality designs. The product uncovered a vast untapped market—apparently nearly everyone has a need to create interesting graphics to communicate and market their ideas. 'Empowering anyone to design' is a simple and powerful value proposition and it is not a surprise that Canva has gone on to become a massive hit.

Online dating took off when people figured out a way to use the Internet to meet people in the virtual world and, if things seemed promising, then meet offline. Dating apps tended to be fairly standard in the early years. Users would create profiles and the algorithm would intelligently match them, after which anyone could initiate the interaction. Whitney Herd, who had earlier co-founded Tinder, decided to rethink this for her next start-up, Bumble. In order to make sure that Bumble stood out from the crowd, she wondered if she could design the platform such that only women could make the first move or initiate a conversation. Empowering women in this way became a very simple, clear and differentiated value proposition and users flocked to the platform, eventually turning it into one of the most successful dating apps ever.

Crafting a value proposition can be hard as customers often misunderstand what you are trying to communicate, and the message can backfire. While Tata Nano set out to build India's most affordable car at only Rs 1 lakh, what most customers heard was that it was an ultra-cheap car and they didn't want to be associated with a cheap product. Tata could have focused on the car's style or fuel efficiency or convenience or some other feature that customers cared about instead of continually harping on about the low price. Similarly, when P&G tried to enter the disposable diaper market in Japan in the mid-1970s, it faced a problem. There was definitely a need for disposable diapers, because parents were increasingly frustrated with the messiness of cloth diapers. So Pampers took off in the US but didn't have the same luck in Japan. Why, you might wonder? It was all because of the way the value proposition was communicated. In the US, P&G ran a hit TV ad showcasing a stork delivering disposable diapers to a happy household. What they didn't realize was that the same ad stumped the parents in Japan. People in Japan weren't acquainted with the common Western folklore of a stork delivering a baby.

Alfred Taubman, former CEO of the A&W restaurant chain and author of *Threshold Resistance*, learnt that lesson the hard way when his company tried to introduce a third-pound burger at the same price as McDonald's quarter-pounder. More than half the customers thought they were being ripped off. 'Why should we pay the same amount for less meat?' they said. The value of the new A&W burger depended on consumers comparing two fractions: ⅓ and ¼. But fractions are difficult for everyone because they're parts of things as opposed to whole objects. We like to count things, and fractions don't equal 'things'. So, we jump to the closest available whole numbers. Four is bigger than three, so we mistakenly infer that a ¼-pounder is a bigger burger than a ⅓-pounder!

At CULT, as we started building the initial set of gyms, we had many different ideas about what the value proposition was. From 'clean gyms' to 'the best workouts' to 'a variety of workouts', everything was under consideration, and we would use all these interchangeably based on whatever may work for a particular objective. After speaking with many customers, we realized that 'the best trainers' was the number one reason why customers loved CULT. Since then, we have internalized this idea, hiring and training the best trainers as well as creating a great work environment for them—the best way we can continue to deliver on this value proposition.

A good value proposition is always simple, and easy to articulate and understand. Too often, a product manager or marketer will use fancy jargon and elaborate explanations. This indicates that the person doesn't have a clear idea of what he is trying to communicate. A good value proposition, like Dominos' 'thirty-minute delivery' or Meesho's 'most affordable fashion' or

Lenskart's 'largest eyewear selection', can be articulated in just a few words, doesn't need any further explanation, and can be understood by anyone from a five-year-old to an eighty-year-old. Never underestimate the power of simplicity. But coming up with a simple value proposition is anything but simple. You often need to go through many options, critically examine each one and keep refining them until you have something that is authentic, that matters to customers and that can be easily and clearly communicated.

What Is NPS and Why Does It Matter?

Businesses have always known that happy and loyal customers lead to strong word-of-mouth marketing and eventually, a very high-quality business overall. But there was no way for businesses to formally measure how well they were doing on this front. This changed in 2003 when Frederick F. Reichheld, a partner at Bain & Company, introduced the concept of Net Promoter Score (NPS) in a *Harvard Business Review* article titled *The One Number That You Need to Grow,* which started a revolution in customer centricity. The key insight behind NPS is that businesses which have a high rate of organic referral tend to have much higher profitability in the long run.

NPS starts with asking a fundamental question: 'How likely would you be to recommend us to a friend on a scale of one to ten?' People who respond nine or ten are considered 'promoters', those at seven or eight are considered 'passive' and those who answer six or below are 'detractors'. Imagine that you ask 100 people this question and find that 70 per cent are promoters, 10 per cent are passive and 20 per cent are detractors. In this case, your NPS is 70 - 20 = 10. Reichheld argued that if you can obsess about getting the best NPS in your category, you will thrive as a business.

As a company, Disney thinks long and hard about what its customers want. They know that the waiting lines for the rides in their amusement parks are long and tiresome. They tackle this problem head-on by ensuring that there are enough grand displays and performers interacting with guests to serve as a distraction from having to wait in line. Another tactic they implement is posting wait times at the queue to every attraction or ride. When they present this waiting time to customers, they always overestimate it, so that when their turn at the ride comes earlier than expected, the customers are delighted. And moments of unexpected delight are sure to boost NPS. At CULT, we wrote down, 'Always exceed customer expectations,' as one of the core values that we strive to deliver every single day.

The story of Doug Dietz, an industrial designer at General Electric, provides a compelling example of how focusing on customer experience can significantly impact NPS, demonstrating the importance of enriching customer lives.[7] Initially proud of his MRI machine design, Dietz's perspective changed when he witnessed the fear and distress it caused a young patient. This moment of realization highlighted a gap in his design approach: while the technical aspects of the machine were prioritized, the patient experience was overlooked. This is a common issue, where businesses focus on product features rather than the holistic experience of the end-user. In response, Dietz assembled a diverse team, including experts from a children's museum and health care staff, to reimagine the MRI experience from a child's perspective. They transformed the MRI suite into an adventure-themed space, such as a jungle or pirate island, turning a frightening experience into a playful and engaging one. This change drastically reduced the need for sedation in children and improved the efficiency of the scanning process. By addressing the fear and anxiety associated with MRI scans for children, Dietz's team not only improved the technical performance of the MRI machine but also profoundly enriched the customer experience. There are numerous pithy sayings about the customer being the king. In India, many small shops have a sign saying, 'Grahak devta hai', recognizing at a very deep level that the businesses exist to service the authentic needs of the customer. Whether it is a B2C or a B2B business, the customer needs to part with their hard-earned money to buy your product or service. They must choose from a plethora of options in a crowded marketplace. If you can build a culture where everyone in the organization obsessively cares about the customers, takes the time to immerse themselves in the customer's context and unearths genuine insights that can lead to clear choices and investments, you will be a truly customer-centric organization. We often complicate business by using complex jargon and management theories. At its root, though, business boils down to whether you have a genuine value proposition that really matters to consumers or not. If you can deliver this value proposition consistently or, even better, exceed customer expectations to create true delight, leading to strong word-of-mouth marketing, you will have the kernel of an amazing business on your hands.

To truly delight the customer, you need sharp insights, but you also need to work very hard to build a product that is head and shoulders above the market. This applies to products as well as services. In his bestselling book *Unreasonable Hospitality*, Will Guidara talks about paying minute attention to the smallest detail to deliver hospitality that customers can't even imagine and, as a result, becoming the top-rated restaurant in the world. Let's dive into the nuts and bolts of building an amazing product in the next chapter.

FROM PAGE TO ACTION

While you might think that everyone is a potential customer for your product or service, you need to narrow down your audience to a relatively small and specific group of people. Here are a few prompts to get you thinking:

a. **Find Your Niche:** Create a customer persona that captures the specific traits, background and needs of your ideal target audience. Who are the people facing the problem that you're trying to solve? Where do they live? How old are they? What are their interests and passions? Be as specific as you can as you create this profile.

b. Still not sure who your customer is? Here are some things you can do:

   i. Spend a day in the field—this could be a mall, a restaurant, a local vegetable market or a gym, wherever your customers hang out. You could also visit a competitor to see how your customers are behaving there.

   ii. Listen to what your potential customers are saying—to each other, to vendors and salespeople, on their social media.

   iii. Take copious notes about everything you see, observe and hear.

iv. For everything you notice, ask 'why' it is the way it is.

v. The next day, review your notes to see if you have stumbled across any customer insights that you could narrow down to find your own niche.

c. Based on the above exercise, try to craft a value proposition that you can communicate in just one sentence.

6

Product Is Marketing

It's not enough to be busy, so are the ants. The question is, what are we busy about?

—Henry David Thoreau

[Apple is] dedicated to building products that make people's lives better, often in ways that we couldn't have even imagined, enabling them to do things that they have never done before.

—Susan Prescott, Apple's vice president of
worldwide developer relations and
enterprise and education markets

The first big challenge that confronts every entrepreneur who is starting up is that of building a product. Building a product is not easy. In fact, it is insanely difficult to create a product that is universally loved, which explains why there are only a handful of outstanding products that are launched each year, cornering most of the investor dollars and market share. Building products is both an art and a science. As a start-up founder, whether you come from a product background or not, you must be passionate about building something that your customers will love, and you must be willing to obsess about this. Kunal Shah uses the term 'product craftsmanship', and I really like the metaphor likening the product-building process to a craft. A craftsman brings a sense of artistry to making a product, chiselling away slowly and patiently until every blemish has been ironed out. That's the mindset cultivated by great product companies such as Pixar and Disney, which produce one hit product after another.

The beauty of outstanding products is that they convert your customers into your marketers for free and guess what—this is the most authentic form of marketing in the world. Imagine seeing an annoying ad on YouTube while you are impatiently waiting for your content to start streaming, versus having a dinner conversation with friends during which someone mentions that you must check out Naru Noodle Bar in Bengaluru. While you can't wait to click on the 'skip' button in the former example, you will probably line up in the digital queue on Monday evening to book your spot at the ramen restaurant before all the slots for the week are sold out. Many brands such as Starbucks, Zudio, Oberoi and others never advertise and they don't need to, as their customers do the job for them. It makes sense to remember the phrase 'Product Is Marketing' in the early days of your start-up journey and approach product building with the same mindset. The moment you have a product in your hand that customers truly love, you will know that you are onto something special.

As Jeff Bezos said in an interview, 'I'm going to put the vast majority of my energy, attention, and dollars into building a great product or service. And put a smaller amount into shouting about it—marketing. Because I know if I build a great product or service, my customers will tell each other.'[1]

Have you ever seen an ad for Sriracha, that famous hot sauce that everybody loves to put on everything? You probably haven't, because Huy Fong Foods, the company behind it, does not advertise. CEO David Tran, a Chinese-origin immigrant from Vietnam, created the Sriracha hot sauce for the Asian community in America. Early on, the company started supplying Asian chefs and restaurants, and that formed the foundation of its word-of-mouth popularity that continues today. Despite the brand not even having a website or social media presence for much of its existence, Sriracha has become a cult product—it has inspired entire cookbooks, Halloween costumes and even tattoos! The brand has survived an onslaught of competitors as well as controversy about its authenticity. A shortage of the chilli peppers used in Sriracha affected production in 2022 which resulted in soaring prices that people were apparently willing to pay to get their hands on the hot sauce. The product is just that loved.[2]

Japan is renowned for building products that customers truly love. From the Sony Walkman, which was once all the rage, to cars that have dominated global markets for decades to fashion brands like Uniqlo and Muji—there is something about Japanese products that connects with customers at a deeper, intangible level. Japanese culture embraces Zen principles of being patient, of perfecting something as in a beautiful, slow tea ceremony, while appreciating nature and minimalism. All this informs their approach to product building and, as a result, the products carry a certain charm that customers can feel at a visceral level.

The Japanese concepts of Atarimae Hinshitsu and Miryokuteki Hinshitsu capture the spirit with which the

Japanese approach the art of making products. Atarimae Hinshitsu is the idea that all products meet a functional requirement. In product terms, it means a level of quality that is essential and non-negotiable. On the other hand, Miryokuteki Hinshitsu is the idea that a product has an aesthetic quality, something that truly sets it apart. Understanding the difference between these two concepts is akin to understanding the difference between products that work versus products that inspire. It means that first and foremost, the product should do its functional job really well and, having achieved that, it should also carry an aesthetic appeal that enables the product to enhance its environment and create a sense of delight for the user with its mere presence.[3] Every Apple product embodies both these principles at its core. While Apple products embed state-of-the-art technology and are carefully engineered to work with very little effort on the user's part, they are also aesthetically striking. A MacBook sitting on the table looks like a piece of art or an installation that you can admire from a distance.

ENTREPRENEURIAL WISDOM

Functionality Versus Delight

When designing your product, be careful to distinguish between the bare minimum functional requirements and the one aspect that will make it truly stand out. Often, companies introduce too many product features. In the ensuing clutter, neither does the product function as it should, nor does it create customer delight!

New York-based pastry chef Dominique Ansel had been obsessively focused on making the perfect croissants, getting the fermentation, the crust, the volume and flakiness all just right. One day, his staff challenged him to make a doughnut, so Ansel decided to draw on his croissant expertise—and, after dozens of taste tests, the cronut was born. A food blogger happened to write an article on this marriage of beloved pastries, which then happened to go viral, and the next morning, Ansel woke up to a line of a hundred people outside his bakery. You've probably read about how the cronut craze unfolded, with other bakeries trying to copy Ansel's creation and even the rise of a cronut black market! And you, like many others, must have wondered about Ansel's marketing gimmicks and budgets, the tricks the bakery must have used to draw the hundreds of people who were queuing up outside at 6 a.m. every day.[4]

The truth, though, is that there was no marketing. At that time, the Dominique Ansel bakery was a tiny, neighbourhood business with a staff of four people. The cronut was the result of a pastry chef paying obsessive attention to detail, a perfectionist bringing his technical expertise to a new product, which customers loved. It helped that customers felt seen and cared for when the bakery staff served them hot chocolate as they waited in line. When Ansel was asked about his next big viral pastry, he said that he wasn't trying to create something gimmicky; he just wanted to make delicious pastries that his customers loved. 'Even with all the money in the world, you cannot recreate the cronut,' he said, on Reid Hoffman's *Masters of Scale* podcast. And this is the truth about most products—you need customer love and devotion, otherwise, no matter how much money or shrewd marketing strategy you pour into it, it isn't going to survive and grow in the long run.[5]

Closer to home, a product that grew incredibly popular largely thanks to its quality, innovation and word-of-mouth marketing is the now ubiquitous Pulse candy, launched by the DS Group in 2015. At a time when candy was just something you got as change from stores, people were buying Pulse in bulk quantities. The company spent two years researching and perfecting the taste of the candy, and it clearly paid off. The familiar *kaccha aam*, or raw mango, flavour of the boiled candy, with its surprising tangy and salty centre, captured the taste buds of an entire population. The DS Group made over Rs 100 crore in just eight months! This is a lot when you think about the fact that the candy costs just one rupee a piece and that the company spent nothing on advertising. Instead, they ensured that Pulse was available in every little corner shop across Indian cities and relied on people loving the taste and telling their friends about it.[6]

Getting to 1000 True Fans

One of my all-time favourite frameworks for early-stage product building is what the author and futurist Kevin Kelly calls '1000 true fans'. It has been over two decades since Kelly's famous blog post about the importance of acquiring your first 1000 true fans as you set out to launch a new product, but the idea remains as relevant today. Who is a true fan? A true fan is someone who loves a product so much that they feel almost responsible for making their friends and family try it out too, because they believe it will improve the quality of everyone's lives.[7] We saw this play out very strongly in the early days of CULT, with every member actively championing the cause and bringing friends and family along, even without any referral incentives because they thought it would have a positive impact on their lives.

The number—1000—is important as it is the right size. It is not so small that it can be composed of just your immediate family members and friends but isn't that large that you will need to find a massive budget to get the message out. You should be able to reach out to a few thousand customers in your community and through online mailing lists or groups that you are part of. As you put your initial product out and start to measure customer reactions, look out for the signs that someone is a true fanatic and try to decode what's behind that. If you can get to 1000 true fans, you can eventually get to a million true fans as well and your product will be amazingly successful. Rameshwaram Cafe is a great example of acquiring 1000 true fans. The cafe just focused on perfecting the taste of the dosas, idlis and other south Indian favourites on their menu, and as soon as they opened shop, word began to spread around Indiranagar and very soon all over Bengaluru. Without any marketing whatsoever, they have become one of the most popular spots for a meal in the city.

ENTREPRENEURIAL WISDOM

Good Products Don't Need Expensive Marketing

The best products are the ones that spread by word of mouth. Customers fall in love with them and can't do without them. If you find that you're spending more and more on marketing each month, you might need to think about your product again. Does it work seamlessly? Have you reached PMF? Does it have a feature that makes it truly special?

Understanding the PMF Journey

A start-up is born twice. The first time is when the founders decide to quit their jobs and the second is when they achieve product–market fit. When we hear statistics about how many companies barely survive for even two years, it is often because they don't have a clear PMF. PMF is the state at which you have achieved acceptance in the marketplace, the product is economically viable and you can see a clear path to scale.

A leading indicator of product–market fit was suggested by Sean Ellis, who headed growth for start-ups like Dropbox and Eventbrite in their early years and is known for coining the term 'growth hacker'. It is now called the Sean Ellis test and involves asking users a simple question: 'How would you feel if you could no longer use the product?' The answers range from 'very disappointed' to 'somewhat disappointed' to 'not disappointed at all'. The general rule of thumb is that if at least 40 per cent of your customers say they would be 'very disappointed' on not being able to use your product, then your company has achieved product–market fit. For example, a 2015 open research project polled the users of Slack and found that 51 per cent said they'd be 'very disappointed' without the product. This doesn't sound like a big percentage, but it was clearly an indicator of the huge success Slack would go on to achieve.[8] At CULT, we often hear that our members, when looking to move house, first check the new apartment's proximity to CULT. This means that the gym has become an integral part of their lifestyle, a reflection of our product–market fit.

Sometimes, we can learn lessons about product–market fit from products that failed in the market. One of the most well-known of these is the story of 'New Coke'. In the late 1980s, the Coca-Cola company had been facing increasing competition from Pepsi and there was a seeming lack of consumer awareness.

So, what did they do? After over 2,00,000 taste tests, they launched a new formula. They were so confident about this taste that they decided to phase out the original Coke and launched New Coke. The launch was followed by an unprecedented response from customers—they were furious. The company was bombarded with angry phone calls and letters—including one addressed to 'The Chief Dodo of the Coca-Cola Company!'[9]

Less than three months after launching New Coke, the Coca-Cola company announced the return of 'old' Coke, and this made front-page news across America. So, what did they get wrong? It seems that they had done a great deal of product research—according to the numerous taste tests they'd conducted, the new formula was superior to that of the original. But what they hadn't considered were certain aspects of the market. For one, nobody had asked for a new taste—customers had never expressed dissatisfaction with the original. Second, customers identified very deeply with the Coke brand and this sudden change made them immediately nostalgic for the product they knew and loved. And finally, customers were not given a choice in the matter. It's not like the Coca-Cola company had just put out a new flavour, they had replaced the original and customers did not want something new forced on them.[10]

Based on everything that I have seen, a good PMF boils down to the following:

- Strong word of mouth: Customers love the product so much that they cannot wait to tell their friends about it.
- Positive unit economics. You can sell the product at a healthy margin.
- Retention: A healthy portion of users keep coming back for more.
- Scale trajectory: You can see a clear path to predictably scale the offering.

Once you have a clear PMF, you are dramatically better placed to build the business. You have proven that there is a clear need for what you are building, and you are able to make a positive impact for your customers.

Doing One Thing 10X Better

Most companies these days know that customer centricity is important. Not only do they pay adequate lip service to this idea, they also genuinely try to address it through internal initiatives, product enhancements and the right pep talks with the respective teams. The problem with this is that it often results in a laundry list of features and unsustainable promises in the quest for creating customer delight. In this way, things never really scale up or become part of the consistent long-term promise. It is important to recognize that you cannot do a hundred different things better than the competition. It is important to distinguish between what is hygiene and what can be done much better. Hygiene refers to all the things that must be consistently fulfilled through quality systems and processes (for example, starting classes on time at CULT, which is non-negotiable) to ensure that these aspects of the product or service are highly reliable, leading to the gaining of trust over time. In order to achieve customer delight above the meeting of basic expectations, you have to try and pick just one dimension in which you are going to truly wow the customer and then invest adequate resources to ensure that you do a very high-quality job of implementing and delivering that feature consistently. Think of IndiGo's promise to always be on time or Netflix's recommendations feature. Customers don't rave about a company meeting the average metric consistently but about a single feature that puts the company head and shoulders above all the other contenders. It requires clarity of thought, elimination of many good ideas and consistent investment to build and maintain an edge in the chosen area that customers also care about.

In an incredibly competitive market, BigBasket understood very clearly that grocery delivery was no longer just about providing customers with a good experience—which is the very minimum requirement. Instead, they zeroed in on the one core need that would differentiate them in a crowded market and focused on getting that right. This is a customer's need to have all the items in an order delivered. Other delivery apps don't keep inventory and instead partner with local stores who do not update inventory or run out of stock, leaving customers disappointed even though the order is delivered in record time. BigBasket focused instead on what they refer to as 'What You See Is What You Get'—everything in your basket will be delivered to your home. The company achieved this by using a combination of an inventory and hyperlocal model to ensure complete fulfilment of orders. They also take punctuality very seriously, and while they may not offer nine-minute deliveries, the time slots given at the time of ordering are almost always fulfilled. This is what made BigBasket the most preferred online grocery delivery company for nearly a decade until they were outsmarted by the players who understood that for many of the items in the basket, superfast delivery is the most important metric. As a result, in the last few years, BigBasket has been consistently losing its share of the market.[11]

At Myntra, streamlining orders, search and timely delivery were all hygiene. We used our data on customer behaviour to find the one thing we could do 10X better. Our teams observed that customers seemed to really enjoy spending time browsing the site, almost like 'window shopping' in the offline world. So, we decided that the one thing we could do significantly better than other platforms was addressing this need, by getting product cataloguing just right and obsessing about the visual delight in the browsing experience. At one time, we even hired a top design firm in LA to help us design a state-of-the-art user interface. No other platform at that time was creating a visual shopping experience the way we were. In time, window shopping Myntra's latest collections became a form of afternoon entertainment for many customers, something that would, every now and then, lead to an impulse purchase.

Good Product Is About Elimination, Not Addition

Deep Nishar, who led product teams at both Google and LinkedIn, offers great advice when it comes to focusing on eliminating features from a product. He offers a framework from one's personal life, which can then translate into how you look at products. According to him, every time you want to add a piece of clothing to your wardrobe, you should ensure that you remove one existing piece. Applying this to products, you should be directing more of your energy into thinking about what you can eliminate rather than what you could be adding. This is easier said than done. Most product managers are good at imagining what new features to add but struggle to remove the old ones. There is always some justification for keeping a feature once it has been launched, on the pretext that some users are still using it. As they say, 'Good is the enemy of great,' and hence it is very important for product managers to watch out and be ruthless when it comes to elimination.[12]

The now popular app Instagram originated as Burbn, which was meant to be a location-based social network, named after founder Kevin Systrom's favourite alcoholic beverage. But even Systrom had an inkling that the product was too complicated and offered way too many features. Systrom kept analysing the data to understand how users were using the product. What he found was that people weren't using many of the product features at all, except for one: the photos. Systrom and co-founder Mike Krieger realized that the most engaging aspect of their app was the ability to share photos. They removed everything from the product except the photo, like and comment feature, and relaunched it as the app we know today: Instagram.[13] As Leonardo da Vinci famously said, 'Simplicity is the ultimate sophistication.' This is one principle every product company would do well to remember and inculcate in their cultures.

One of the most ubiquitous objects that readily comes to mind is the humble Post-it™ note. What sets this product apart is its sheer simplicity, and therein lies its primary selling point. The invention of the Post-it™ note, however, was a stroke of serendipity. It all began when a chemist by the name of Spencer Silver inadvertently stumbled upon the creation of a weak, pressure-sensitive adhesive, contrary to his original pursuit of a powerful adhesive. Interestingly, it was several years later that another scientist, Art Fry, recognized the latent potential within this seemingly weak adhesive. He envisioned using it to craft bookmarks that could delicately cling to paper surfaces without causing any damage. Customers quickly caught on to the beauty of this simplicity. The Post-it™ note gained immense popularity for its remarkable ease of use and its versatility in an array of tasks.[14]

Building a Product-First Culture

Amazon, known for its innovative strategies, once adopted an interesting approach for new product launches and redesigns. They would start by crafting a hypothetical press release,[15] outlining the vision for the new product and how it would enhance the customer experience. All product managers were expected to draft a formal press release long before the first line of code was even written. It ensured that instead of simply having an internal rationale, every product manager was very clear on the exact benefits that would accrue to the end user. If the press release was not compelling enough, there was no need to go through the other stages of product specifications. This strategy prioritizes outcomes for the users, rather than the output of the product itself.

Walker Lockhart, who previously worked at Amazon, brought a variation of this concept to Nordstrom. He transformed the press release idea into a customer letter format. In this approach, a fictional customer persona writes a letter to the CEO, expressing their satisfaction with the product and explaining the reasons for their contentment. This method provides a customer-centric view of the product, emphasizing its impact from the user's perspective. For decades, Nordstrom has written the playbook on what it means to have an incredible customer-first culture and is a great role model for any company that wishes to imbibe this.

If you don't inculcate a product-first culture, you will very soon fall out of touch with what the customer needs, which is what happened to Kodak. In 1975, an engineer at Kodak developed the first digital camera, marking a groundbreaking innovation in photography. However, Kodak's executives decided against pursuing this digital path. Their reasoning was based on the company's profitable film sales; they feared that venturing into digital photography would undercut their lucrative film business. As a result, Kodak chose to focus on its existing film products, setting aside the digital camera invention. Fast forward to 2012, and Kodak found itself in financial turmoil and declared bankruptcy. The primary cause of their downfall was the global shift from film to digital photography—a transition that Kodak had initially pioneered but chose to ignore. Their reluctance to adapt to the emerging digital market, which they themselves had once been at the forefront of, ultimately led to their decline in an era where digital cameras became the norm, rendering film nearly obsolete.[16]

We are now part of a giant global village in which information flows at the speed of light. What that means is that we don't have to start from scratch as we look to define the initial set of features for a new product or when we are looking for ways to enhance a product. Consumers around the globe all have fairly similar problems. When an idea's time has come, due to various technology breakthroughs, it takes off simultaneously across the world. When Uber started to take off in the US, we had Ola come up in India and many ride-hailing apps in nearly every country of the world. Similarly, DoorDash in the US and Meituan in China triggered the rise of food delivery. The benefit of this is that you can study similar players in other geographies and take plenty of inspiration from them about how to build your product. In the early days of Myntra, we obsessively studied Zappos, Zalando and Asos in the US. Similarly, when we were building CULT, we studied all the emerging group fitness players in the US such as Crossfit, Barry's Bootcamp, Orange Theory and Soul Cycle.

While it may seem obvious, many founders still approach a problem as if they are the first people in the world to attempt to solve it. This is nearly impossible unless you are doing fundamental research and looking for completely new breakthroughs. What most entrepreneurs engage in is applied problem-solving, and in nearly every case, there are people in other geographies who have either already solved the problem or are actively trying to. A lot of these companies have many smart people obsessing about a problem every single day. By studying how they are approaching the problem and then mapping it to your local context, you can make major strides in a matter of days, avoiding a lot of dead-end approaches. Sometimes it also helps to ask, 'Who else has tried to solve this problem and why did they fail?' When we were trying to build Care.fit to approach primary care in a completely different manner, we looked at many other players in India who have tried to build primary care-first solutions but couldn't scale. We created a very different customer-first approach and were off to a decent start until Covid put paid to the nascent effort.

Three brothers from Cologne in Germany—Oliver, Mark and Alexander Samwer—pioneered this copycat business model, which worked beautifully for a while. They would study companies in America that had become hugely successful and then build replica companies in Europe. Once these companies grew successful, they would often sell the copycat company to the original—for huge sums of money! For example, they created Alando, a copycat of eBay, which they sold to eBay for $43 million within a hundred days of launching it. In other cases, they held onto their businesses which went on to make them large sums of money—such as Zalando, billed as the 'Zappos of Europe', which was worth over $25 billion at its peak. The Samwer brothers eventually launched a start-up studio, Rocket Internet. While the Samwers did a great job of creating fast copies, they failed to build entrepreneurial teams with sufficient ownership and long-term orientation and hence a majority of their copycat businesses didn't work out.[17]

In India, D2C aggregators like Mensa, Goat Brands and Global Bees were all inspired by the rise of the D2C platform, Thrasio, in the US. But one must remember that copying is just the start. Each market has several local nuances that need to be understood. While e-commerce and ride-hailing might have been inspired by players in the West, the execution playbook in India had to be completely different.

According to Walter Isaacson's biography of Steve Jobs, when the iPhone was in development, Jobs was very particular about the aesthetic elements of the device. He believed that the design of a product was not just about how it looked but also how it felt to the user. This philosophy extended to the smallest details, including the curvature of the iPhone's corners. Jobs was reportedly so focused on getting the corners just right that he summoned the design team to discuss the radius of the curves. He felt that the original design wasn't quite perfect and insisted on making slight adjustments until it felt right to him. This level of detail might have seemed excessive to some, but it was part of Jobs's approach to creating products that were not only functional but also beautiful and enjoyable to use. It also reminded the teams periodically that small details matter and that no detail was too small for Jobs himself to obsess over. Over time, this became an integral part of product culture at Apple.[18] Similarly if you read about the evolution of Tesla as a product, Elon Musk would time and again obsess about small details and challenge his engineers to make the impossible possible. In one such example, he insisted that door handles should automatically pop out at the touch. This was received by the team with a lot of resistance. In the end, they executed the idea, which became one of the most loved features of Tesla cars.[19]

Attention to detail is the essence of a product-first culture. You need to obsess over the tiniest things to really create a product that is one of a kind. In fact, it's often the unexpected little things that you build into an app that draws people in, and not its basic functionality, which is expected. Duolingo's success story highlights the importance of attention to detail in the competitive mobile app market. The company has mastered the art of user engagement and brand identity through a meticulous focus on seemingly minor elements, such as notifications. Duolingo's approach to notifications stands out; they are crafted with humour, cheekiness and occasionally a nudge of guilt. Imagine a user neglecting their lessons for a bit, only to receive a playful reminder from Duolingo: 'Miss us? Your Spanish tree is getting lonely.' This clever strategy fosters a personal connection between the user and the app, demonstrating how small touches can significantly impact user experience and brand perception.[20]

Fallacy of the Fail-Fast Approach—You Are Not Facebook!

Facebook had a dream run from the very beginning, with users lining up in college campuses waiting for the platform to launch, and then non-college goers waiting for the service to be available to them as well. So, wherever Facebook launched, people flocked to it, providing another fresh (and free) burst of growth. This went on for nearly five years until growth started to peter out. This was about the same time that Facebook was considering going public, so it was crucial for them to keep growing. Facebook had a very strong tech-first culture and Mark Zuckerberg thought that engineers should solve the problem of growth. And thus, the concept of growth hacking was born. The team was empowered to make fast decisions, launch quickly, learn from feedback and then iterate again. This approach resulted in numerous incremental improvements and Facebook went from 100M users to 500M users in less than two years. During this phase, Zuckerberg would use the phrase 'fail fast' and it caught on not only in Facebook but across the entire digital world. In fact, his motto was: 'Move fast and break things.'[21]

Very soon start-ups started chanting the same mantra and it became an accepted approach. But I don't think the fail-fast approach necessarily works for an early-stage start-up. There is a huge difference between Facebook trying to fail fast and a brand-new start-up trying to do so. Facebook had their core value proposition figured out and all their experiments began with only 1 per cent or fewer of their users. Hence, the fallout of failure was quite limited and the feature could be easily rolled back without any impact to the core business. For a new start-up, though, the entire product is on the line every time it tries to 'fail fast'. Start-ups need to focus on just a few things, putting in enough thought and refinement to ensure a 'wow' experience for the early adopters. If something is not working, one needs to keep making incremental improvements and give it a long runway. If start-ups choose to fail fast, pretty much every start-up will fail. A big part of the initial product journey is about building collaboratively with users, with continuous feedback from an initial set of customers. If you reach the conclusion that it is a complete dead end, you will have to obviously think about a pivot, but a pivot too early is as bad as a pivot too late.

In 2014, Microsoft launched an AI chatbot called Tay on Twitter in an experiment on 'conversational understanding'. Unfortunately, in just twenty-four hours, Tay had been corrupted, and turned into a racist and misogynistic conversationalist. Unfortunately, Microsoft had not put enough thought into the design of their chatbot, or else they would have blacklisted certain words, or hard-coded certain responses to sensitive questions or comments. Especially since they were putting this 'experiment' on an extremely public forum like Twitter, Microsoft ought to have been more careful. This is one example of how short-term, fail-fast thinking can cause actual damage.[22]

Most start-up journeys involve one or more pivots somewhere along the way. One critical reason for this is that start-up founders know so much more twelve to eighteen months into the journey than they did on day one. But after more than a year of hard knocks on the ground, wrestling with real problems and interacting with customers, you start to develop a much deeper understanding of the market potential, the other players who are trying to solve the problem (or have already solved it!), as well as a much better appreciation for what you are good at (and what you're not good at!) and what the customers are willing to pay for (or not pay for!). Every piece of feedback can lead to incremental improvements or just the acceptance that there are areas of improvement. If there are too many of the latter, you might have to eventually ask yourself if this is a lost cause and whether your dwindling resources would be better put towards a fresh start.

Most early-stage founders struggle with the choice of when to make a pivot. After you have invested considerable energy into building a product, testing with hundreds of users, making many changes to the product and spending a significant amount of the capital raised, founders often feel deeply invested in what has been built. With every iteration and positive piece of feedback, there is renewed hope that things might start inching up in the coming months. At the same time, when one zooms out, there may not be any strong sign of a product–market fit, or the product may have low retention rates with no core group of truly loyal fans emerging. At this time, you may feel like you're at the crossroads and not sure whether to keep marching along or to completely change your product and strategy. There is no easy answer here and it largely boils down to a judgement call. Founders can contemplate the following questions to arrive at a decision about whether to pivot or not to pivot:

• What was the initial hypothesis? Based on all the learnings and data so far, does the initial thesis seem more valid or do many factors not stand any more?

- What is your own sense of excitement about the initial thesis? Are you getting more convinced or is the data starting to stack up against it?
- Have you learnt any new insights about the space that you were not aware of before? Do these insights strengthen or weaken the original thesis?
- Are there any companies in this space that are doing well? If so, do they have any significant advantages that you cannot replicate? If there is no one doing well, that might imply a very shallow market or a market that's quite mature and settled.
- Do you feel energized going into work every morning? Do you have clarity about the problems that you need to solve?

After pondering these questions, you will have to make a judgement call on whether a pivot is the right thing for you. If you have no clear sign of product–market fit in sight after having given sufficient time to the current thesis and have new insights that strengthen an alternate thesis, it might be a good idea to pivot. A general rule for pivoting is to choose a hard pivot rather than trying to keep one foot in both boats. Sometimes, there is a tendency to want to keep both options alive, but this reduces the chance of success for either approach. A start-up has limited resources, a short runway to make things work and, with a dilution in focus, neither path will get sufficient chance to shine.

Once you decide to pivot, it is best to get the whole team together, explain the rationale behind pivoting and get everyone's buy-in and commitment to make the new strategy work. Take a few days off to reset and clear your mind, before returning with renewed commitment to go all-out and test the new thesis. Pivots are a very legitimate part of the start-up process. At Myntra, we tried to make the personalization business work over four years with good customer love and differentiation, but almost no signs of meaningful scale. When we finally decided to pivot to fashion, things really took off as we were now in a much larger market with excellent market timing, as e-commerce was starting to take off, fuelled by the rise in mobile Internet use. Similarly, at CureFit, the pandemic presented a completely new challenge—many of our products which had green shoots suddenly ran out of any meaningful runway and many other opportunities for consolidating the fitness industry opened up. As a result, we had to make many hard pivots that set us up well to navigate the pandemic and emerge as a much stronger company.

Another general rule of thumb is that it is easier to pivot earlier on in the start-up journey, when the company is still small, rather than later. In 1998, Peter Thiel, Max Levchin and Luke Nosek founded Confinity as a mobile encryption company. They soon pivoted to mobile phone cash and then to PalmPilot payments using infrared beaming to transfer money. Unfortunately, this market of PalmPilot users who wanted to pay each other was very small, so they pivoted a third time to add email payments.[23] Finally, seeing an emerging market in the need for settling eBay transactions, they pivoted a final time to serve this market, becoming PayPal as we now know it. The ability to start a company and then pivot four times in just one year came from the fact that the company was still small and could quickly adapt by changing focus and tactics.

But remember that pivots are expensive and demoralizing. You are effectively writing off all your efforts and restarting from scratch. A company ideally shouldn't have to pivot but rather keep making minor course corrections along the way. If at all a pivot does need to be undertaken, it should be done after a lot of deliberation and should be definitive. There is no point pivoting and continuing to maintain the old business. At

Myntra, we started getting real traction in the fashion space only after we completely shut down the personalization business.

Live and Die with One Product—Don't Hedge in Early Days

When you start up and launch a product, you begin to get feedback from customers, and while watching what the competition and other players around the world are doing, you might start to get ideas about many different possibilities. There will be temptations to add more features or even build different products for different segments or expand into adjacencies as soon as you see some signs of a product–market fit. We made a similar mistake at CureFit. Since we were well funded and had the ambition to resolve health issues holistically, we went after all aspects of health in our early years, building products for fitness, food, mental health and even primary care. It diluted our focus and when the pandemic struck, we had to make hard choices to kill many of these products. Today we are 100 per cent focused on fitness and the business is much larger and more profitable. Given the current scale, we are now in a much better position to think about adjacent opportunities, compared to earlier stages.

Apple is the ultimate icon of the most disciplined company in the world. Tim Cook, the CEO of Apple, shared this important message with his shareholders:

> We are the most focused company that I know of or have read of or have any knowledge of. We say no to good ideas every day. We say no to great ideas in order to keep the number of things we focus on very small in number so that we can put enormous energy behind the ones we do choose. The table each of you is sitting at today, you could probably put every

product on it that Apple makes, yet Apple's revenue last year
was $40 billion.[24]

Product Makes a Brand

As a start-up gets some traction, founders need to think about
the process of building a brand and consider spending money
to do so. Many people see billboards or even iconic TV ads of
rising start-ups and that becomes an aspiration. Who doesn't
want to see their creation on national television? But advertising
should be one of the last things one thinks about when building
a brand. I like to compare building a brand for a product to how
each of us creates our own personal brand in our social groups.
We don't do this explicitly by advertising what people should
notice about us. Instead, our behaviour reflects how we are
wired, and people take notice. Some may like our personalities
and become close to us, while others choose to maintain their
distance. If people see us being consistent through ups and
downs, they start to see us as more reliable and trustworthy. If
people see us hold steady during tough times and strive even
harder for a solution, people perceive us as resilient and so
on. In other words, our personal brands are formed through
consistent action over a period. Product brands are no different.

People pay a premium for a good brand because a brand
promises to deliver time and again. People have believed in
brands such as Lifebuoy for over a hundred years now because
it has kept pace with progress and people continue to believe
that it will keep them safe from germs. Similarly, Apple fanatics
expect the brand to deliver a unique combination of amazing
aesthetics and great functionality time after time. If you want
to build a brand that customers love, you will have to work
on earning that love through diligent and consistent action. In
today's world, a brand interacts with customers at numerous

touch points digitally and sometimes offline. Each interaction is an opportunity for brand building by delivering a consistent experience, maintaining consistent design language and evolving to stay in touch with the emerging needs and tastes of the consumer. As consumers learn to trust the brand for its value proposition, loyalties will be strengthened and you will have earned a permanent place in their minds, at least until you falter on your promise.

While a student at the University of Oregon, Phil Knight ran track under coach Bill Bowerman who used to hand-sew sneakers for his runners, experimenting with lighter shoes. When Otis Davis won the Pacific Coast Conference in Bowerman's home-made shoes, many athletes wanted a pair, and this struck Phil. He co-founded Nike in 1964 with an investment of $500 each from himself and Bill. Their laser focus was on building an ultra-high-performance pair of shoes. They didn't care how it looked, only on how much speed it enabled and its superior performance on the track and, in due course, Nike came to be deeply trusted by top athletes around the world. Nike has continued to live by this philosophy and in each generation of product evolution, the brand has kept pushing the bar on how they can help athletes achieve superior performance.[25] Even when they sign on someone as renowned as Michael Jordan or LeBron James, Nike doesn't just use the superstar athlete to shout about how great the brand is. Instead, Nike works closely with these athletes to design unique products that give consumers an edge on the field while the brand uses the product superiority to further deepen customer loyalty. Product is indeed marketing for many of the leading brands in the world.

Building a start-up is all about building a product that customers love. This requires a commitment to product craftsmanship, generating unique insights and practising minimalism to build few things, and then iterating furiously to achieve true customer delight. Only then can you think about scale. A good product sells itself and a little marketing boost goes a long way. All entrepreneurs need to be great product managers and put themselves wholeheartedly into building something that stands out. This is the only way you can earn the right to be a real start-up!

FROM PAGE TO ACTION

When you have a really great product on your hands, it does your marketing for you. So, your product really is your brand. Spend a little time thinking about how you can build a product that people fall in love with:

a. **Write a Press Release:** Imagine that your product is ready to go live, and write a press release describing it in as much detail as you can. What is your product vision? What should customers look out for? Why should they be excited? What problems will your product solve?

b. Minimalism is 'in' for products. So, imagine that you were only allowed one new feature for your product—what would it be? Why? Write a page about this single, outstanding feature that will draw in a thousand (and more) true fans.

7

Growth Engine

Many start-ups die within the first twenty-four months of launching. While many don't find a convincing product–market fit, some die even if they do because they fail to figure out how to grow their business. While some founders might be happy to bootstrap a business and get to a minimal scale that can support a good lifestyle, this doesn't work for venture-funded start-ups where scale is paramount, in order to generate the returns that the VC investment requires. While PMF requires obsessing about product and customers, the growth journey requires all of that and more. In this chapter, we will look at what goes into building a very compelling growth engine.

How Big Is Your Market?

Start-up growth is determined largely by what your total addressable market (TAM) is and what the current growth rate of that market is. Many start-ups begin with wildly ambitious estimates of the potential market and, once they get to the growth stage, they realize the folly of their assumptions. Let's look at the fitness market in India as an example. One can start top-down and say that in the US, 20 per cent of the population regularly subscribes to a gym membership. India is early in its journey so let's assume it can have a penetration of 5 per cent. With 1.4 billion people, this translates into seventy million potential users. At $150/year on an average, this will translate into a $10 billion market. This is a nice big number which may look good in an investor deck. Except that it is totally wrong.

ENTREPRENEURIAL WISDOM

On a Bottoms-up Approach to Growth

While understanding TAM is important, it can be a very top-down approach. Your success actually boils down to how many customers you are focusing on and how much they like your product. This bottoms-up approach will give you much more clarity on the growth and success of your company.

Market size must be calculated based on how many people are currently paying for a service. As we look into this in more detail, we realize that India has only eight million people who pay for gym subscriptions today and, on average, they pay about $150. So, this translates into a market size of $1.2 billion, dramatically less than the previous estimate. If the market size is $1.2 billion, one cannot build a $1 billion business in this category but one can aspire for a 30 per cent market share which would be a business of $350 million. That's what CULT is gunning for. To build a larger business, we will have to find other categories or help grow the market.

The next thing to look at is growth rates. When conditions are ripe, growth rates can take off and the magic of compounding can inflate markets dramatically. The last twelve years have seen e-commerce grow at a compounded annual rate of 40 per cent. As a result, the total market which was less than $1 billion in 2010 has now grown to be worth over $60 billion and is still growing at an annual rate of 20 per cent. Rising tides indeed lift all boats, and you will be better off picking categories with high compounded annual growth rates (CAGRs).

One of the most important things to keep in mind while dealing with market size and growth rates is not to read too much into averages but look at the distribution. What I mean by this is that you can divide the entire market into relevant segments and look at the size and growth rates by segment. When we look at fitness markets by cities, we realize that Delhi and Mumbai are both about 20 per cent of the market each and growing at 10 per cent annually, while Bengaluru is about 10 per cent of the market and growing at over 20 per cent CAGR. Starting CULT in Bengaluru gave us the advantage of playing in a market that was growing rapidly and hence there was a significant organic demand, and we were able to hit our PMF goal really fast.

Customer Acquisition Makes or Breaks a Start-Up

Sustained customer acquisition is the most important activity a start-up needs to focus on after achieving product–market fit—and it is often the hardest part of the journey. Customer acquisition for an early-stage company can be very expensive and I know of many start-ups that are never able to overcome the hurdle of acquiring a customer at a reasonable acquisition cost (CAC). Early-stage start-ups have no brand or organic traffic, so all acquisitions tend to require paid marketing through Google and Facebook. Since a new start-up is not known at all, the click-through rates on ads and the conversions both tend to be significantly low, leading to very high acquisition costs. This is where a start-up needs to think hard about how to build a customer acquisition engine that has some unique advantages. One should almost think of this as building a differentiated product and go through a new CAMF—Customer Acquisition Market Fit.

Having a microfocus on a very small slice of the market that you have some leverage in is generally a good place to start. For many start-ups, this may mean focusing on a city or, better still, focusing on a very small market within a city. At CULT, we only focused on a small part of south Bengaluru for our first two years. FMCG companies have a standard playbook of launching a product in a city like Pune, which is a good representation of India as a whole, and gauging market receptivity by how the product fares there. The same can also be extended to an online environment. Say, your product is relevant for new mums with kids below the age of five. Instead of just advertising, you can focus on building a very strong content-led community for this group, create better content than your competitors do and work on organic placement of products only after you see healthy engagement within that community. Or you can become a very active participant in other such communities online. FirstCry has done an amazing job of building a community for first-time mums where they can share and learn from each other during what can be a harrowing few years before and after birth.[1]

A huge challenge for an early-stage start-up is getting noticed. Just like real life, you need to be bold in order to get noticed, and that means being over the top and having at least some feature or story that becomes a show-stopper. This is easier to do if you are a well-funded start-up. Once you feel confident about your PMF, you can think of a one-time strategic investment to make a splash and get widely noticed. But note that this strategy will only work if your product is sure to stand out and make an instant impression on first-time users, otherwise it will end up being an expensive mistake. If you haven't raised significant capital, you are better off being patient and investing in various organic means of acquisition before considering significant spends.

When Uber first entered the Indian market, they knew they were coming into a culture of regular autorickshaw and local taxi usage—thanks to the many people in big cities requiring transport for their daily commute. Instead of spending their budgets on TV advertising, huge billboards or even social media ads, Uber focused entirely on customer acquisition through referrals, outstanding service and steep discounts. They first hired a fleet of super premium vehicles including the Mercedes S Class and BMW 7 series.[2] When someone booked a cab and saw the car that showed up, they were always blown away and made sure they told everyone in their circle. Suddenly everyone wanted to try the 'Uber experience'. Facing stiff competition from their homegrown rival, Ola, Uber managed to acquire customers by becoming almost indispensable to them. Anyone who downloaded the app in its early days in India might remember paying almost nothing for rides, getting exciting discounts and points, and constantly receiving nudges to invite more users to the platform. This understanding that customer acquisition was the key to success helped the company become deeply entrenched in India.

The success story of Figma, a highly recognized software in the design world, underscores the pivotal role that customer acquisition can play in building a successful business. They took a strategic approach, first focusing on understanding and integrating what their users truly needed into their product. This ensured that upon launch, the product resonated strongly with their target audience, making customer acquisition more effective. Figma made a strategic choice to build a browser-only interface that made it easy to work on the designs from anywhere instead of having to download cumbersome software. They also enabled real-time collaboration so that multiple users could work on a design simultaneously, enhancing each other's output.

Prior to the release, Figma smartly built a community, creating a ready and receptive audience for their product. This pre-launch community building was crucial in overcoming initial customer acquisition challenges. They also hosted demos to generate buzz, engaging potential customers early and gathering valuable feedback to refine their product. The community was further extended by building a plug-in ecosystem so that many other developers could participate in enhancing the product. This freemium model enabled Figma to acquire early adopters who could experience the product features and talk about this in the designer community for word of mouth to build up.[3]

ENTREPRENEURIAL WISDOM

On Gaining and Sustaining Customers

Drawing first-time customers and turning them into loyal users are two very different things. If you understand this very clearly, you will better understand your company's CAC and LTV.

Understanding CAC and LTV

More often than not, it is the Customer-Acquisition-Cost (CAC) that breaks the back of many a fledgling start-up. You obviously need to acquire customers to grow and since no one knows an early-stage start-up, by definition, it is very hard to acquire customers unless you spend money. Thus, CAC becomes a super important consideration. Let's look at what CAC is and how to calculate it. The simplest and most accurate way to calculate CAC is to take your total marketing spends and divide that by the total customers acquired in that month. Let's assume you spent Rs 10 lakh and acquired 500 customers. Then your CAC is Rs 2000. Now, some companies might leave out their brand budgets from the calculation which might be okay in later years, but early-stage start-ups should use the entire marketing budget or else you get an inaccurate picture. It is a good practice to track your CAC on a month-over-month (MoM) basis and track the trend line. Ideally you will want to see your CAC come down at some point as you get better at targeting your customers.

Now, let's assume that the product that you are selling retails for Rs 3000 and your margin on the product is Rs 2500, including all direct costs such as logistics. So, your net contribution margin (CM) in this case is Rs 500. You acquired a customer for Rs 2000, but the CM on this transaction is only five hundred, which is clearly going to leave you in the red—not a great place to be. What's the way out? It all depends on how frequently this same customer will come back and buy from you again. Let's assume that the customer will buy four times a year, and let's pick a five-year period to compute the lifetime value. So, over five years, the customer will make twenty transactions, and your CM is Rs 500 every time, adding up to Rs 5000. So, the lifetime-value (LTV) of this customer is Rs 5000, and you spent a CAC of Rs 2000. The LTV/CAC ratio is then about 2.5 which effectively means that you will make 150 per cent of your original investment on this customer. This is not bad, but given the many other costs also involved in running a business, most people consider an LTV of 3–5 very healthy and above 5 is when you are really killing it.

While I have used the LTV of one customer as an example, you need to consider LTV for the average customer, as not everyone will stay on the platform doing five transactions. When you factor in the churn rate and compute the average number of transactions across the entire user base, you get a true picture of the LTV. The higher the churn rate, the lower the LTV. Most people obsess about unit economics but don't pay enough attention to the churn rate, which has a huge bearing on the overall LTV. Building a strong foundation for healthy retention can go a long way in ensuring sustainable LTV/CAC. In the early days of e-commerce, the CAC for most companies was over Rs 1000 and clearly unsustainable, given the very thin margins. But as some players differentiated themselves with quality of service and strong word of mouth, CAC began to fall. At Myntra, when we were able to bring CAC down to Rs 400, growth really took off. Flipkart did even better with CAC below Rs 250, enabling hyper-growth for many years.

Getting to Contribution Margin Positive Before Growth

One of the most important factors in figuring out whether you are growth ready or not is to see if you are contribution margin positive or not. Simply put, contribution margin is the amount that a customer has paid you minus all direct variable costs that go into fulfilling that order, including all the direct marketing costs such as performance marketing. The idea is very simple and we can illustrate it using the example of a simple grocery shop. Let's say, you source a loaf of bread at Rs 50 from the provider and retail it at Rs 100. So, your gross margin is Rs 50. But you also need to pay rent to run the shop as well as staff salaries. If you divide your monthly rent and salaries against all sales, you may realize that rent is about 20 per cent of sales and salaries are 10 per cent of sales. With this data, for your bread sale, you are paying Rs 20 in rent and Rs 10 in salaries. After subtracting all this, you are left with Rs 20 which is your contribution margin or the money you earned on one transaction.

Initially, almost all start-ups will have a negative CM and that's fine. Sometimes you need minimal scale to be able to make sufficient CM as some economies of scale are needed to be able to amortize certain costs over a larger number of orders. But if you don't have a positive CM, you are not recovering any money to start paying back the CAC. A negative CM also means that the more you sell, the more money you lose. I often tell the teams that I work with that if you multiply a negative number with a large negative number, you will get an even larger negative number!

In the early days of e-commerce, everyone was rapidly scaling negative-CM businesses. In hindsight, it's clear that I was deeply involved too, driven like everyone else by the land grab mindset and fuelled by the unprecedented amounts of venture capital coming into the category. Every company was scaling spends in marketing and offering unsustainable discounts, all driven by market share and growth numbers, without paying much attention to CAC, LTV and retention rate. As a result, many companies ran out of runway, crashed and now we don't even remember their names. When we started CureFit, while we were able to achieve significant positive-CM for our CULT business, our food business eat. fit continued to have negative CM, mostly because of very low

AOV (average order value). If a product AOV is below Rs 300 in India, it becomes extremely difficult to make the CM work. This is why companies like Meesho are truly impressive, managing to make money on every transaction despite a very low AOV of Rs 300.

When you are operating a CM-negative business, you need to make certain choices. First and foremost, put an upper limit to the scale, as a higher scale means more burn and a shorter runway. Calculate the minimum scale you believe you need to be CM-positive. Next, articulate a set of initiatives—a walk between your current CM to CM 0 (1st milestone) and eventually to a CM in-line with your long-term LTV targets. Work on these initiatives diligently, continuously iterating and finding what works. You will have many levers, from increasing prices, reducing the cost-of-goods (COGS), optimizing fulfilment costs, optimizing marketing spends and more. This could be a prolonged and frustrating process for many companies and failing to figure out how to make CM turn positive may mean either shutting down or, if you have energy and money left, pivoting and trying something else instead. Trying to make your business CM positive is one of the most challenging problems you will face, but it is also crucial if your business is to survive for the long run.

We have seen the rise of the digital economy in the last fifteen years. From virtually no transactions online to tens of millions of daily transactions, online retailing has come a long way along with categories such as ride-hailing and food delivery. As these platforms were being built, many players were in a significant negative economic zone. A particularly hard category is grocery retailing. Grocery is a category where both the AOV and product margins are very small and, as a result, it is extremely tough to make the unit economics work. In the recent past, the category has become even more competitive with many players entering the market. This is a category with the largest TAM and hence many larger commerce players find it attractive to gain market share. But simultaneously, it is also very difficult to create differentiation, such as when you are buying a staple such as bread: customers want the best product at the lowest price. Most of these players have tried to gain market share with deep discounts and so, the category continues to be very challenging. Despite its size, no one really makes money in this category.

WeWork, founded in 2010, quickly became a leader in the co-working space, targeting tech start-ups and entrepreneurs with its shared workspaces. The company's business model involved leasing large office spaces, transforming them into stylish co-working areas, and subleasing them. However, WeWork faced substantial challenges in achieving a positive contribution margin. Its strategy of long-term leases against short-term subleases created a financial imbalance, with high upfront costs for property acquisition and renovation not being sufficiently offset by the growing revenue from subleasing. This model led to continuous investment requirements without corresponding profitability. The company's focus on rapid expansion and market dominance over immediate profitability further compounded these issues. WeWork's aggressive growth in many cities and countries dramatically increased its operational costs. The belief was that scale and market presence would ultimately bring profitability, but the reality was a struggle to achieve a positive contribution margin amidst soaring expenses. Not able to make the unit economics work, the company eventually ran out of luck and fresh funding and had to file for bankruptcy. This inability to reach CM-positivity can often end up being very costly and it is best to be mindful about sustainable unit economics from day one.

Building One Channel at a Time, Not Carpet-Bombing

As companies start to focus on growth after achieving product–market fit, there is a tendency to start doing everything simultaneously. From building online communities to cultivating influencers and from paid marketing on both Google and Facebook to trying to build organic traffic through SEO and other brand-building efforts—founders and growth teams throw everything and the kitchen sink at the problem in the hope that something will work. Often, however, nothing does, and it is not a surprise either. Building a channel carefully requires understanding its nuances and intricacies in the context of your business. Just as you are better off building only one product in the beginning, you are also better off focusing on only one main channel based on what you deem most relevant in the context of your products and customers.

Once you choose a channel, you need to develop context about how the channel works, and how the best in the world approach that channel. You need to get relevant experts on the team and drive continuous experimentation and iterations. At CULT, after many experiments, we realized that driving walk-ins through hyper-local digital marketing and conversions at CULT centres yielded the best possible ROI on marketing spends. Today, a bulk of our marketing dollars are spent in this fashion. Flipkart initially rose to prominence because of its incredible SEO work, resulting in its website always showing up at the top of any product search results and hence driving huge amounts of free traffic. Nykaa built a significant community around beauty to draw its initial set of loyal customers. If you can master one channel, you know that you have product–channel fit. That one channel alone can power predictable growth for some time while you can slowly start dabbling in and figuring out alternate channels.

In his bestselling book *Zero to One*, Peter Thiel says that the 'kitchen sink approach', or trying several distribution channels at once, doesn't work. In fact, most companies do this and don't manage to get even one of them to work. But if you figure out just one distribution channel and make it work for you, you have a good business on your hands. Distribution follows the power law.[4] According to the power law, if you have figured out one channel and achieved product–channel fit, that channel will contribute to 70 per cent or more of your company's growth. This explains why focusing on one channel at a time, rather than carpet-bombing, is so important.

While carpet-bombing is never the right answer, you also can't be married to a single channel forever; you need to keep evolving with the times and adapting to what is most current and relevant. Look back on the evolution of dating apps, for example. Match.com relied on banner ads, having launched during the early days of the web, and then Plenty of Fish grew with the rise of SEO marketing, eventually followed by Tinder, which found its product–market fit in the era of mobile apps.[5] Each time, the older product tried to copy and paste its model from its old channel into a new channel, but lost to a new player that figured out a better product–channel fit.

What Is Growth Hacking?

We mentioned earlier in the book how Facebook pioneered the idea of growth hacking in 2008. Until then, most companies had a culture in which engineers built the product, while sales and marketing teams drove user acquisition and retention. This model worked well for building physical products for which competence is very different from the competence required to unlock sales channels. In the digital world, however, the boundaries start to overlap quite significantly and things like data, real-time analytics, personalized targeting and A/B testing become very important. Realizing this, Zuckerberg concluded that to be able to build an efficient growth engine, engineers needed to play an active role in tweaking product features quickly, measuring impact and then discarding or scaling accordingly. Thus, growth hacking came to become a standard part of all Internet-savvy companies.

The specialized group responsible for catalysing growth at Facebook was known as the Growth Circle. This small, diverse team comprised individuals from various fields, including product management, data analytics and marketing. Their approach to driving the platform's international growth marked a departure from traditional marketing strategies. One of their most notable innovations was developing a translation engine to make the platform accessible globally. At that time, Facebook had around 70 million users, predominantly in North America, indicating a vast potential for attracting users from other regions.[6]

The conventional method would involve targeting the top ten languages and gradually translating the platform by hiring teams specific to each country. However, Facebook's growth team, led by Javier Olivan, chose a more innovative path. They engineered a translation system that leveraged the power of crowdsourcing, enabling Facebook's user base to translate the site into various languages. This approach exemplified growth hacking, focusing on scalable engineering solutions rather than traditional, resource-intensive strategies. Andy Johns, a prominent figure in growth hacking who was part of Facebook's growth team, highlighted this strategy as instrumental in Facebook's global expansion. He emphasized that the key to growth was not about employing numerous people across multiple countries but about creating systems that could scale and allowing users to contribute to the product's growth. This method was a pivotal factor in expanding Facebook's reach worldwide.

I remember starting a group at Myntra which we called sales-tech at the time because it was staffed with engineers with the goal of growing sales rapidly. The team was empowered to make rapid changes and launches in production, bypassing the standard product release process. This team would pore over data, try to discern patterns, and launch features such as personalized offers, shop-a-look together, showing items that people were more likely to buy, or trying to convert the previously saved but not checked out shopping carts, among other things. The efforts of this group led to the challenging of all standard assumptions and asking what new things we could do—which ultimately culminated in the creation of India's largest fashion sale, which is known as EORS (End of Reason Sale) now a big part of fashion enthusiasts' annual shopping calendar. Incidentally, I hated this name and asked the team to reconsider it, but they overruled me. Clearly, there are benefits to empowering teams so they can overrule the founders, as founders are often wrong!

Rapid feedback is essential for any product. It is a bad idea to wait till the day of the launch to decide if a product is a success or failure. Think about stand-up comedians. They don't go from writing a set to directly performing it in front of a huge crowd. They have multiple iterations of the set, based on the reactions they get from smaller crowds, at bars or local comedy clubs. This is how they perfect their punchlines. The same applies to building products. There is a common saying among product managers: 'Eat your own dog food.' Getting your employees to be heavy beta users of the product much before it is launched publicly is a great way to get quality product feedback. At Myntra, nearly all employees became regular shoppers—which not only led to everyone looking stylish but also brought in fresh, insightful customer feedback to all discussions, leading to rapid iterations.

Similarly, at CureFit, most of our early employees were regular users of both CULT and eat.fit and that was a critical factor in getting the product right. If you can deliver what customers want and keep pace with them, growth automatically takes care of itself. I suppose this brings us back to the idea of 'Product Is Marketing'. If you want your product to fly off the shelf (and who doesn't!), make sure it's at the core of how you approach growth. These days, even enterprise software companies, who were known for cut-throat sales cultures (watch *Glengarry Glen Ross* for an iconic sales team meeting scene!), are starting to embrace what's known as 'Product–led-Growth' (PLG) to build product features from the get-go that encourage sustained usage through better features in the hopes of viral growth.

Another example of rapid product iteration is Zara, launched in 1975, a brand that made its founder Amancio Ortega one of the richest men in the world. Speed and fast fashion are at the core of Zara's strategy—and can be summarized with the following sentence: 'Give customers what they want and get it to them faster than anyone else.'[7] Zara takes only two weeks to design and launch a new product in stores, something other companies take much longer to do. As a result, they launch over 10,000 designs a year. It also holds only sixty days of inventory when, for example, H&M holds ten times as much. Rather than move to China for cheaper manufacturing, Zara still manufactures most of its clothing in Spain—in highly automated factories that turn out 'greige goods' that aren't whitened and dyed. They are then sent to a partner network of over 300 small shops across Spain and Portugal to process into finished apparel. This allows for high responsiveness and speed. Feedback from stores comes in daily, designers then create new patterns on the spot (up to three a day per designer!). Zara has clearly found its own version of growing at a significant pace, consistently.

Predictable Growth vs Hustle Growth

Steve Jobs famously said, 'Why join the navy when you can be a pirate?' While there was a time when the swashbuckling swagger of pirates was what start-up founders wanted to emulate, we have now shifted beyond this idea. Facebook's 'Move fast and break things' worked, but these days, growth at all costs just isn't acceptable anymore. By 2017, Uber was in the news for all kinds of infamous reasons, from accusations of sexual harassment to shady ways of undercutting their rival, Lyft, and various other issues.[8] They finally hired Dara Khosrowshahi to turn things around. This was their period of shifting from being pirates to behaving like a more responsible and ethical navy. In a LinkedIn post, Khosrowshahi wrote: 'As we move from an era of growth at all costs to one of responsible growth, our culture needs to evolve. Rather than ditching everything, I'm focused on preserving what works while quickly changing what doesn't.'[9] I recently had an opportunity to interact with Khosrowshahi and was highly impressed with his clarity of thought as well as his focus on building a strong foundation that will lead to long-term sustainable growth. He mentioned that his core asset is the network of 6.4 million Uber driver partners. He even stealthily drives customers around as an Uber driver every now and then to keep a finger on the pulse of what's going on at the ground level.

Sometimes start-ups get carried away with too much hustle and the mindset of doing whatever it takes to drive growth. While aggression and a fire in the belly are necessary ingredients for any start-up, they need to be tempered with critical analysis of whether a growth initiative is genuinely improving the lives of customers or if you are just making the sale with irresistible discounts, catchy marketing or baiting the customer into clicking on the 'buy' button. Customers are not stupid. Far from it. They understand the value of their money and unless you can deliver genuine value for money, ensuring that they are better off with the product than with having their money still in the bank, they will not come back. And without a loyal customer base, you will neither have a brand, nor a business.

In 2011, Internet entrepreneur Jason Goldberg launched Fab, a platform selling curated selections of rare and beautiful products from boutiques, with flash sales inspired by daily design inspirations. Within just five months, Fab acquired one million customers—growing faster than even Facebook or Twitter had.[10] In its first year, sales also increased, which in turn drew more investors, and by the end of 2012, Fab had raised over $170 million, while being valued at over $500 million. Having spent huge amounts of money on inventory, logistics and expansion, Fab came under pressure from investors to expand faster globally. As a result, Goldberg acquired three copycat companies in Europe for a large sum and lost its USP of curation by expanding inventory from a select 1000 items to more than 11,000. In its early days, Fab had almost no products that were listed on Amazon—selling itself as a curator of rare objects. But by 2013, almost 90 per cent of products were also sold on Amazon where they were cheaper and could be delivered in two days! This is an example of a start-up losing sight of its product in favour of hustle growth. This reckless pursuit of growth led to Goldberg selling his company—which had once been valued at $1 billion—for $15 million.

Building Unique Growth Capabilities

When a company tries to be great at everything, it often ends up being just 'ok' at everything but great at nothing. True excellence requires identifying strengths and focusing disproportionately on them to consistently deliver something amazing—and much better than the competitor. If you think of some of the most successful companies in the world, you are likely to very quickly be able to identify their unique capabilities. Amazon excels at customer service and satisfaction. Since it doesn't list just one product but offers users an incredible selection to choose from, the company has strategically made customer service its core growth capability. Think about Dropbox, which has focused on unmatched value for money in its file sharing and storing service. For both these companies, success has come because of their sharp focus on their unique capabilities, leveraging them for growth. A growing start-up is tempted to put its eggs in many baskets—attempting to make everything its strength— but it would do better to focus on the capabilities that set it apart from the competitor.

Building Strong Word of Mouth

It is every founder's and marketer's dream to have incredible word-of-mouth marketing for their new offering. Imagine how cool it would be to acquire customers who love your product so much that they go out of their way to champion your offering, raving about it on any platform that they have access to, and becoming unofficial brand ambassadors as they pester everyone within their circle to give the product a shot. That is some seriously deep and authentic marketing—and all for free! Well, most companies can only wish for this, but some manage to create an engine that makes this dynamic happen. What's their secret?

Let me start with an example of a boutique product—a weighted blanket. Now, if you are into health and understand the critical importance of sleep, you might have come across the idea of the weighted blanket. It's a very heavy blanket that can weigh anywhere between five to ten kilograms and, trust me, you do feel the weight when you sleep with one. The theory is that you feel cosier and more supported, and as a result, your quality of sleep goes up significantly. My yoga teacher happened to mention a vendor in Rajasthan who makes these custom weighted blankets. I tried it and really liked the experience, so I mentioned it to some colleagues in the office. All of them happened to buy and like the product and, in turn, recommended it to others in their circles.

Let's try to break down how this plays out. First, let's see this from the customer's point of view. We are all social beings, sharing our lives and experiences with those around us. Being able to share something new, cool and interesting makes us cool and interesting too—at least in our own eyes! And so, most of us have an almost innate need to find the next cool thing that we can brag about to our close friends and social circles and appear to be in the know. Good brands tap into this latent human need by creating unique experiences that customers feel good about sharing with others. The rise of the Huberman Lab podcast from its quiet beginnings to become one of the world's top podcasts in just a couple of years, is thanks to word-of-mouth marketing. Similarly, products like the Whoop band continue to grow in India through strong word of mouth.

What does it take to have this strong word-of-mouth marketing? It starts with the intent. What is that one feature of your product that truly delivers customer delight? Something that is so cool that people feel compelled to share it with the world. Early iPhone models had such cool packaging that unboxing it became a phenomenon and people started uploading these videos by the million, leading to incredible free marketing for Apple. Unless there is someone in the company who is obsessing about what that one feature is and continuously iterating and measuring it, it is not going to happen in an instant. At Myntra, we figured out that the most delightful feature we had was delivering a product within two hours of receiving a customer order. Most people expected it to take a few·days at least and so, when the product showed up almost immediately, they were totally blown away. At some point, we created a process to ensure that 1 per cent of all orders would be delivered within two hours and this led to sustained positive word-of-mouth marketing.

To find that feature to bet on for driving word of mouth, you need to have a finger on the pulse of your customer. A lot gets lost in averages. While your average NPS might be fifty among all your users, there might be 10 per cent of users that truly love your offering. If you can't tell who these users are or why they love your offering so much, you are missing out on a massive opportunity to pick something and double down on it to scale word-of-mouth marketing. If you can realize that, then you have found the most powerful and cost-effective way of building a brand and acquiring customers at nearly zero cost. But someone needs to own this, design it intelligently and continuously iterate on this.

A word of caution about paid referrals. This is a common go-to tool for many marketers. As sales start to plateau, someone in the company will likely have an ingenious idea about launching a referral programme where users are paid an incentive for bringing in more users to the platform. I have rarely seen these programmes work as there is no deep authenticity to this. It effectively boils down to being spammed by your own friends and even if some users do come, there is no stickiness. There are exceptions to this rule, when the referrals are more prestige-driven rather than offering a monetary incentive. In the early days of Gmail, for example, the only way to get access to an account was if a friend were to refer you and this led to huge organic demand for the product.

Product-Led Growth

Until recently, the standard playbook for all enterprise software was to build version One of the product, then hire a team that comprises pre-sales and sales teams with the former going to the client site to understand requirements and quickly putting together a demo that is impressive enough to be taken seriously. Once the pre-sales team has found interest, the sales representative takes over and tries to figure out the right pricing and other details to be able to get a purchase order from the customer. Back in my enterprise software days in the Bay Area, I remember literally waiting by the fax machine for the PO to show up on the last day of the quarter so we could make our quarterly numbers!

As consumer Internet companies grappled with growth issues in the last couple of decades, they kept refining the art of acquiring customers via digital mediums and invented many sophisticated techniques to acquire customers. For the most part, these techniques remained confined to the B2C world, while enterprise companies stayed with their tried-and-tested sales methodologies. With the advent of SaaS, or Software-as-a-Service, this changed, as many innovative start-ups whose founders had B2C experience started to apply the tools that they learnt or borrowed from the B2C world to start making inroads into the enterprise space. One of the most widely adopted practices was to offer the base version of the product for free, so that some proactive enterprise users would start to adopt it for basic use cases. These users would invite their colleagues to join them for a collaboration and before long, there would be a significant organic demand in the enterprise, eventually leading to bulk adoption and licensing without any pre-sales guys having to put together a klutzy demo!

In a typical sales-led company, the reliance on star salespeople is very high. More often than not, the company is heavily dependent on the Rolodex and the sales capabilities of the salesperson, rather than the inherent strength of the product. The salesperson might be able to save the day through her relationships, charm and sheer determination, but there is no evidence that the client really needed the product or—even if the sale has been made—whether the client will see meaningful adoption. But with product-let growth, the only way the product gets traction is when some users start using it and organically become superfans, slowly roping in more users and championing the product internally. This ensures strong adoption of the product by the time widespread use is achieved and, as a result, the product is extremely sticky.

Most traditional companies used to be sales-led and top-down, requiring sales representatives to speak to senior executives and key decision-makers in companies to explain the product's benefits and guide them through the sales cycle. On the other hand, most SaaS companies today are product-led and bottom-up. Product-led companies give consumers the 'keys' to their product, focusing on improving the customer's lives through the product so much that the customer will almost automatically upgrade to a paid version. When Slack was first launched, for example, it spread very organically in companies, with colleagues inviting each other using the free version. Eventually, entire teams were using Slack and it became so indispensable that managers had no choice but to buy paid versions of the product.

It used to be that enterprise software deployment would cost millions of dollars and, as a result, the cost of sales would also be very high. It was common for companies to pay 6–8 per cent of the total sales to the sales team as an incentive for making the sale. But, with the advent of SaaS, where each licence may cost as little as ten dollars, this option doesn't exist. Instead, by giving a product away for free for the first few months or up to a certain number of users, the cost of sales is effectively zero. You still might have to spend some money to generate enough initial leads to drive early users, but the CAC in these situations will be dramatically lower than what it might have been otherwise.

. Another benefit of product-led growth is that users train themselves on the product. Enterprise software of the past used to be very clunky, with thousands of menu options and shortcuts that would require many weeks of training and even certification in the products. This contrasts with product-led growth which necessitates that a product be designed in such a simple manner that users can figure it out on their own fairly quickly or else they will lose interest. As users learn more and more features, they start to become more proficient and become the go-to person for other folks who are adopting the tool, hence effectively becoming a free trainer for your products.

Understanding Various Growth Channels

Today whether you are a B2C company or a B2B company, you have a plethora of growth strategies to pick from. It all depends on what stage of growth you are in, what your current expertise is and also which strategy is best suited for your product. As mentioned earlier, you cannot hope to master all the channels simultaneously, so you need to carefully pick what is best suited for your unique situation.

One of the easiest places to start to drive growth is performance marketing—where you create personalized ads on Google or Facebook for keywords or topics relevant to your product category. For example, if you are building a new organic protein bar, you can target keywords such as 'health', 'fitness', 'muscle building', 'organic food' and so on. While platforms like Google and Facebook are very effective in targeting users with interest in these keywords, these platforms are highly competitive and there are probably many other companies out there also competing for these keywords, driving up the per-click rate that you will pay. Starting with performance marketing is easy, but it takes a lot of fine-tuning and specialized skills to achieve a healthy respect of ROAS, or returns on ad spend. A good rule of thumb is not to have an ROAS of more than three to four times your CMs for new acquisition so you can recover the investment in three to four transactions. For repeat transactions, ROAS must be below one, or you are losing money on each transaction.

Search engine optimization, or SEO, is every marketer's dream. When someone searches for a keyword in Google—let's say, for a 'healthy protein bar'—Google will show them a long list of search results, but the first three results will end up getting nearly 80 per cent of all the clicks, and hence free traffic. If you can show up in the top three or top five search results for your relevant keywords, you will have a very powerful growth engine, nearly for free! Flipkart, in its early days, mastered SEO for the books category so that for virtually any book, Flipkart would be the first result, and therefore they had massive traffic for free and their first wave of growth came from this. In recent years, 1mg has perfected SEO for the health category where they get nearly 40 per cent of all health-related searches in India. The way Google's search engine works is that it tries to show the most relevant results at the top for any search category. It recognizes the relevance based on the content of the web page and how many other credible sites are linking to this page (backlinks). To be good at SEO, you must aspire to have outstanding content for each page and build cross-linkages from various credible sites over a period of time. SEO requires a lot of patience and time and may often take years to see meaningful results.

Another growth strategy that has seen traction in recent years is the idea of content-led marketing. As a product or brand owner, you try to create relevant and useful content that can educate and engage the prospective customer so that you start to build familiarity and trust with the user as an expert in that category long before making your first sale. If you are an online beauty retailer, you can start creating content around 'How to Prevent Acne', 'Five Tips for Indian Skin Types' or 'Ideal Skin Care for Teenagers'. If you create high-quality and differentiated content, you will start attracting users. In its early years, Nykaa did a great job of creating relevant content for the beauty space in India, which created a strong social media following for the brand.

Like content-led marketing, another growth strategy that some companies use is to build a highly engaged community in which the brand and the users have an active dialogue around their mutual context. In the early days of Notion, the marketing team observed users of Notion on Reddit and Twitter helping other users out.[11] One of their fans, Ben Long, was moderating a Notion Facebook group and had a website where users could upload templates! The company decided to leverage this to start a formal community, hiring Long as their Head of Community. He implemented unique community-based programmes that allowed these power users—who were passionate about the product—to gain early access to features, create content about Notion and even teach courses on how to use the software. This led to immense user engagement, at workplaces, on campuses and within localized groups all over the world. The community leaders are volunteers but get early access to features, while the company gets almost real-time feedback that helps them improve the offering. Their community-led growth strategy led them to be valued at $10 billion.

Sometimes, finding the perfect growth channel suited to your product or service can transform your start-up journey.

A now well-known example is Airbnb. When they launched, they thought about where their target audience was currently seeking solutions—in their case, Craigslist, where people were renting out or seeking rooms in apartments or temporary housing. They began advertising directly on the Craigslist site—and with better photography and graphics—redirecting users to their own new website.

How to Hire a Strong Growth Team and Build a Strong Culture

In a start-up's early years, the entire company usually functions as a growth team, with everyone aligned on goals. However, once product–market fit is achieved, it's important to have a dedicated growth team to really leverage that PMF and amp up growth when it matters most.

Growth happens to be a highly cross-functional responsibility. On the one hand, you have the traditional marketing team that will manage different marketing channels according to the ROI. If you are investing in content or community, you will need team members who can write good-quality content and engage community members in genuine conversations. Any effort towards SEO requires product managers and engineers to be deeply involved. You might also have a dedicated growth team which will typically comprise a growth product manager, a couple of growth engineers and growth data scientists. Not only does this team focus on driving growth in competitive environments, they also act as a first line of defence when something is off with a new feature or launch—they are able to identify the root problem and respond immediately, so the impact is restricted.

Facebook was one of the first companies to set up a dedicated growth team—they realized that if they didn't assign growth of monthly active users to a single team, then nobody would take full ownership or accountability for this critical focus area.

Growth teams must have their finger on the pulse of the customer—what the customer needs, what will convert them into loyal users and what more they might want from a product. Dropbox's growth team, for example, figured out early on that one of the best ways to encourage referrals was to offer free storage space.[12] This worked incredibly well, resulting in a huge number of new users. Closer to home, Swiggy also has a strong growth team in place. This team's work is not straightforward as theirs is a three-sided marketplace, working with customers, delivery partners and restaurants. Swiggy follows a bottom-up approach, where teams come up with ideas and possibilities, rather than having instructions being handed down from above. Clearly, they have got something right, having achieved 30X growth between 2016 and 2019.[13]

A good growth team requires a combination of many diverse skills. While they need to have the competence in the core skills required to do the job, that alone is not enough. Growth focus requires the ability to keep coming up with new insights, generate lots of new ideas, try things quickly and scale what works while discarding others. Often teams need to drop what might have worked until a point as growth strategies keep evolving with the scale of the organization.

While most efforts in a company require a long-term orientation, growth teams often need to be on the ball daily. Monitoring numbers daily to allow for swift interventions creates a culture of high accountability and continuous iterations. Growth teams often face regular crises as numbers are rarely where they need to be, and most surprises are often in the wrong direction. Any sudden change in steady growth numbers requires immediate problem-solving to stem the problem. Recently, at sugar.fit, due to some algorithm changes at Google's end, the ROI on performance marketing dropped by half and it took many months of persistent effort to recover and return to the same level of performance.

Growth is life for start-ups and making a choice to build a best-in-class growth team can go a long way in ensuring steady progress. Growth continues to be a mix of art and science, but the attitude of the teams towards being data- and action-oriented goes a long way. As growth channels mature and the company starts to have a clear line of sight to be able to plan monthly and even quarterly numbers in advance, they can develop confidence in the delivery, a huge luxury which can enable the company to start thinking truly long term. In a strong organization, the CEO shouldn't have to worry about quarterly numbers, focusing instead on more strategic and foundational topics which we will cover in the next two chapters.

FROM PAGE TO ACTION

Once you have reached the PMF stage, you need to shift gears to focus on growth and scale. There are many aspects of this journey to think about so you can build a consistent and powerful growth engine:

a. Now that you have a product in your hands, think about a unique feature or aspect of your offering that you think customers will love. List out the top three channels you can leverage to turn it into a word-of-mouth hit (building a community online, customer referrals, etc).

b. Understanding these concepts is essential to your growth journey. Spend some time researching and gaining a deeper understanding of the following:

    i.   Total Addressable Market (TAM)
    ii. Customer Acquisition Cost (CAC)
    iii. Lifetime Value (LTV)
    iv. Contribution Margin (CM)

8

Organization Is Product

An Organization Is More Than a Collection of People

Steve Jobs famously said that his greatest creation at Apple was the culture itself, one that would keep generating great products long after he was gone. That's exactly how it panned out—90 per cent of today's Apple valuation was created after he died.[1]

Culture has been an integral part of human societies since time immemorial. It is what binds a group of different people together. It's a common identity that not only creates a shared sense of purpose but also lays down norms that dictate what is expected and what isn't. This creates a very strong bond, helping people navigate the ups and downs of their experiences as one unit. At its core, culture is what the group collectively agrees to adhere to. It should be rooted in the group's deeply held beliefs and a deeper understanding of what the group is trying to achieve. In most of the eastern world, societies have a collectivist culture in which the overall well-being of the group is prioritized over that of the individual. America, in contrast, is a highly individualistic society which stemmed from the fact that as settlers arrived from Europe, they relocated to far-flung, remote areas, and were left to fend for themselves. As a result, they ended up becoming fiercely independent.

Whether an organization recognizes this or not, a group of human beings ultimately ends up coexisting in a shared culture. In healthy societies and companies, this culture is carefully engineered and nurtured, while in toxic groups, the culture is completely unmanaged and grows based on whatever helps people survive and take care of their narrow interests. Culture is both the biggest enabler of human potential as well as something that can drown any hope of progress and impact. Just imagine a new age start-up like WhatsApp: a twenty-person company that changed the world. Now imagine a large, slow-moving government organization that creates more harm than benefit for society. At the heart of it, it all boils down to culture.

Culture is also a huge factor in the longevity and renewal of an organization. Universities are a type of organization that can survive and thrive for centuries as they are often built around a key central idea and have a very distinct culture designed around that idea. Think about the coveted MIT. It describes itself as: 'We are fun and quirky, elite but not elitist, inventive and artistic, obsessed with numbers, and welcoming to talented people regardless of where they come from.' This comes through in something as elemental as the way they send acceptance letters. Instead of a typical acceptance letter, they send the students an acceptance tube which has a fridge magnet, a poster and some confetti. To make things even more interesting, they announce their results on 14 March which, in the US calendar format, is written as 3–14, the first three digits of the number pi—a fundamental number of geometry. Clearly MIT's culture is deeply embedded in the organization, reflected in every action and decision.[2]

Culture Eats Strategy!

Peter Drucker is arguably one of the foremost strategy experts of the last century and his books and ideas continue to influence many generations of business leaders. While he is best known for his work in strategy, he famously remarked that, 'Culture eats strategy for breakfast.' What he meant was that culture is this invisible driving force behind the company, and no strategy can have any impact unless there is a strong shared sense of culture that can support the strategy and its outcomes. Even the best strategy will make almost no impact if it is held back by people who do not have a healthy, well-defined culture.

Culture is not about nap pods at the office or Friday evening happy hours. It is what determines how employees behave in crises, how they respond to difficulties and how they treat each other, as well as their customers and stakeholders. Culture has been described as the soil or the habitat in which strategy will either thrive or die. Think about one of the biggest corporate downfalls in history—that of Enron. Once considered a disruptor that had taken on the monopoly of traditional electric utilities, it soon became known for its insidious, toxic culture. This culture allowed fraud and misconduct to run rampant, leading to Enron's collapse in 2001.[3] No amount of strategy could save it.

Crafting Culture

Many leaders, particularly those in the early stages of company building, don't pay enough attention to building culture proactively. As the organization grows, more people join the team and each brings their own way of thinking about and doing things, and the culture starts to grow organically. If no one is orchestrating it proactively, it will develop on its own in this way, but this may not be conducive to what the organization's goals are. The early stage of a company is a great time to deliberately engineer a culture that the founders and early teams believe in. This requires deep thought, designing and implementing cultural artefacts—taking time away from the task of recruiting and product building. But that's what makes start-ups both very hard and very exciting—you must do a lot to get things right!

In order to prioritize and actively nurture a unique culture, you will have to dedicate consistent bandwidth towards shaping it. I believe that the first twenty or thirty employees and the first one or two years are crucial, as these set the tone for company culture, which is very difficult to change once set. The thing about human groups is that a culture will form whether you engineer it or not, so if you are not actively shaping it, you may end up with a culture that you don't like.

In an interview on the podcast *Masters of Scale*, Reed Hastings, founder of Netflix, talked about his first company, Pure Software, a debugging tool for programmers that was initially successful. As the organization grew, it acquired other companies, and as CEO, Hastings was entirely focused on the product. He worked long hours, writing code all night and focusing on pushing more sales through marketing. Not only was culture not a priority, but the acquisitions meant that different teams based on different values were suddenly working closely together. While the teams at Pure were very good at following processes to a T, there was no culture of independent thinking or agility to adapt to new landscapes—because there was no culture at all. When the market environment changed, Pure simply could not keep up. Hastings eventually had to sell it. He went on to put the lessons he had learnt into practice at his new start-up, Netflix, which is well known for its carefully crafted and intentional company culture.[4]

ENTREPRENEURIAL WISDOM

On Crafting Work Culture

As a founder, remember that the most important thing you will build is your organization's culture. If you aren't deliberate about crafting the culture you want, you will find yourself with a culture you didn't sign up for; one that is the result of random ideas and accidents.

If one isn't mindful about the company culture in the early days, it can have disastrous consequences. Take, for example, the company, Theranos. While the company has other, bigger problems, its culture wasn't well thought out either. There was an atmosphere of secrecy and a very strongly entrenched hierarchy in place. So much so that it was impossible for employees from one department to get information about the work being done in another department. As a result, while the company was engaged in blatant fraud, most employees were unaware of what was going on and had no way to challenge the decisions being taken.[5] In India, Byju's had a similar culture of secrecy. While the company was an early pioneer of online education, its culture didn't enable the company to identify and address problems early enough. This eventually led to massive issues for the company.[6]

What makes culture so powerful is the fact that it is highly self-replicating. Once a culture has been set, it is nearly impossible to alter it. When a new employee joins an organization, they initially observe how things happen there and how different people behave, slowly starting to imbibe the same language, mannerisms and values. At Flipkart, people had this habit of writing on the white tabletops during meetings and I just hated it. But before long, even folks at Myntra started copying this and, much to my chagrin, soon it was everywhere. This is a trivial example, but it applies to pretty much everything. Human beings are highly adaptable and a key survival skill that all of us have is observing and incorporating habits and mannerisms from any new environment. It is not for nothing that the adage, 'When in Rome, do as the Romans do,' works all the time! Founders who want to build a company that lasts will do well to accept that the building of culture is a big part of their job description. While I may not have personally liked the writing on tabletops, it was a signature Flipkart element and even now when I see someone writing on the table, I ask them if they worked at Flipkart and more often than not, it turns out that they did. I hope by now Flipkart has writable desks to actively support this behaviour!

Codifying Your Culture in a Constitution

By the time we started CureFit, I had adopted the process of writing a constitution for the organization, which is very similar to a country's constitution. This document codifies shared beliefs and is an explicit agreement that everyone in the organization undertakes, to act within certain guidelines and shared mutual expectations. The act of writing down the constitution itself brings out the belief system of the group and, in doing so, encourages debate about what to include and what not to, developing a bond and shared context among early employees. While there is no universal template for writing a good organizational constitution, I have come to use the following broad structure:

- Purpose
- Core Values
- Beliefs/Principles
- Policies
- Rituals

Purpose—Everything Starts with Purpose

In the chapter on purpose, we talked at length about how critical it is to clearly articulate why an organization exists. Purpose becomes a core driver of culture, and it is paramount that the founders spend a considerable amount of time thinking deeply about purpose. While at Myntra, we took some time before we arrived at the purpose of 'helping people look good'. We made sure that in the first six months of CureFit, we spent a significant amount of time debating our purpose before settling with: 'Making health easy.' Similarly, in my new venture studio, MerakiLabs, we have been iterating through various articulations of possible purpose statements.

Your purpose is that North Star that affects nearly everything that happens in the company. Without a clear purpose that everyone believes in deeply, the culture is likely to evolve into an 'anything goes' environment that helps navigate the challenges of the day. But there will be no coherent soul or identity that emerges for the company. Tools and suggestions for crafting a credible purpose are covered in chapter three— Start with Why. A shared purpose that everyone truly believes in creates a shared sense of identity and belonging that bonds the group together. As different policies and rituals take hold, one can use purpose as the filter to gauge whether every move is in the right direction or not.

When Howard Schultz was a young boy, a life-altering incident set the course for his future ambitions. At just seven years of age, Schultz watched his father lose his job due to an injury sustained from slipping on ice. This resulted in the loss of their family's health insurance. The experience was particularly challenging as their financial stability crumbled with Schultz's pregnant mother and the family being left devoid of any savings. Witnessing the hardships faced by his father, who juggled multiple strenuous blue-collar jobs, Schultz was deeply impacted by the struggles of working-class families who were often left without support or opportunities. Motivated by these early experiences, Schultz was determined to create a different kind of company—one that his father would have been proud to work for. He envisioned a workplace that not only recognized the contributions of its employees but also treated them with dignity and respect, regardless of their educational background or where they came from. This vision was crucial in shaping the culture of Starbucks, the company he would go on to lead. Under Schultz's leadership, Starbucks became a pioneer in providing comprehensive health benefits to all employees, including those working part-time. This decision was not merely a policy change; it was a statement of trust and respect, strengthening the bond between the company and its employees. Schultz's commitment to his values transformed Starbucks into a global entity, renowned not just for its coffee but for its inclusive, people-first approach, connecting the well-being of its staff directly to its broader business success.[7]

Crafting Values That Matter

How does one create a shared code of conduct, especially when an organization grows with hundreds or even thousands of people? Everyone is unique, with their own belief systems, and different things have worked for different people in the past. Most people who join a company have worked in different organizations and have inadvertently absorbed ways of working—both good and bad—from those places. Have you noticed that when people join a new organization, they keep referring to how they did things a certain way in their previous company? This is because we absorb something from every environment we have been part of and carry this with us wherever we go.

A big part of how people make choices is through shared core values that are either deliberately created or that evolve organically. At Flipkart, 'bias for action' was a key core value and you could see it in action during all the hyper-growth years at the company. At CureFit, one of our core values is 'nurture your mind and body'. We take this very seriously as we believe that only when folks inside the company see the difference that a healthy lifestyle makes for them, can they appreciate the products we are building and create more solutions that make the pursuit of a healthy lifestyle fun and easy.

Now, there is a bit of an art and science to the process of crafting your core values. There is no right or wrong answer here. What you want to avoid is ending up with a long list of values to please everyone. There are things like 'integrity', 'honesty' and other obvious values which are table stakes, assumed to be present in any professional environment but don't need to be spelt out. Once you have clarity on your purpose, thinking deeply about what core values you can emphasize will have a disproportionate impact on the business you want to build. At MerakiLabs, we want to be a deep tech lab and hence 'first principles thinking' can be an important core value for us.

To arrive at your list of core values, you should have a series of discussions involving all the early team members on 'What values must we live by that will help us achieve our purpose to the fullest?' Initial brainstorming sessions might generate a very long list which is okay as it will help you to get all ideas on the table. Then you can filter these based on various criteria like relevance to purpose, whether it helps with differentiation, reflects deep shared values among group members, will be relevant in ten years or will help make key decisions. After all this analysis, try to filter down to just four or five core values that do the most justice to the above criteria. This doesn't mean that other values are not important, but just that the listed ones will have a disproportionate impact on the long-term outcome. This set of core values will help to create a sense of cohesion in the organization, forming the bedrock of a strong culture. One key question to ask is if we were to live this core value in its true sense, is this going to make a major difference to who we are and help us make strong progress towards our Purpose.

Having the core values written down creates explicit expectations for everyone who works at the organization, including the founders. Founders who openly flout their core values will stand out and, if they have a good team, someone will stop them from doing so, doing the company a great service in the long run. For a while, there has been this popular notion of start-ups and their founders as ruthless—almost selfish in their pursuit of disruption, where they can do whatever it takes and treat people however they feel like in the relentless pursuit of economic success. Unfortunately, there are examples of companies with famously toxic work cultures which have contributed to this myth. In my opinion, this is indeed a myth. Moving fast and breaking things is one way of doing business, but I do not believe that it is the only way, or even the most effective way for lasting success. This might produce results for a short period but, just like over fertilized land, the company will be left fallow in the long run.

Professor and bestselling author Adam Grant has an interesting perspective on this. He says that people assume that start-up founders have to be 'takers' in order to achieve true innovation and disruption. For example, Uber had to take what they wanted, regardless of the consequences to achieve success, tackling local taxi driver unions and transport laws alike. However, Grant says this isn't true. What you need to be is a 'disagreeable giver', someone who might enjoy conflict and questioning the status quo, but does so in service of other people's success or a larger organizational goal.

Core Beliefs and Principles

As you work on your core values, you will realize that a lot of things come up which seem relevant and are difficult to keep off the list. One simple tool I have adopted over a period is to make a longer list of core beliefs or principles that I believe are important to guide the operating environment but don't make it to the list of core values. Companies such as Google and Amazon have what they call 'what we believe in' or 'core principles'. For example, in the CureFit constitution, we had a core belief that said the top one percentile of people can make up to 50 per cent of the organization's impact. Google has a core belief that states: 'Focus on the user and all else will follow.' Once you write down these core beliefs based on what the shared beliefs of the group are, you will be able to translate them into specific policies and choices.

A good way to evaluate a core belief is whether it might influence a policy choice. For example, if one of your beliefs is: 'When people feel empowered, they will go above and beyond to help contribute to the larger mission.' Now, to really put this belief into action, you need to seriously consider what kinds of policies you want to institute. Do you want to have separate cabins for managers? What kind of titles (or not!) will you choose within the organization? And so on.

It is important to understand the historical context that has a huge bearing on established organizational patterns. The largest organizations in history have always been in the military. The size of an army can range from a few thousand to a few hundred thousand. The army of the Persian King Xerxes is supposed to have been three million strong. Managing such a large group of people requires a lot of structure—chains of command and communication protocols will be needed for the whole army to behave as one unit and perform in a coordinated manner. The vocabulary of 'reporting', 'chain of command', 'signing authority', 'call of duty', and others, all come from this long-established military history.[8] With the advent of the Industrial Revolution, there arose a need to hire thousands of people for each factory. People found it convenient to borrow the language and many of the structures from the military to organize factories. This has continued for a couple of hundred years, right up to the emergence of very large companies that needed significant top-down organization to steer its affairs.

In the Seventies, a new type of company, relying on the knowledge economy, began to emerge. In such companies, the biggest asset was an employee's ability to use her own mind and knowledge. This was very different from the older command-and-control models of the past in which decisions in large companies were taken at the top and would slowly flow down through the organization hierarchy to be executed on the ground, with information also slowly making its way back to the top. This wasn't going to work in the knowledge economy where everyone had to use their brains, especially people who were closest to the ground reality. Hence the organizational models started to go through major changes through the Seventies and Eighties, led by the emerging new culture of Silicon Valley.

Codifying Culture in Policies and Rituals

Writing down your purpose, core values and beliefs sets a strong foundation for the culture, specifying why the organization must exist, what the principle guiding values are and what the deeply held beliefs are that will inform everything that will govern culture. But so far, this is only a paper document and unless this is translated into what happens daily, it will only exist in theory and become a distant memory in some time.

Once you start to define your core values, start thinking about ways in which you can make these a default part of organizational culture so that people not only remember them but also actively practise them through rituals and policies. In the early days of Amazon, Jeff Bezos wanted to promote a culture of frugality within the organization. Instead of lecturing people about this, he created a ritual which came to be known as the door desk.[9] Bezos figured out that if employees were to buy a door from Home Depot and then fix four legs on it, it would cost a tenth of the cost of buying a premade desk and be bigger. And so, this became an initiation rite at Amazon with all new employees heading to Home Depot to pick the door that would become their desk. In the process, the ethos of frugality was etched deep in their psyche, working in countless ways so that they kept making choices to reduce costs for customers.

Google borrowed many of its original cultural norms from academia, as the founders appreciated the freedom of the academic setting. They wanted a culture of transparency and autonomy and, to engineer that, they created a TGIF (Thank-God-Its-Friday) ritual—an open house with the entire organization, during which anything could be shared or discussed, including asking the CEO any tough questions that were on people's minds.[10]

At CureFit, we did away with titles and permanent reporting structures in order to promote a culture of equality and transparency. We also got rid of fixed office hours; people can take as much time off as they feel the need for. Employees can also approve their own reimbursements, as we wanted to convey the message that we trust people's judgement, and no one needs to police them. Obviously, such radical empowerment requires a lot of accountability, and deliberate violations must be dealt with decisively.

Mostly, culture is about people, and people care a lot about their growth and compensation. You need to pay a lot of attention to how you want to design your hiring process and performance appraisals. Now, this might sound boring, and you may be tempted to outsource most of it to your HR department but that would be a mistake. As we will discuss in the next chapter, the primary work of all leaders is centred on people. One of the most important things that a leader does is hiring. Just one good hire can cut down your work by half, freeing you up to focus on more strategic ideas and decisions.

Amazon wanted to have a culture of small teams working collaboratively. They evangelized a concept that has come to be known as the 'bar-raiser'. They observed, over a period, which people in the organization had a track record of hiring top-notch people, thus raising the calibre of the whole team. They then began to designate these people as 'bar-raisers'. Every interview panel at Amazon has one bar-raiser who has the power to veto the panel outcome, even if the rest of the members are keen to hire the candidate. There is an adage in company building which says: 'A players hire A players, while B players hire C players.' Unless you have a strong mechanism in place, the quality of teams will get diluted very fast. This leads to a bloating in the payroll and a drop in the overall productivity of the team.[11]

Often, you get to know the true potential and performance of a person only after you have seen them in action for six to twelve months. The few hours of the interview process are not enough to form a completely well-informed opinion of the person's capabilities. This is why Netflix has a policy known as the 'keepers-test'. What this test means is that, after working with someone for a year, you ask, would you still rehire this person? If the answer is not an unequivocal 'yes', you have a problem on your hands and you may want to think about a different role for the person or transition them out. You must remember that a team is only as strong as the weakest link, so carrying a lot of people who are not able to raise the bar will dramatically lower the overall team's performance.[12]

Another area in which to design good-quality policies and rituals is in facilitating collaboration between teams. Some of the best examples come from Amazon, which has thought long and hard about how to make teams most collaborative. Bezos noticed that small teams tend to be way more productive than large teams and hence he informally instituted the 'two-pizza rule'. What this means is that a team's size should not grow beyond a point where they cannot have a proper lunch with two large pizzas! This translates into a maximum team size of ten to twelve people. The genius of such language is that it creates a unique and memorable vocabulary specific to the company, which becomes part of its cultural identity.[13]

Bezos also noticed that most meetings were a waste of time, and I wholeheartedly agree. My estimate is that at least two-thirds of all meetings, through the course of a person's career, are not a good use of people's time. Bezos's insight was that most meetings are subpar because people come unprepared. So, he instituted a ritual which came to be known as the 'six-pager' rule. The person organizing a meeting would write a six-page-long note detailing the overall context relevant to the meeting, what the decision to be made was, and what the key debate points and recommendations were. The first fifteen minutes of the meeting would be devoted to everyone going through the document silently, and post that the group could debate from an informed vantage point.[14]

It takes a lot of effort to think, design and experiment with a policy or ritual. But that's the only way to design cultural artefacts one policy or one ritual at a time. And it is also a lot of fun! You can create your own language, challenge the conventional way of doing things and design a way to collaborate and communicate that's truly unique to your context.

Leaders Need to Role Model Culture

Once you have defined a set of core values, founders and leaders must embrace them wholeheartedly. Otherwise, these will come across as shallow and superficial, defeating the entire purpose. At Myntra, we wanted to promote a culture of equality where policies and rituals for all team members would be the same. Despite my best efforts, I realized that the security team had assigned a parking spot for my driver which was always reserved for my car! Now, that wouldn't imply the true spirit of equality. Once I got to know about this, I had to go out of my way to undo this and release the parking spot—if I hadn't, whatever I said about the culture of equality would have been quite meaningless.

Hubert Joly, the former CEO of Best Buy, spent the first few days on the job working at one of their stores in a small town near Minneapolis. He wore the same T-shirt as the sales staff, with a badge reading 'CEO in Training', and went out for a pizza dinner with the team. By doing this, Joly was setting the cultural tone for the company which was in crisis when he took over. It showed people that the voices of frontline workers were essential in solving problems and that every job was equally important, irrespective of designation or seniority.[15]

Leaders often exemplify culture without even realizing it. That's why it's not important just to articulate culture, or assign a team to do so, but to live the company culture in every action. When Angela Ahrendts, former CEO of Burberry, joined Apple as the head of retail, the PR and HR teams at Apple came to her with a draft of a formal email about her recruitment to circulate with the entire global organization.[16] Wanting to reach out to the 60,000-odd employees in a more personal way instead, Ahrendts chose to record a short video on her iPhone—three thoughts in one, unedited take. In the middle of recording, however, her youngest daughter called. Ahrendts answered the phone to check if her child was all right, told her she'd call her right back and then went back to finishing the video. Despite the PR team offering to edit this out, Ahrendts said she wanted to be authentic and sent out the video exactly as it was. The next day, she received a flood of emails from employees thanking her—not only for sharing a video that helped them connect with her better but also for answering her daughter's phone call, because it showed that she was human. This became an important activator of culture—leaders being recognized as one of the team, as parents and humans with similar problems, hopes and dreams.

Hiring for Culture

It has been said that people are your 'cultural co-founders'. Aneel Bhusri, founder of Workday, personally interviewed his first 500 employees![17] Increasingly, people believe that while skills and technical expertise can be taught on the job, culture must be intentionally articulated and even hired for. It is especially important in the early years, when the people you hire will be shaping the company culture. Since it can be extraordinarily difficult to dramatically change culture, it can be easier to initially set the tone for a company's culture by filtering it in the hiring process.

Adam Grant says: 'It is nice to have the right people on your bus but it is even more critical to keep the wrong people off your bus.' He adds that, while hiring, founders should have a list of qualities that they absolutely do not want to let into the organization. Netflix's now famous Culture Deck, which they have made public, is a truly authentic piece of communication that encapsulates the company culture without trying to make it sound more appealing than it is. What's amazing about it, though, is that while some people who would never have thought about applying to a job at Netflix might identify deeply with the company's principles and end up working there, others might be turned completely off by the same deck—it clearly either is or isn't the right fit.[18]

Another fun test that hiring managers often consider when hiring for culture is the airport test. The idea behind this is simple. You just need to ask yourself if the candidate in front of you is someone you would want to be stuck with, at an airport. In the early days of Google, the founders talked about this a lot. One of their key criteria in hiring was whether they enjoyed speaking to the person they were potentially going to hire. This is rooted in a deep insight that when you enjoy conversation with a colleague, you are more likely to reach out and have engaging conversations, including a healthy give-and-take to push and build on each other's ideas, which is a much more effective way of problem-solving while having fun in the office. The workplace is the largest part of our social lives, and we might as well work with people we like. Kunal Shah also uses something he calls the 'energy test'—what he means by this is that when the interview is done, he asks himself if he feels more energized or less after the interview. If his energy increases, it is a positive sign that the conversation was stimulating and energizing. Otherwise, it is a strong negative signal. I have started to incorporate this in my interviews as well now and find it very effective.

Zero Tolerance for Culture Transgressions

Culture is made of how people behave daily. In general, people can be polite at a superficial level, but their true colours start to emerge when things go wrong. One of the key things to watch out for is how people react when things are not going well. People who have a true sense of ownership will stand up and own up to mistakes, while those who myopically think of self-preservation will try to come up with an excuse and pin the blame on someone else—preferably someone not in the room! That's a major cultural red flag. You should not tolerate someone throwing a colleague under the bus behind their back, or you are sending a signal that it is okay to act in this manner. Soon enough, others will start to behave in the same way, and that's a disaster for culture. Sometimes, managers blame their team members, which is another major red flag. The job of the manager is to make sure that the team can deliver and to intervene proactively to solve problems. If something does not work out, the manager must take direct responsibility, especially in a public forum. This is why, since time immemorial, the captain of a ship goes down with it when it sinks!

It is also important to watch out for hypocritical behaviour, when people interact with senior members in one way—which is polite, deferential and even sycophantic—and in a totally different way with their own direct teams, being bossy, rude and demeaning. People like this shouldn't be on your teams, as they end up creating an environment that is very toxic for others. The team is unable to perform at its full potential; good people are discouraged and they leave. It is said that 'People never leave a job; they leave their manager.' As a leader in the company, you must ensure that every employee has a good manager.

Sometimes, there are team members who are good at their jobs but are rude and arrogant with their team members. Unfortunately, no amount of excellence can mask the detrimental effects of an uncooperative team member or a manager who puts down other people or shouts at them. Robert Sutton is a professor at Stanford who has written a bestselling book *The No A**hole Rule*. As the title of the book implies, Sutton argues that you should have no tolerance for someone who is a jerk at work. Numerous studies have shown that when you let go of such a person, the overall morale and productivity of the team goes up significantly.[19]

According to Adam Grant, there are four deadly sins of work culture—toxicity, mediocrity, bureaucracy and anarchy. These sins are the result of what Grant calls the two fundamental tensions in organizational culture: one is relationships versus results, and the other is rules versus risk. Toxic cultures, which research shows are the number one driver of resignations—even more so than burnout and low pay—result from companies valuing results over human relationships. Companies with a toxic culture allow or even enable disrespect, discrimination, abuse and exclusion. On the other hand, mediocrity arises in companies that place relationships above all else, including results. People are so focused on being nice that there is no accountability or honest feedback system. What ends up happening in mediocre cultures is that people get promoted to their level of incompetence—known as the Peter Principle. When a company tends to cling to rules and is obsessed with red tape, it ends up with the sin of bureaucracy, too scared to question the status quo, thus suffocating creativity. This is the problem of too many rules and not enough risk-taking. At the other end of the spectrum is anarchy, when risk overtakes any heeding of rules, resulting in total chaos.[20]

There is absolutely no question that culture is at the heart of why some companies succeed while many fail. Consider two contrasting situations. One is what Bezos calls 'tap dancing to work'—when you enjoy your work and the work environment so much that you are filled with joy on your way to work every morning, super pumped and energized, looking forward to solving problems and collaborating with your colleagues.[21] In the other situation, every morning you frantically search for an excuse to avoid going to the office, even hoping you fall sick so you can miss another day! I have been in such a situation while I was working for a start-up in Silicon Valley. The culture was so bad that every morning when I drove into the parking lot, I wouldn't feel like going in. I'd end up just staying in my car in the parking lot, listening to audio books, which was infinitely more fun than having to go inside the office building. It's no surprise that I left that job in less than a year!

In most cases, more than the bad behaviour itself, it is management's tolerance of bad behaviour that makes a culture toxic. This makes it more important to call out transgressions, even when it is uncomfortable to do so. If it comes down to a trade-off that involves tolerating a behaviour that visibly dilutes the culture versus letting go of a star employee, the choice shouldn't be difficult. Culture is the most important asset that an entrepreneur builds, and it continues to live on well past even the founder's stint. After all, Jeff Bezos and Bill Gates no longer run the companies that they founded.

Building High-Performing Teams

Building an organization and culture is not only about individuals but also about teams that are able to collaborate and create magic together. I have often observed that teams go through a life cycle that, in organizational psychology, has been described as the Tuckman model. The four stages in the Tuckman model are Forming, Storming, Norming and Performing. Initially, when a group comes together, people are very cordial and accommodating, based on generally accepted social norms. As work gets underway, sooner or later, problems develop as differing work styles, different opinions and different competencies start to surface and people start speaking up. At some point, this leads to contentious discussions and even full-blown arguments or a lot of stewing behind the scenes. This is a very critical stage for a team's formation.

People go through the third stage, known as Norming, when they decide to work through all the issues, table everything and find ways to work out differences, identify complementary strengths and acceptable methods of resolving differences. This is a good outcome. But in other teams, people form clear boundaries, and when they learn what the hot button items are, they decide to just avoid bringing those up. They learn how to skirt around issues so as to not cause friction or end up in uncomfortable situations. Some even resort to completely ignoring some team members, barely even making eye contact. This creates a situation where things appear normal on the surface but there is very little deep collaboration.[22]

ENTREPRENEURIAL WISDOM

On Hiring for Excellence

A good rule of thumb, when hiring, is to look for people who have been in inspiring, high-growth environments, irrespective of their role or position. This matters because once people have been exposed to excellence and experienced it first hand, they begin to set a very high bar for themselves. They will then bring this quality with them wherever they go.

The teams that figure out a way to norm in a healthy manner, so that they can have open dialogues about problems and come together to resolve issues, go on to the Performing stage. They keep building mutual trust and confidence through each win. When good leaders see friction building up, they proactively intervene, get all the actors on the discussion table and make sure issues are resolved at the root level. If this isn't done, teams will never get to the Performing stage.

Crises are a great way to bring teams together; a company will go through many crises in its lifetime. When a crisis occurs, if a leader or manager can bring teams together and recruit everyone to double down to help solve the problem as one unit, the teams will end up being really close, developing the confidence that they can deal with a similar situation in the future. When people go to war together, they forge friendships that last a lifetime. Similarly, wins are very important for any new team. One of the things I look for in a new team is when they can get their first win together. When people start winning together, their confidence in the team as well as in their own contribution goes up and they want to win more as a team.

In his book *The Five Dysfunctions of a Team*, Patrick Lencioni narrates the struggles and eventual turnaround of a fictional company to highlight the main causes of politics and toxic cultures in organizational teams. His framework of 'dysfunctions', as he calls them, is an elegant one. A lack of trust is at the heart of a dysfunctional team—as it prevents members from being genuinely open and vulnerable with one another. Trust requires a commitment to transparency, having equal access to information and having as many open-door conversations as possible. I have followed one rule throughout my career which is that I completely avoid talking about a person if that person is not in the room. It does lead to uncomfortable conversations, but everyone knows that everything is discussed in front of them and there is no need for second-guessing. Project Aristotle was a five-year study on highly productive teams conducted by Google, and its most important finding was that psychological safety was what set the most successful teams apart from the rest. This refers to team members feeling safe enough to take risks and be vulnerable with one another.[23]

The absence of trust often leads to a fear of conflict and a lack of healthy debate, because people can't engage in truly honest arguments without a foundation of trust. If people are unable to voice their opinions in passionate debates, they often don't buy into decisions, and thus teams only reach superficial consensus. Remember Intel's culture of 'disagree and commit'? Most reasonable people don't want to just get their way, but they do want to be heard. Once they feel that their opinion has been heard and considered, they're happy to buy into the decision that the team takes as a whole, even if it differs from their idea. Good leaders should encourage getting conflicts out in the open and force debate so that tensions don't keep simmering below the surface until they get to a point of no return.

If consensus is just superficial—without buy-in from every member of a team—there is a false sense of harmony, leading to the next dysfunction, which is a lack of commitment. When there is too much ambiguity—because people have not expressed their thoughts and concerns—teams cannot commit to a specific course of action. Many teams have members who seem to think, 'I will do only what I am told to,' or have an attitude captured by that popular acronym 'CYA' (or 'cover your ass') which is all too pervasive in most dysfunctional environments. Unless people have full and sincere commitment, the efforts of the group will never add up to an outstanding outcome. Start-ups can't survive unless people are able to punch way above their weight.

This lack of clarity then extends into a lack of accountability. People hesitate to call each other out or hold one another accountable because they want to avoid interpersonal conflict. Good teams must be willing to 'enter the danger' with each other. If not, standards fall, and teams descend into mediocrity. It is critical that the accountability framework be clear; the buck must stop with someone. One of the telltale signs I look for is when people start explaining failures or the absence of results in terms of 'we'. While on the surface, 'we' sounds very collaborative and team spirit-oriented, it is often the most convenient way to mask accountability because if the group has failed, there is no one who has individually failed and hence no one is directly responsible for rectifying the issue. Accountability enables teams to get to the bottom of an issue, identifying who is individually responsible, making it easier to learn from the failure.

Finally, teams often lose sight of the overarching objectives and results when they are too focused on individual career advancement or their own teams rather than the good of the entire organization. Inattention to results is a sure sign of a dysfunctional team. I have often seen a team in which the individual performance assessments are very good, but there is not much to show for the overall team's outcome. If the company culture doesn't highlight the overall lack of results or have a way of identifying bottlenecks and right accountability, the company will keep chugging along, everyone looking after their own interests but as a whole failing to achieve the organizational objectives.

Changing Culture Is Hard, But Not Impossible

IBM, before Lou Gerstner became CEO, was steeped in a legacy culture, characterized by rigidity, bureaucracy and an inward focus. The company was losing ground due to its inability to adapt quickly to market changes and customer needs, largely due to its entrenched ways of operating. Gerstner, upon joining IBM, recognized that the company's biggest challenge wasn't just strategic or technological, but cultural. This was manifest in various ways, from the strict dress code to the siloed approach to business units. Gerstner understood that culture change could not be decreed; it had to be cultivated. He started by questioning the status quo, challenging the existing norms and emphasizing the need for a customer-focused approach.

He addressed the bureaucratic culture by decentralizing decision-making, thereby empowering employees closer to the customers and markets. Gerstner took symbolic and tangible actions to signal change. He initiated large-scale lay-offs and restructuring, not just as a cost-cutting measure, but also to reshape the organization into a more agile and responsive entity. Gradually, as IBM started to stabilize and then grow, the new culture began to take root. This was marked by a more collaborative environment, quicker decision-making and a greater focus on market realities. By the time Gerstner left IBM, the company had not only recovered financially but had also undergone a significant cultural transformation. IBM had become nimbler, more focused on the customer and better equipped to handle the rapid changes in the tech industry. The success of IBM under Gerstner's leadership serves as a testament to the fact that while altering a company's culture is a daunting task, it is indeed achievable, with focused leadership, clear vision and consistent actions.[24]

Dara Khosrowshahi took over the reins at Uber when it was in the news for all the wrong reasons, most stemming from a very toxic work culture. Khosrowshahi recalls attending an all-hands meeting early on when someone asked how they were going to solve the 'PR problem'. Khosrowshahi quickly stood up to say that what Uber had wasn't a 'PR problem' but an 'us problem'. Acknowledging in front of the entire company that the issue lay with the culture was the first step he took towards change. Khosrowshahi focused on listening, getting to the bottom of what was wrong in Uber's culture as well as what had worked for the company in the past, developing deep insights in the process. He had to make massive changes in the leadership team as culture stems from people in senior leadership positions and often, a clean slate is a much better way to initiate cultural changes rather than trying to change people, which is very hard.[25]

Arianna Huffington, as a member of Uber's board, had already stated that the company would no longer allow 'brilliant jerks', which was one step towards changing the culture. But Khosrowshahi came in to provide the leadership and guidance that the teams needed. Because, as he recalls, there were still many employees who were good workers, had a strong sense of ethics and truly believed in what Uber could do. What Khosrowshahi did, that Uber had lacked before, was to focus on being radically honest and transparent, on earning the trust of teams, and listening to all stakeholders to create a culture that truly supported the company's original mission.

Winning Culture Makes Everything Easy and Fun!

Very few people ever get to build a company from scratch. It is a rare privilege that happens because of numerous things going your way over many years or even decades. This is only the start of the journey. Going by start-up statistics, most companies will die in the first two years and the ones that do survive will go through a lot of ups and downs throughout their journey. And yet, some companies do make it and then continue to thrive for many decades. These companies were built to last, and the founders took pains to ensure a very strong foundation despite all the pressing needs of an early-stage company.

For an early-stage founder, the entire company is a blank slate. You have a choice to build the company however you choose to. There are many companies out there. Some are a nightmare to work for, while others have people raving about their time in that company as the best time of their career. I used to tell my teams at Myntra that I want to see three things happen during people's tenure there. People should grow at a much faster rate, they should have an accelerated learning curve and have a lot of fun in the process. I hoped that when people left, they would recall their Myntra tenure with a lot of fondness, rating it as one of the best experiences of their lives.

In the foundational stages, you get to be the architect of your company. What is the dream environment that you had always wished for? What did you like in the companies that you worked for, what did you hate the most and what are the companies that you admire as role models? You can pick the features that you like, you can design policies to counter the things that you don't, and you can create totally novel policies and rituals that will create a unique signature for your company's long-term success. If you can adopt a mindset of approaching the organization as a product and yourself as the master architect, you will not only have a lot of fun in making design choices, but you will also pave the way to eventually have hundreds and thousands of people join and do the best work of their lives. This is one of the many privileges that comes with choosing to build your own company and you should embrace the opportunity wholeheartedly.

FROM PAGE TO ACTION

Culture might not be a priority for you when you're focused on product and growth, but it should be something you spend time thinking about. Culture is what will transform your company into one that endures. Here is an exercise to spend some time on:

a. **Draft an Organizational Constitution:** To codify the culture you want. This should include:

    i. Purpose
    ii. Core Values
    iii. Beliefs
    iv. Policies and Rituals

9

Leaders Lead

Seek first to understand, and then be understood.

—Stephen Covey

In the past, jobs were about muscles, now they're about brains, but in the future, they'll be about the heart.

—Minouche Shafik, former director of the London School of Economics and president of Columbia University

Management is doing things right. Leadership is doing the right things.

—Peter Drucker

In the 1980s, the AIDS epidemic was raging. While the medical establishment had very little understanding of the disease, young men in America and Europe were filling the

213

wards of hospitals and dying from all types of complications, each unique in terms of the stages of deterioration. Since most of the people who were contracting AIDS were homosexuals, it was termed by the popular media as the 'gay disease' and there were many misconceptions and a sense of stigma around it. People suffering from AIDS were not only ostracized, they were also actively targeted, blamed for having contracted the disease and shunned by society. It was also widely believed that there were many ways to contract the disease, including something as simple as shaking someone's hand. As a result, people avoided all physical contact with AIDS patients, making an already difficult situation even more difficult, as those suffering were in dire need of support from caregivers around them due to the drastic deterioration in their immunity and strength.

Princess Diana was one of the most famous people in the world during this time, with her every move and appearance being recorded and splashed across international media. In 1987, thanks to the Princess, Britain opened its first AIDS unit, and she visited the centre. During her visit, she went out of her way to shake hands with many of the patients without wearing gloves. The picture went (what we would now describe as) 'viral' and caused massive consternation, the event being broadly covered and debated. This one simple gesture did so much to educate the public about the fact that AIDS didn't spread from simple physical contact, helping to slowly change the misconception. This is what leaders do. They lead through action and not just words. Leadership is about behaving in line with deep principles, self-awareness, clarity about one's objectives as well as living authentically. People notice, they get inspired, they follow the leader and end up doing amazing things together. Leaders lead through action. We have incredible examples of leaders ranging from Rosa Parks to Malala Yousafzai to Greta Thunberg, each of whom took a stance for an issue they cared about and, in the process, ended up inspiring millions of people, and became exemplary leaders.

I really like this John Quincy Adams quote: 'If your actions inspire others to dream more, learn more, do more and become more, you are a leader.' This really gets to the heart of what being a true leader is. Leadership is never about an individual in the leadership role. It is about the cause that you believe in and the method through which you can get a group to perform at a level that they themselves cannot even conceive of. Steve Jobs repeatedly got his teams to deliver at such high levels—with people finding ways to do things they thought were impossible.

No One Is Born a Leader

Teams thrive most when they are guided by a leader. Without a leader, groups often disintegrate into chaos. Even in traditional societies, there are elders who are the designated leaders of hunting parties who direct the group's actions. All sports teams have a captain who calls the shots during the ebb and flow of the game and gets a disproportionate share of both the glory of a win and the ignominy of a terrible loss. So how does one become a leader? Who are the privileged ones who get to play the role of a leader? I believe that no one is born a leader. Leadership is a skill that is only learnt with deliberate practice and experience. It takes decades before an ordinary person can be considered an outstanding leader.

Not everyone needs to be a leader either. Many people prefer to focus on being outstanding individual contributors and find that most fulfilling, as dealing with other people can be quite frustrating. In the initial years of starting up, founders have almost no choice but to be leaders. However, over time, they might have the self-awareness to realize that the company would be better off with someone else in the leadership role, while they focus on building things for the long term. But, if founders choose to lead the organization into the future, they will have to learn on the job, along with numerous other things they will need to manage as the head of a fledgling company.

Know Thyself First

One can have no smaller or greater mastery than mastery of oneself; you will never have a greater or lesser dominion than that over yourself; the height of your success is gauged by your self-mastery, the depth of your failure by your self-abandonment. Those who cannot establish dominion over themselves will have no dominion over others.

—Leonardo da Vinci

The journey of leadership starts with self-reflection—building a deep understanding of who you are and why you want to be a leader in the first place. This takes time to develop, as you learn from the ups and downs of life and go through many intense experiences. Many key leadership traits are forged when you hit rock bottom. This is when you are forced to think deeply about who you are and why you are here, finding that inner strength required to dig yourself out of a bad situation. If you're able to do that, you can dig deeper to discover what you are capable of and how you can conduct yourself in a difficult situation.

ENTREPRENEURIAL WISDOM

On Entrepreneurship as Leadership Training

Founders, whether they want to or not, undergo the most gruelling training in leadership simply by virtue of leading their companies. They are tested almost daily in everything from making tough decisions to managing people in crisis. These lessons are invaluable and often turn founders with no formal management experience or education into the finest leaders.

The book *Diary of a CEO*[1] offers great advice when it comes to looking at the self. No one can do great things and become a leader until they focus on building their own skills and capabilities. The five questions one needs to keep in mind are: What do you know? What can you do? Who do you know? What do you have? What does the world think of you? Now, this may sound easy but is very difficult to arrive at in practice. How do you even begin to answer these questions? This will require a lot of reflection, contemplation, taking notes, asking questions, asking for feedback from people around you and analysing your past journeys and choices, over a long period of time. In my case, by the time I was twenty-five, I had already taken many major risks, many of which failed spectacularly. But I realized that adverse outcomes didn't bother me as much as I enjoyed the learning and adventure that came from choosing an unconventional path. With that, I knew that I would always be comfortable taking a reasonable amount of risk and be at peace, no matter what the outcome.

The journey of self-discovery often involves some kind of proverbial exile or wandering in the wilderness, much like Nelson Mandela's twenty-seven years in prison, which often involved solitary confinement and long stretches of deep contemplation. When asked how he survived those twenty-seven years in prison, he replied, 'I didn't survive, I prepared!' Mahatma Gandhi had a similar period of preparation or wandering, in South Africa where he fought on the ground for basic rights, and later in India, travelling the length and breadth of the country and spending time with the people on whose behalf he was going to mount a totally new freedom movement—the likes of which the world had never seen before.

According to Guy Kawasaki's classic business book *The Art of the Start*, good leaders should use four phrases often: 'I don't know,' 'Thank you,' 'Do what you think is right,' and

'It's my fault.'[2] This is because great leaders are not afraid to admit their shortcomings or take responsibility for mistakes. They are also able to trust their teams to make decisions and show genuine appreciation. These phrases encapsulate things that all of us might struggle with, no matter what our position may be within a company, but it is something we can learn and practise. True leadership requires a lot of authenticity. Without being able to see the situation as it is and calling a spade a spade, even if it means admitting your mistakes publicly, one is just an imposter who will never have the kind of following that people who are willing to go to war for you will have. Leaders that demonstrate vulnerability and own their mistakes publicly not only keep growing but also inspire confidence in others.

Many leaders are known to emphasize 'think time' or 'reflection time' in their schedule. Bill Gates famously used to take 'think weeks' during which he would go deep into the wilderness to think deeply about Microsoft's big picture and come back with unique new realizations. Similarly, Jeff Bezos talks about how he likes to keep his mornings free to do what he calls just 'putter', leisurely drinking his morning coffee, perusing the newspapers, having breakfast with his kids[3] and doing other things that allow his mind to be in a relaxed state before he goes into the office where he has his first meeting at 10 a.m. His mental model is that if, as a leader, you can make just one or two good decisions every day, it is a very productive day. I have now come to believe that senior leadership roles require up to 50 per cent of the time to be free of meetings. Instead, leaders should use this time to think deeply about the topics at hand, consuming all relevant inputs to develop a comprehensive picture. I see way too many leaders continually busy with everyday firefighting, running from one fire to another—which may seem heroic in the moment but leads to just shallow work on a regular basis. These leaders need to remember to 'Beware the busyness of a barren life.'

Leadership Is about People

Let's face it. People are complex, mercurial, unpredictable; each one is unique in his or her own way. As a leader you must deal with a lot of people, all the time. If you are an introvert, this can be very daunting at first. You would probably rather go to a corner and do your work, but leaders don't have that luxury. It doesn't help much if you are an extrovert either. Extroverts thrive on social companionship and unfettered conversation, but in a leadership situation, you can't afford to be too friendly with your teams or you will struggle to take a firm stance when needed.

Above everything else, you need to be a good listener. There are numerous examples of leaders who would only hear what they wanted to hear, create an environment of fear around themselves or surround themselves with sycophants who might boost their ego for a while. But these leaders don't create anything worth noting. Learning to just listen and understand people is a key hallmark of a leader. Winston Churchill's mother, Jenny Jerome, recounted the time she met Benjamin Disraeli and William Gladstone who were both running for the position of prime minister of England.[4] Gladstone was known for his brilliant wit and polymath knowledge of just about everything. Jerome recounts that when she dined with Gladstone, she thought that he was the cleverest man in England. But when she dined with Disraeli, she left the meeting thinking she was the cleverest woman! That's what great leaders do. They listen with so much intent and focus that they can develop a deep understanding of the people around them and make them feel truly heard.

Leaders need to take a keen interest in people. People have different motivations, different communication styles, different strengths and weaknesses. A good leader will know how to leverage someone's strengths to the maximum and not let their weaknesses come in the way. If a message needs to be communicated, it needs to be tailored to the personality of the person being addressed. For some people, just a mere hint is enough, and they will move heaven and earth to rectify the situation while others need to be sat down and the concern spelt out in black and white.

This is the keen understanding that made Steve Jobs such a great leader. The basic understanding that humans have an insurmountable desire to do meaningful work helped him convince John Sculley to leave his very lucrative job at PepsiCo and come join Apple as the new CEO.[5] While John was vacillating about whether to give up his high-profile role at Pepsi to join a much smaller company, Jobs famously asked him if he wanted 'an opportunity to change the world or to spend the rest of his life selling sugared water'. That did the trick and John took the plunge. Leaders have this ability to inspire people about the vision that makes the work truly worth investing a portion of their lives into. They can convince people that they have the ability to contribute at a far larger level than they might have done otherwise.

Jim Sinegal, co-founder and CEO of Costco, exemplified a leadership style that valued employees as the key to long-term business success.[6] Known for offering higher wages and better benefits compared to rivals, Sinegal's approach contributed to Costco's low employee turnover and high job satisfaction. He maintained a personal touch by keeping a modest salary for himself and interacting with staff during his annual visits to every Costco store. Defying Wall Street's short-term profitability pressures, he prioritized employee welfare, believing that workers who are treated well provide superior customer service, fostering customer loyalty. Sinegal's hands-on, egalitarian approach not only shaped Costco's strong corporate culture but also proved that investing in employees can drive sustainable financial growth and create a resilient business model. His leadership remains influential at Costco, demonstrating that ethical management and care for employees are compatible with corporate success.

Putting people first doesn't mean sacrificing excellence or performance—in fact, companies that do so are more stable, innovative and successful than their competitors. Good leaders don't see people as a commodity to be managed to make money, but instead see money as a commodity to grow people. One of the most fulfilling aspects of being a leader is that you get to help people achieve their full potential. Naresh Krishnaswamy started working with me in 2012 when he joined as a business analyst at Myntra and now, twelve years down the line, he is the CEO at CureFit, which speaks of phenomenal growth. He is now nurturing multiple leaders who could possibly take on his role in a few years.

Many Different Leadership Styles—They All Work!

A leader's style defines the tone and environment of the entire company—it can have a true multiplier effect. There are many different styles with different advantages, better suited to different personality types. Some leaders tend to be heavily content-oriented, which means that they invest a great deal of time building depth in relevant subject areas, are very aware of the bigger picture, and spend considerable amounts of time outside the company to have a 360-degree view and hence they can bring very unique perspectives and insights to their decision-making. I am often amazed when I hear a CEO add a unique perspective to a discussion—one that teams who are much closer to the action have failed to see, probably because they didn't zoom out of their immediate contexts to see the larger picture.

Some leaders are genuinely people-first. What this means is that they realize that their strength lies in bringing the best out of the people they work with. These leaders spend time getting to know their teams, setting ambitious goals that are suited to their individual strengths and then providing enough space and autonomy for them to do their thing, intervening only when necessary. This style works very well when you have a highly competent team around you, as most competent people want the freedom to express themselves with the space to make their mistakes without being constantly watched.

A hard-charging leader is someone who runs rigorous daily and weekly meetings, is on top of all the numbers and demands an explanation for any deviations on the spot. This style works well in heavily sales-driven companies as well as operations-oriented companies but is not very well suited to product-oriented companies. Some people need to be in the loop all the time and the whole company culture revolves around the brilliance and charisma of the leader. Some of these companies work very well but don't ever become leadership factories as other people never get the space or opportunity to sharpen their own skills. In fact, even very talented and capable people come to rely more and more on the wisdom of the charismatic founder.

Some of the best leaders can combine hard and soft styles— having high expectations of their teams but also constantly building them up and having their backs. Such leaders spend considerable amounts of time helping build strategy, setting long-term goals, defining clear ownership and accountability frameworks, and then letting their teams do their own thing, not reacting too much to short-term ups and downs. But when they see that a situation is starting to unravel, a crisis is building up or a gap is growing too large to be bridged, then they jump into the trenches and get involved in the firefighting until the crisis is solved. In my own experience, I have seen that I am able to create a lot of space when things are going well but tend to get involved at a fairly granular level when things are not working.

In his cult classic *Beyond Entrepreneurship*,[7] Jim Collins says that good leaders must be comfortable with paradox—not subject to the 'tyranny of the OR' but believing in the 'genius of the AND'. It is amazing how often this idea comes up in leadership. There is no real either-or when it comes to profit versus growth, long-term versus short-term thinking, product versus sales, high talent bar versus closing open positions and so on. One of the top leaders I worked with used to say that if you can operate with an OR mindset, then leadership is very easy; anyone can make an either-OR choice for mediocre outcomes. What makes leadership difficult is that often you must manage and deliver both sides of AND. Let's take the recent example of Zomato. After going public in 2020, the company saw a decline in stock prices of two-thirds of its peak value. Their burn was continuing to increase, and growth was starting to taper down. Zomato's founder Deepinder took some major calls in 2022, significantly changing the management team, giving a lot more responsibility to younger managers and encouraging them to make sweeping changes in product and operations. The company increased prices in many areas, leading to much better unit economics, but also raised service levels and introduced many features to delight customers. As a result, the company grew much faster in 2023 while also hitting profitability goals, and the stock recovered nearly up to its previous high.

While there are many leadership styles and every leader favours a particular one, they will often be required to adapt their approach to the situation at hand. For this, they must be flexible and agile to some extent. There is an adage: 'If the only tool you have is a hammer, you will treat every problem as a nail.' Leaders need to be able to read a situation, choose how they want to respond and pick an appropriate style for the environment. For example, a soft, open and vulnerable style might work for some leaders most of the time, but when a sudden crisis arises, taking a tougher stand and becoming a hard-charging leader for a period of time might be necessary.

Wartime versus Peacetime Leadership

Andy Grove, the former CEO of Intel, is known for having turned the company around in the face of immense competition, even leading a drastic pivot away from its core business. He is often cited as an example of a strong wartime leader, with his famous quote: 'Success breeds complacency. Complacency breeds failure. Only the paranoid survive.' This captures the approach of wartime leadership, of staying constantly and aggressively on edge.

Winston Churchill is famous for being a strong leader during World War II. But some people, like leadership expert Gautam Mukunda, think that without Hitler, we might not have remembered Churchill much, or we might have remembered him for not being very good at his job.[8] Before 1940, many people thought Churchill made decisions too quickly, was too aggressive, and didn't treat some people fairly. For example, he wasn't kind to Mahatma Gandhi and didn't do much to help during a big famine in Bengal in 1943, where millions died.

But the same qualities that led people to criticize him were what enabled Britain to keep fighting in the war when things looked really bad. This toughness and stubbornness played a part in the victory over Hitler and the Nazi Party. This could mean that Churchill was the kind of leader who was good during war but not as good when things were peaceful. The same Churchill who people didn't like before the war was praised as a hero after it. If Britain had been led by Neville Chamberlain, who was a good leader in other ways, they might not have made it through the war. The voters of Britain showed their astuteness in voting Churchill out of power despite having enormous respect for his wartime grit and savvy. They realized that he was a mediocre peacetime leader.

Many employees at Uber have written and spoken about how every day at the company felt like there was a crisis unfolding. There was a sense of urgency, emphasized by vocabulary used at the time, such as the 'war room' or 'code red'. Travis Kalanick worked like a wartime CEO all the time—sparing little time for niceties, violating protocol, engendering a culture of paranoia defined by the 'war'. This constant wartime attitude contributed to the notoriously toxic work culture at Uber. When Dara Khosrowshahi took over as the leader, despite the company being in one of its worst crises ever, he was able to bring in a much more balanced approach. In an interview on the Greylock podcast, Khosrowshahi said,[9] 'There's this push and pull. During easier times, I'm much more consultative. During tough times, I'm much more hardcore.' This illustrates the need to recognize and adapt to wartime and peacetime in business.

You must be able to recognize whether a company is in a war phase or a peace phase. It is not that hard to figure out. When you are beginning to lose sleep over one crisis after another, when you are losing your star employees and customers together, when your market share continues to erode consistently and when you are staring down the barrel, you know that you are not in peacetime at all. Wartime calls for major and drastic action and there is not much time to think. When the pandemic hit, all our CULT centres shut down and our revenue essentially went from 100 to 0 while all costs were intact, leading to an incredible amount of burn with no end in sight. In the ensuing months, we cut down costs significantly, shut down many businesses, exited Dubai and many smaller cities, spun off eat.fit as an independent business, made a few acquisitions and started two new business lines that were more conducive to the situation—in other words, we took more decisions in twelve months during the first two phases of the pandemic compared to all the other years before or after put together.

A wartime leader has the licence to be bold. In fact, smart entrepreneurs will use this time to wipe out all the mistakes of the past, including hiring the wrong senior managers, starting too many businesses, having unsustainably high levels of burn and so on. Tough times allow leaders to take bold decisions and make major course corrections with the support of those around them; these calls will pay back great dividends in peacetime. The Indian start-up ecosystem between 2022 and 2023 resembled a battlefield. All the growth stage funding had dried up and start-ups had to radically alter their cost base and business plans in order to have a credible plan for profitability.

Peacetime playbooks look very different. These are times when there are no major existential threats. There is steady, predictable growth. Teams are fully aligned, competent and charged up about future prospects. Peacetime is when the CEO should step back more and use the time to think about the long run. This is a time to flesh out multiple year strategies as well as to give a long rope to key leaders, allowing them to come into their own. Leaders should ensure that this time is used to strengthen processes and automation to bring in a lot of efficiencies that will all flow to the bottom line. This is also when you can think deeply about building long-term moats. The beginning of 2024 was that time for us at CULT, when everything was going quite smoothly. We had grown consistently over the previous eight quarters, were nearly profitable and had no major competition in sight. We spent that period thinking about how we could grow the culture of fitness in India to drive consistent growth of 25 per cent over the next ten years and beyond. There is no question that at some point in the future, a new crisis will hit us and we will have to switch back to wartime mode, but while this lasts, we are making the most of it.

Most leaders are naturally inclined to either a wartime mindset or a peacetime one and find it very difficult to switch between them. Elon Musk, for example, is hardwired to think in terms of wartime and even when things are going well, he stays in this mode. He drives surges to create an atmosphere of war which, while it leads to dramatic results, also ends up burning out a majority of his team members. To grow as a leader, one needs to develop both wartime and peacetime skills to be able to take advantage of both phases which are an inevitable part of any start-up journey.

Leaders Are Consistent, Not Opportunistic

Consistency is paramount in leadership. Before you become a leader with full faith in your instincts, you need to learn and practise every day. Demosthenes, a Greek statesman, was widely renowned for his oratory skills, but he didn't become a great orator overnight. It is said that he practised reciting every day with pebbles in his mouth, trying to speak over the roar of the waves. That is the kind of discipline and dedication one needs to have in order to become an effective leader.

Sir Alex Ferguson is often hailed as the epitome of football management excellence.[10] His remarkable twenty-six-year tenure at Manchester United was marked by an impressive number of trophies and awards won by the club. Ferguson's journey with Manchester United began in 1986, at a time when the club was facing challenges. He held a strong conviction that a team's triumph depended not just on its players and tactics but more fundamentally on its culture and values. Ferguson's legacy was grounded in his belief that a strong and cohesive club culture was the key to achieving sustained success on the field. A critical aspect of his approach was his insistence on prioritizing the team's ethos and values over individual players. He famously asserted that no player is greater than another or would come before the club. This philosophy was evident in his decisions to transfer players who did not align with the 'United way', irrespective of their current performance, fame or the important role they played within the team.

To be consistent, you need to know who you truly are as a leader. Deep down, what do you believe in? What are your core values that you will not compromise on, no matter what? What kind of delegation do you feel comfortable with and what are your natural tendencies and biases? Once you have clarity on these, you can act in accordance with these traits as much as possible. Most leaders succeed and fail in their own ways. Just as there is no perfect batting stance in cricket and many players do well with highly unorthodox stances, similarly many different leadership styles can work, as long as you are true to yourself. By staying true to yourself and acting in accordance with your core values, you will be a lot more consistent and people around you will notice and trust you. Even when you make tough decisions, people will know where you are coming from and back you. But if you try to be someone else, it will only lead to disarray and the disintegration of trust. There are choices available at times to completely reinvent yourself or make a major change, but it needs a sustained amount of work, preferably with a leadership coach.

Level 5 Leadership—Personal Humility, Indomitable Will

Jim Collins is one the foremost business scholars in the world and his books have had a profound impact on our understanding of what it takes to build an outstanding company. In his book *Good to Great*[11] he talks about Level 5 leaders which he posits as the highest form of leadership, the hallmark of companies that create lasting shareholder value over a very long term. He uses the phrase 'personal humility and indomitable will' to describe leaders who inspire the whole group to aspire for something much larger than any individual could achieve, and yet never make the work about themselves. The CEOs of some of the most valuable companies in the world, from Satya Nadella at Microsoft and Sundar Pichai at Google to Tim Cook at Apple or Andy Jassy at Amazon, are never at the forefront of their companies trying to promote their personal brand or position themselves as heroes, and yet they have all created incredible amounts of shareholder value.

Speaking about leadership, Theodore Roosevelt famously said, 'Speak softly and carry a big stick; you will go far.' This is what great leaders do—negotiate peacefully while being firm in their stance. They are calm, measured and great at listening, but simultaneously deeply committed to the mission and will pull all stops to steer the organization in that direction. Abraham Lincoln was unflinching in his ideals and convictions. He stayed the course throughout the Civil War, through ups and downs and personal tragedies, to score a massive win not only for America, but for humanity as a whole. Mahatma Gandhi is another example of a person who was humility incarnate in every sense of the word and yet his commitment to the cause of freedom was unflinching. As a result, he gave courage to millions of people to follow in his footsteps.

Genuinely Caring for the People You Lead

People don't care how much you know until they know how much you care.

—Proverb

The Spartans of ancient Greece were considered the strongest and most courageous warriors. Surprisingly, though, it wasn't the sharpness of their spears that they were known for, but the strength of their shields.[12] The worst crime a Spartan could commit was losing his shield—he could be forgiven for losing a helmet or breastplate, but never a shield. That's because a warrior carried a helmet and breastplate for his own protection but a shield for the safety of the entire line. In the same way, a leader at the forefront of a company must have her employees' backs. In the context of the workplace, it is the responsibility of the leadership to extend what Simon Sinek (in his book, *Leaders Eat Last*) calls the 'Circle of Safety' to every employee in the organization. Once inside the Circle of Safety, people and teams feel valued, cared for and confident in their colleagues and leaders.

Good leaders protect the organization from internal rivalries that destroy the culture. People shouldn't have to protect themselves from each other within an organization— trust and cooperation are essential for us to thrive. Biologically, if we feel threatened, we go on the defensive, but if we feel safe, we're more willing to cooperate. Our inherent need to cooperate arises from our primal survival instinct, because evolution has taught us that we are most likely to overcome danger when we face it together. Unfortunately, many leaders think that piling on pressure and a sense of urgency within an organization will motivate people to overcome the external pressures and difficulties. In fact, it is a deep sense of safety and a bond of trust that will allow people to cooperate and thrive in the toughest of times.

Helping People Grow at a Faster Pace

In order to help their teams and people grow, good leaders sit down with them to understand where their strengths lie—where their contributions are most valuable. This happens through open and honest discussions, as well as close observation. Once identified, these leaders place team members in positions in which they can find their flow, positions that allow them to add the most value. In his book *The New One Minute Manager*, Ken Blanchard advises leaders to, 'Catch people doing things right.'[13] This is much more valuable than focusing on where people might be making mistakes, because it will help you empower them and enable them to grow.

Peeyush Ranjan, the VP of Engineering at Google Pay, gives an excellent analogy for thinking about people and growth. He urges one to think about the people you lead as a sports team. One can make the locker room as comfortable as possible, but even then, every athlete has to show up, has to be super-fit, has to play like a winner and go win matches. If these things don't happen, it is not going to matter how comfortable you make the locker room. The environment is not the primary defining factor. It is how you can inspire people to show and display true sportsmanship.[14]

In my experience, I have often found that two methods work well in helping people grow. One is actively solving a real-life problem. If you see an emerging leader struggling with a particular issue, and if you, as a leader, can roll up your sleeves and work alongside them over weeks or months, a good leader will pick up on your approach to the problem and will make this part of their standard repertoire. Another tactic that often works (but can sometimes backfire) is when you take a major bet on a promising candidate. Nothing motivates someone as much as a leader taking a big bet on them by giving them a larger portfolio when they are doing well. It inspires people to raise their game and operate at a very different level. I have done this many times in my career and I have seen it work at least four out of five times. When you can take a bet on people, everyone benefits in a big way. When people are promoted internally, you also avoid the risks of culture misfit, and you already know their strengths and weaknesses. If you are considering giving someone a larger portfolio, it also means that the person has a strong track record. This then sends a signal to others that if you perform well, there is a way to secure a much larger role at the organization.

But this too can backfire. When given a larger role, people need to make many adjustments very fast. Their previous role needs to be delegated quickly, which requires two things. First, there must be people on the team who can rise and take on the role, and the new leader must have the ability to let go, which is not always easy. The person given a larger role also needs to ramp up very quickly as they will face different challenges. Sometimes, when people take the larger role for granted and don't put in the effort to learn the ropes and build new relationships, the whole thing can unravel very soon. It is great to get additional responsibility, but if you are given such an opportunity, you must double down and work as if you have two roles for the first six months until you are able to notch some new wins.

Showing the Way, When Needed

A leader is one who knows the way, goes the way and shows the way.

—John C. Maxwell

Some of the finest leaders know when to allow their teams to take the reins and steer the company forward, and when they need to roll up their sleeves to get their own hands dirty. They also epitomize the company's values in every action and behaviour. Anne Mulcahy became CEO of Xerox at a critical time, when the company was on the verge of bankruptcy, with $18 billion in debt.[15] She demonstrated exemplary leadership by personally visiting employees, customers and stakeholders, fostering open communication and trust. Instead of laying off staff as a quick fix, she opted to protect jobs and maintain morale, believing in the long-term value of her workforce.

Mulcahy took a pay cut herself and sought cost-saving measures that wouldn't sacrifice employee positions. She remained committed to innovation and customer service, even when finances were tight, ensuring that Xerox continued to invest in research and development. Her approach not only steered Xerox away from financial ruin but also transformed the company culture, emphasizing community and sustainability over short-term gains. Her leadership style was characterized by her unwavering commitment to her principles and her workforce, proving that with integrity and strategic thinking, even the most daunting corporate crises can be navigated successfully.

In a leadership role, one gets to define strategy and long-term goals while holding people accountable for high levels of performance, but sometimes things just don't go well. There is no point yelling at people from up above to raise their performance. As a leader, if you are able to get involved and directly contribute to problem-solving, you are not only able to help move the team forward, but you also earn their respect and contribute to their learning. In cricket, when the captain directly contributes to a win through bat or ball, the headlines go the extra distance to laud them for 'leading from the front'. This is my favourite way of engaging with teams. I don't like review sessions or status updates. I encourage the teams that I work with to engage me in problem-solving sessions. Now, this doesn't mean that I always have the solution, but by engaging at a detailed level, I am able to have a deeper appreciation for the nuances and trade-offs and occasionally I might also suggest moving the problem forward.

ENTREPRENEURIAL WISDOM

On Leadership and Accountability

A big part of leadership is accountability. Good leaders own up to their mistakes and don't shy away from saying, 'I was wrong.' This fosters a culture of transparency and a feeling of shared ownership.

Give and Take: Leaders Are Always Generous

In his book *Give and Take: Why Helping Others Drives Our Success*, renowned author and professor Adam Grant describes our different styles of reciprocity—takers, givers and matchers.[16] In business, one might assume that being a taker will be most beneficial, especially as you rise into leadership positions. Interestingly, however, studies have found that while it is true that givers score lowest on measures of success initially, they also score the highest in the long term! For example, in a study of 160 professional engineers in California, those who reported giving more than they received were the least successful on measures like tasks, reports and drawings completed. Apparently, helping others prevented them from getting their own work done. However, especially over time, the benefits of giving begin to outweigh their costs, and it turns out that some of the most successful and productive people are givers. This makes sense when you think about the fact that we live in an age of collaborative work, where being able to work well in a team, build people up and share knowledge is valued immensely. As a leader, it is even more important to keep in mind what your reciprocity style is, as it will have a profound impact on the way your company functions.

In his early years, Abraham Lincoln—who was very obviously a giver—struggled to enter the arena of politics, and some might say he was too nice to survive that cut-throat world. Lincoln himself famously said, 'If I have one vice—and I can call it nothing else—it is not to be able to say no.' However, he eventually won the presidency in 1860, and when he did, he invited his three rivals in the Republican nomination to be his secretary of state, secretary of the treasury and attorney general. This was a highly unusual cabinet, as the three were far more well known, better educated and more experienced than Lincoln. Yet, instead of worrying that they would overshadow him, Lincoln recognized that he wanted the strongest men in his cabinet. Takers would want to surround themselves with 'yes-men' while matchers might return favours to allies who had supported them. But Lincoln felt that he would be depriving the country of the services of three great leaders, if he did not invite his rivals into his cabinet. Historian Doris

Kearns Goodwin, in her book *Team of Rivals*, says Lincoln's 'success in dealing with the strong egos of the men in his cabinet suggests that in the hands of a truly great politician the qualities we generally associate with decency and morality—kindness, sensitivity, compassion, honesty, and empathy—can also be impressive political resources'.[17] Leaders, therefore, do not always need to be cut-throat, ruthless or unfeeling. In fact, compassion, generosity and kindness can truly serve a leader well, setting them apart from everyone else.

Retaining the IC Skill Set

Most people in the tech world start their career as an Individual Contributor (IC), writing code, building product specs, creating marketing collateral or getting sales done. One can even argue that the real work only happens at an IC level, as everyone further up in the chain of command is merely shouting orders. As you do well in IC roles, you get more responsibility and at some point, you are asked to manage a team. In the early stages of becoming a team lead, you are first among equals—you are responsible for managing the work of the team, even as you continue to do IC work. As people start reaching mid- to senior management, they stop getting so involved and nearly all their actual work is done through other team members. Before you know it, you lose all ability to do any IC work at all. While there are many leaders who are still very effective without being able to do IC work, I personally believe that leaders are more effective when they can do some.

Every engineer respects a CTO who can code or a sales head who can still close the most challenging accounts. I personally feel that taking the time out periodically to flesh out a concept and articulate it clearly in a word document or a PowerPoint presentation helps me clear my head and organize thoughts that might otherwise be unorganized and scattered. This also helps communicate ideas clearly to the teams and presents a possible path forward that can be debated. I have seen way too many leaders who can't even write a one-page document to save their lives; I feel that something fundamental is lost if you get to that stage—and it will only hold you back. As a rule of thumb, I believe that if leaders can keep 30–40 per cent of their time for IC work, they will be significantly more effective than those who lose that ability entirely.

Dealing with Crises and Momentum

There are two pivotal moments that inevitably arise in every company's journey. Recognizing and seizing these moments are extremely important and can lead to the complete transformation of a business. It's difficult to predict when these crucial phases will arise, but it's good to know that they will, in fact, occur with regular frequency. If you can identify them and adapt your strategy and execution dramatically, you can really reap the benefits.

The first of these is momentum. This is when things are falling into place and everything seems to be going your way, including maybe a lucky break of some kind. Like the concept of momentum in physics, it is much easier to accelerate when you have some momentum, as against starting from a place of inertia when you may encounter friction. I have found that there are three effective ways to make the most of your momentum:

1. Double Down: When you sense momentum, you must strengthen your resolve and really double down on the course of action. When the news of demonetization hit India at the end of 2016, Paytm found itself perfectly poised to take advantage of the situation—and they went in for the kill.
2. Focus on Strengths: During periods of momentum, it's important to reflect on what is working so that you can zero in on and amplify those strengths. All too often people

238 · The Start-Up Code

have great results and celebrate without ever realizing what was working in the first place. Then, when the momentum stalls, they are left scratching their heads. During this phase, you should focus and double down on whatever is working.
3. Identify Speed Breakers: Proactively thinking about what could slow or stop the momentum and ensuring that situation doesn't come to pass is essential. If you can maintain the momentum for twelve to eighteen months, you will create a significant gap between yourself and your competition. On the other hand, if you don't look out for the bumps in the road, they will slow you down and the momentum will fizzle out.
4. The Long-Term View: Given that things are going well, you have the luxury of taking in the larger picture and investing in capabilities that will let you ride the momentum for a long period of time.

One of my favourite sayings is 'Never let a crisis go to waste.' In fact, I have come to love crises and embrace them when they confront me. The most dramatic revolutions and big changes in human history have come about as a result of crises. Think about how the 1992 financial crisis in India led to economic reforms that completely changed the path for the country, paving the way for the resurgence of modern India. Start-ups are more prone to crises than established companies, or even countries, are. At Myntra, I faced two major crisis periods that resulted in dramatic transformation. One was in 2010, when our original niche business just wasn't scaling, and we ended up having to pivot to fashion. Then, in 2013, when our funding dried up completely, we were forced to make big changes in our organizational size and marketing budgets, which resulted in inspired execution, making it one of our best years yet. These are my favourite ways of making the most of a crisis:

1. Call a Crisis a Crisis: Too many companies bury their heads in the sand and are in denial when they face a crisis. Calling out a crisis loudly and acknowledging it honestly save precious time and resources.

2. Start from First Principles: Go back to the drawing board and let go of old strategies—what worked in the past may no longer be relevant in a crisis. Flipkart derived a great deal of success from its mobile-exclusive strategy in 2014, but to keep returning to the same plan years later wouldn't make sense. Remember how Intel shut down its memory business as soon as it sensed the threat from the microprocessor industry—this is first principle thinking in action.

3. Make Bold Moves: A crisis is a time to do the unthinkable—making radical changes in business model or team constructs, implementing entirely new strategies, making deep cost reductions, shutting down a product or a business unit are all good options. When Apple had its back against the wall in the late Nineties, Steve Jobs's first move was to shut down 90 per cent of all products.

4. Fight in the Trenches: A crisis is a time to get your hands dirty, engaging in hand-to-hand combat on the field and focusing on survival. The companies that refuse to die often go on to become great. Those that don't make it past a crisis will never get that chance. Paying attention to detail and focusing on the every day will help you make it.

5. All Hands on Deck: All too often, crises lead to infighting, pointing fingers, shifting blame and CYA behaviour which can spell death. Instead, crises should bring teams together, so they are on the same page and fighting as a single unit.

Being able to seize the opportunities presented by periods of momentum and crisis can truly be a game changer for a company.

Power of Radical Transparency

Ajeet Singh, co-founder and executive chairman at ThoughtSpot and co-founder at Nutanix, spoke to me at length about the importance of running companies in a very transparent manner. During ThoughtSpot's early days, he took a very unconventional route by deciding to have board meetings that were hands-on. At one point, he had about 110 employees all huddled in a room for a board meeting. Of course, as the company grew, it was no longer possible to do this, but the essence of Ajeet's philosophy remains intact. He wanted everyone in his company, who had left great jobs elsewhere to come work with him, to feel a sense of ownership. In fact, one of his objectives and key results (OKRs) in life is that ten people who work at a company he started should go on to start their own companies. Google maintains the practice of sharing the full board deck with the entire company right after the board meeting ends to ensure that everyone is truly on the same page.[18]

I have come to believe that the information in the company belongs to everyone. It empowers people and acts as a very strong antidote to any possibilities of petty politics within the company. In the companies I have worked for, I have encouraged a culture of transparency—if anyone feels that they need access to some information, they should be able to ask for it and people have the obligation to share it unless there is a valid reason not to, such as safety or privacy.

Leaders Communicate

A big part of leadership is communication with various internal and external stakeholders. This may not come easily to those who have been great individual contributors, doing their jobs by hunkering down and focusing completely on a task with excellence. As one manages larger teams, one of the biggest challenges is how to get the whole team to work towards one coherent goal, despite differences of opinions, or gaps in skill sets and motivation levels. Communication is the answer to all these issues. Leaders must develop a method to continuously communicate across all of the following:

- What is the big picture and the external perspective? Let's say, the company is dealing with a situation like the pandemic. Leaders need to talk to a lot of experts and translate what they say for the company.
- There may be a strategy that the company has decided to pursue, but to keep the strategy top of mind, it needs to be continuously and repeatedly communicated. You may feel like a broken record, but unless you parrot the same message and choices again and again, it will not seep into every part of the organization.
- If you are driving cultural change, you must explain the rationale in as many forums as you can, engaging people in a constructive dialogue and bringing up the issue at every possible opportunity.

There are many methods to communicate and there is no right or wrong way. You need to embrace your own style of communication. I have found writing to be a very effective way of communicating and have been using a tool that I call Top-of-Mind (TOM). In this weekly ritual, I write a one-page note on any topic that I think is relevant to the company and share it with the whole organization. Every meeting is also an opportunity to communicate, so instead of diving into things right away, you can see if there are any recent developments that you should share with the group. Various all-hands forums, off-sites and workshops are other opportunities to communicate with the larger group. If you prepare well and deliver the key messages consistently, teams will internalize them and further debate these among themselves.

Communication is obviously not meant to be one-way. Leaders need to listen as much as they speak and leaders who are not good at listening miss out on the most important insights that might help them develop a more holistic perspective about what's working and what's not. Asking a lot of questions and giving people space to think is very important. One of the things I have struggled with is that I expect very well thought-out and structured answers, and don't react very well when people give half-baked responses. But this leads to a vicious cycle in which teams end up being more guarded about what to say and not to say for the fear of being judged. This is something I need to work on so that I can create an environment in which people can speak up, without having to come to each meeting with a prepared speech!

Communication doesn't mean that you must always have a well-prepared answer for every possible question about the company. Very often, just saying, 'I don't know,' is the best possible response and creates the opportunity to find new information and have many perspectives aired. It is equally important to be able to say, 'I was wrong.' Most leaders never ever publicly state that they were wrong, and this inability to publicly acknowledge mistakes promotes a similar culture in the company. This not only blocks growth and course correction but is also a lost opportunity to learn from failures. Whenever a leader can say, 'I was wrong,' in a public forum, it sends a very strong signal that what matters is the right choices and not managing optics about who was right or wrong.

In corporate settings, people talk about HiPPO culture— Highest Paid Person's Opinion. This is all too pervasive and very dangerous. In most meetings, the senior-most person in the group will hog most of the talk time, the next few people in the hierarchy will have some, while the rest of the attendees will be silent bystanders. This leads to a very lopsided conversation in which the pertinent points never surface, and the group misses out on the opportunity to have a much richer dialogue. McKinsey has a great cultural value that they call 'Obligation to dissent'. This is drilled into even the junior-most people of the firm that when they are part of a group discussion, they must find ways to challenge the mainstream opinion in the group, just to ensure that all viewpoints are considered and debated. This also ensures that everyone gets an opportunity to speak up. As a leader, you will do well to observe the dynamics in the room and create space and opportunity for as many people to participate as possible.

Leadership is a privilege. Very few people ever get to lead a large group of people, but it is also a privilege that is easily squandered by not being fully prepared for the role. It is very demanding, and you have to put in constant effort to become better at leadership. We have covered some of the tools and mindsets that are relevant in shaping your leadership journey, but this is a vast topic and it may take a lifetime to truly become a leader worthy of the people you serve. As a founder, you should embrace the opportunity and embark on the journey to deliberately cultivate your leadership skills. This will go a long way in determining the eventual outcome as well as ensuring that the company enriches the lives of customers and employees alike.

One of the biggest deliverables of all leaders is to have a winning game plan, also known as strategy. It is the hardest thing that you will do as a leader but the one with the maximal bearing on the outcome. In the next chapter, we will dive into the art and science of crafting a strategy that will create a huge advantage for your company.

FROM PAGE TO ACTION

Nobody is born a leader. Leadership is an extraordinarily complex skill that takes practise, essential for a start-up founder, at least in the early years. One of the most important parts of growing as a leader is the ability to introspect and understand yourself.

a. **Contemplate Who You Are:** Questions to ask yourself on your leadership journey

    i. Why do you want to be a leader?

    ii. What kind of leader do you see yourself being? (content-oriented, people-first, hard-charging, hands-on, etc)

    iii. What are the values you will not compromise on as a leader?

    iv. How much of delegation are you comfortable with as a leader?

    v. How do you think you will handle moments of crisis? How will you take advantage of momentum?

10

Strategy: Where to Play, How to Win

I am not afraid of an army of lions led by a sheep; I am afraid of an army of sheep led by a lion.

—Alexander the Great

. . . strategy isn't always a rational enterprise.

—John Lewis Gaddis, author of
On Grand Strategy

Most Strategy Comes from War History

Strategy, as we understand it in modern business, has deep roots in military history. The word 'strategy' itself is derived from the Greek word 'strategos', which means 'army leader'. Until the end of World War I, the sole focus of strategy was teaching military officers the nuances of combat, defined as the 'art of the general' or 'art of war'. Wars are unpredictable.

Even when one army seems to overwhelmingly outweigh the other, victory is never guaranteed. This uncertainty underscores the importance of strategy. A skilled strategist can influence the outcome by carefully planning and positioning their resources well before the first sword is drawn or the first shot fired.[1]

In the business world, these military strategies have been repurposed. Modern business leaders, akin to the generals of the past, study historical military strategies to navigate and conquer market landscapes. The ancient principles of warfare translate into business strategies for competition and growth. Sun Tzu's *The Art of War*, for example, is considered essential reading for every business leader and strategist.

The language of business strategy is filled with military metaphors: 'moats' represent significant competitive advantages, 'guerilla tactics' are unconventional market approaches, 'Trojan horse' signifies deceptive tactics, and 'chain of command' is clear hierarchy—all terms that have transitioned from military to business contexts.

Strategy, as a field of study, took a significant turn after World War II, with the onset of the nuclear age. The focus shifted from winning battles to preventing them, and consequently, the essence of strategy began to evolve. It became less about direct combat and more about broader planning and foresight. Strategy soon emerged as a distinct academic discipline, expanding beyond military applications to include business, politics and social sciences. It's now a key part of curricula in universities and business schools worldwide, signifying a move towards strategic thinking that encompasses long-term vision, resource management and ethical considerations in decision-making. Its core principles, shaped by millennia of military history, continue to influence modern strategic planning and execution in the business sector.

In his book *On Grand Strategy*, John Gaddis draws lessons from a historical encounter between King Xerxes of Persia and his adviser Artabanus. As they led an enormous army to face the Greeks, Artabanus pointed out the potential problems they might encounter, from hostile territories and the immense task of supplying their army with food, to the risk of their forces being worn out before the battle. Xerxes, however, was determined to achieve his goal and chose to overlook these concerns, focusing on his grand vision of victory. Gaddis uses this anecdote to illustrate the contrast in strategic thinking. Xerxes embodies a leader who is focused on the ultimate goal, willing to face any challenge that arises. His strategic mindset prioritizes end goals, sometimes at the expense of the practical steps needed to get there. This can be effective but also risky, as it may ignore smaller, yet critical, details. On the other hand, Artabanus symbolizes the strategic approach of being attentive to the realities and complexities of a situation. He is cautious and considers various factors that could derail their plans, emphasizing a more measured, detail-oriented approach to strategy.

The tension between these two perspectives highlights a fundamental aspect of strategic planning: the balance between ambition and pragmatism. Understanding strategy requires recognizing the importance of both the ultimate objectives and the means to achieve them. Gaddis's recounting of Xerxes's march underscores this balance, teaching that a good strategist must be both a dreamer like Xerxes, envisioning the larger picture, and a realist like Artabanus, mindful of the practicalities. This balance is crucial for leaders in any field, whether in ancient warfare or modern business, to be able to successfully navigate their way to achieving their goals.[2]

Strategy is the ability to align the organization's grand aspirations—the vision and distant destination—with its current capabilities. Put differently, strategy is the ability to connect the dots between your current situation and the desired destination.

F. Scott Fitzgerald famously said that the measure of a first-rate intelligence is 'the ability to hold two opposite ideas in the mind at the same time, and still retain the ability to function'. The best strategists can hold a larger plan and vision in their minds, even as they pay close attention to the resources available and the dangers of the journey, improvising and adapting to the ups and downs on the way.[3]

Choosing What Game to Play

There's an old Wayne Gretzky quote that I love. 'I skate to where the puck is going to be, not to where it has been.' And we've always tried to do that at Apple.

—Steve Jobs

The leading strategy firm McKinsey often frames strategy as, 'Where to play, how to win.' Where to play is a crucial element for any strategic move. In an early stage of a business, all possibilities are open and a start-up can choose to build anything and compete with anyone. Figuring out what choices you can make so that you give yourself a disproportionate chance of winning is half the battle won before you even start.[4] Let's take the example of the early days of e-commerce. Among all the possible consumer categories, Flipkart chose to focus very heavily on smartphones. Smartphones as a category checked numerous boxes: the product size is small and hence easy to ship, the ticket size is higher which leads to better absolute margins, the demand for smartphones was growing rapidly and yet offline distribution wasn't built out. All this combined to create favourable conditions that Flipkart was able to leverage to create a dominant market share. If Flipkart had chosen grocery instead, a category in which the market size is massive but is riddled with numerous challenges, its growth would not have been anywhere close to what it achieved.

When thinking about business growth, entrepreneurs need to be aware that there are two kinds: linear growth and exponential growth. With linear growth, you will meet all the deadlines and meet customer expectations, but a quantum leap will only happen when you step out of the day-to-day running of the business to execute something exceptional. Focusing on business development and operating systems will feed into your linear, incremental growth, whereas planning the next innovative campaign and leadership development will lead to exponential growth. Linear growth requires consistent, high-quality execution, while exponential growth requires breakthrough thinking. Now the allure of steady execution is very addictive as you see your efforts translate into actions almost immediately, whereas thinking about radical moves often amounts to idle castle-building in thin air and doesn't feel that productive. As a result, most entrepreneurs are drawn to action which is certainly helpful in building a good execution engine but can become a handicap in terms of thinking of major strategic moves that can have an outlier impact. Entrepreneurs aspiring to become good at strategy need to first allocate time to step out of their day-to-day concerns to be able to think about the big picture and arrive at genuinely original insights.

ENTREPRENEURIAL WISDOM

On Generating Luck

Luck plays a big role in the success of your start-up. However, you can think of entrepreneurship as choosing to invest your time on activities that give you the maximum returns on that time. If you focus on your strengths and on doing the things that you are most skilled at, you increase your odds for getting lucky. Because no matter how lucky you are, there is no substitute for plain old hard work.

In his book *Good Strategy, Bad Strategy*, Richard Rumelt describes the three components at the heart of every strategy—diagnosis, guiding policy and coherent actions. Before you choose which game to play, it's important to first analyse the complex set of circumstances that your company faces in its efforts to come up with a diagnosis. Next, the guiding policy will define the approach to tackle the specific diagnosis. The final step is the outlining of coherent actions towards ensuring that the policy is effective. The word 'coherent' is significant here, as every action needs to be in service of the same policy—consistent and coordinated—and one cannot contradict another. When choosing a game plan for your company, keep in mind that a strategy is not a random set of actions but a set of coordinated actions designed to solve a specific challenge.[5]

A Game Plan to win

Jeff Bezos applies a strategy called 'regret minimization' whenever he is trying to make a decision. What this means is that he projects himself into the future and forces himself to think about what decisions he might theoretically regret not having taken. This ensures that he can take calculated risks. When faced with a dilemma in 1994 on whether to quit his very lucrative Wall Street job and try his hand at entrepreneurship, he thought about what he would regret more when he was an eighty-year-old—quitting his Wall Street job or never trying his hand at entrepreneurship, and the answer was obvious, launching him into a cross-country drive back to Seattle to start Amazon. The rest is history. I find this framework very helpful whenever I face a tough decision. I try to think about what I will regret less a few years down the line when I have the benefit of hindsight, and this often provides clarity that might otherwise get masked in day-to-day concerns.[6]

Strategy is often about making clear choices and saying no to many possibilities. Continuing to straddle many avenues simultaneously is often a bad strategy and leads to many mediocre outcomes rather than one outstanding outcome. Sometimes, a winning game plan is all about making a tough decision to move in a very specific direction, against all the odds. This means prioritizing and focusing your resources in this direction, even if it results in damage to other areas of business and opposition from other teams. Intel's decision, under Andy Grove, to shift the company's focus from manufacturing memory chips to producing microprocessors, faced immense resistance, and caused turmoil within the organization. Struggling in the face of stiff competition from Japanese manufacturers, Grove was forced to make this difficult choice, seeing it as their best chance at survival. It was a strategic decision, however, focusing all the company's resources and energy on an entirely new business, because by 1992, Intel was the world's largest semiconductor company. 'Burning the bridge,' which again comes from the military exploits of Alexander the Great, is a very pertinent piece of strategy advice. If you keep too many options open, you are not fully committed to any and will not be able to give your best possible shot at winning any of them. [7]

Building Moats

Moats once defended forts from adversarial attacks and the concept has found great traction among modern practitioners of strategy. Even after struggling to achieve product–market fit and feel like you've reached the top, you are always vulnerable to attack from new start-ups who would like nothing more than to disrupt your current business. Jeff Bezos famously said, 'Your profit is my opportunity,' and if you are making fat, predictable profits consistently, rest assured that sharks will start to circle from all corners. And that's where moats come in. These are competitive advantages that will defend your business in the long run.

Unlike forts, economic moats come in all colours, shapes and sizes. Let's look at Reliance's oil business. Reliance has exclusive rights to some of the most prominent oilfields in India and that moat cannot be taken away, ensuring that Reliance has a very powerful cash engine that they can keep using to build other businesses. For FMCG companies, brand equity and distribution can be the biggest moat. Think of a brand like Surf Excel or Lay's or Maggi. Consumers will not buy detergent or chips or noodles from another brand, even if it claims to offer identical products, because they have an emotional bond with these brands and, therefore, deep trust. Moreover, these brands have slowly built distribution that reaches nearly every remote corner of the country which is incredibly difficult to replicate for a new consumer brand start-up.

In the retail business, once you have built a sufficient density of offline footprints, it is difficult for a challenger brand to replicate that footprint. Not only will it require massive capex, but it will also require being a lot more efficient compared to the entrenched brand. At CULT, we now have a footprint spanning 600 centres which took seven years, massive investments and many acquisitions to create. We now think it is a very strong moat that will deter new players from trying to build a similar footprint in terms of a network of gyms. Since we can give access to all gyms in the network for the price of one gym membership, any single gym or small gym chain cannot match the value proposition that we can offer.

In the digital world, two types of moats are often used. One is a deep data tie-in that companies can build over a long period of time. Think of packaged software like SAP or Oracle financials. These are cumbersome software, requiring months of training, deep customization and many integrations to be truly effective. Now, on the surface, these sound-like handicaps, but once these players are in, companies are deeply invested, and everyday processes are completely dependent on them. The cost of switching vendors would be massively disruptive to the business and hence most will continue to renew their subscription by default. Companies like TCS have a similar moat. The IT services company often implements a complex software solution and then maintains and upgrades it for years. While the employees in the client company keep churning every few years, the services companies end up building a deep knowledge about the software, processes and workflows. As a result, companies have no choice but to continue to renew their annual maintenance contracts worth hundreds of millions of dollars.

Another very powerful moat is what's known as network effects. Network effects have two sides to their equation and one side creates a virtuous feedback cycle with the other. Let's take an example of a business like Uber. If Uber had only a hundred cars in Bengaluru—which they did at the time of their launch—the chances are that you would have to wait for up to an hour to get your ride. As they increase the density of cars and spread out across the city, chances are that there is going to be a vehicle close to you. They now have close to 20,000 vehicles in the city, thus ensuring that you can find a ride within a few minutes. As the numbers of cars increased so did the consumer demand and with the increase in demand, Uber could afford to deploy more vehicles, creating a virtuous loop until a point where it is prohibitively expensive for new entrants to break this cycle. The same dynamics are at play on social network platforms. Once everyone you know is on Facebook, Instagram or WhatsApp, you have no choice but to be on the same platform, eventually leading to an almost monopoly-like situation for many of these which is very hard to unsettle.

Strategy Is Not Your Goal or Project Plan

Many companies have an annual strategy and planning process as part of which senior leaders come together to hash out the strategy for the next year or the next few years. Most people come armed with ambitious goals—for example, saying that they will double the revenue in three years or gain market leadership in two years or go public in eighteen months. These are not the same as strategies—they are just the goals that the company would like to achieve. Strategy is about what moves you can make today and orchestrate in the future to increase the odds of your success. I have been in numerous strategy discussions over the last many years that revolve around what goals one can aspire for, what investments are required and what the intermediate milestones are. Most of these plans don't go anywhere as there is no depth of thinking and no clarity about how these goals will be achieved beyond the enthusiasm to get things done.

Sam Manekshaw was the head of the Indian Army when the India–Pakistan war broke out in 1971. Indira Gandhi wanted him to march on Bangladesh right away to assist Bangladesh in its independence movement, but Manekshaw chose to just do nothing and wait for six months. His rationale was that if they were to march in June, his army would be bogged down in the monsoon floods while the Himalayan passages would all be open for the Chinese army to possibly come to the defence of the Pakistani army. But in winter, the situation would reverse. Floods would have receded, and the Himalayan passes would be closed due to heavy snow. So, he did just that—he waited for six months and eventually led India to a famous victory in the winter. The goal might have been to win the war, but the strategy stemmed from reading the chessboard well and making choices (in this example, to do nothing) to dramatically increase the odds of success.[8]

Renowned strategy guru Michael Porter explains that strategy is about clear choices—choosing to pursue certain activities that are likely to benefit the intended outcome. For example, when Southwest decided to take on the more established airlines, they didn't simply decide to lower their prices to become a low-cost airline. They looked at ways in which they could dramatically reduce the cost. One of the biggest changes they made was to fly to much smaller airports that had significantly lower costs, allowing them to tap into a different set of customers. Porter says, 'The essence of strategy is choosing to perform activities differently than rivals do.' It is not about outdoing the competition, but out-thinking them and then committing to a path that is decidedly different from established industry practices.

ENTREPRENEURIAL WISDOM

On the Art of Planning

In business, as in life, things very rarely go to plan. Yet, planning is of utmost importance. The simple act of sitting down to think about the future and how you're going to face it is one that will teach you discipline, no matter the eventual outcome. Don't ever underestimate the art of planning.

A strategy move that remains iconic is Steve Jobs's decision to take on the music industry to help boost the usage of the iPod. By the early 2000s, the music industry was a behemoth that had perfected the business model of selling a bundle of songs, first in a cassette tape form and later in a CD. This allowed them to charge $10–20 for an album. Most users really liked just one or two songs, but they were forced to buy the whole CD. Jobs completely upended the business model, allowing a listener to buy just one song for $1. This made it easy and convenient for listeners to buy only the music that they loved. The same applies to how Netflix made a critical change in the film rental business by doing away with late fees and offering monthly subscriptions, unlike Blockbuster, which allowed you to rent DVDs for a fixed duration but levied hefty late fees—a big part of the bottom line for the company. CRED has spotted a similar opportunity in India, recognizing that if you are late in paying your credit card bills, credit card companies start charging exorbitant late fees as high as 2–3 per cent per month. CRED offers to pay your credit card bills on time and charge a more standard interest rate for the money they will be lending to you, leading to a massive growth in its user base.

The next time you are participating in a strategy discussion, ask your team to list the major activities that the business already performs today to grow the business. For example, at CULT, we open new gyms on our own or with franchisee partners, acquire users through local marketing and try to deliver outstanding experience. Next, ask your teams to list down which of these activities should be stopped, or dramatically altered (let's say, a focus only on franchisee partners and not own gyms) or new activities that can be started (let's say, building gyms in Tier 2 towns). If there are not going to be any new major activities, that means that you are only changing the goals, but the strategy will continue to be identical to what you are following today. It is apt to remember Einstein's admonishment here that, 'The definition of stupidity is to keep doing the same things again and again and expect a different result.' Far too many companies make this mistake of doing too many things. They are too vested in the current way of doing things and are not able to allocate enough runway and investment to new choices. So, despite the best intentions and lip service, their strategy doesn't change much.

The Big Picture: Full Context to Choose Your Strategic Moves

Strategy is difficult. Most people are never taught how to think strategically. They do other things well—operate with lofty goals, a lot of hustle and resourcefulness, and do their best to execute better than the competition to win—but this approach is neither reliable nor sustainable. Doing strategy well requires a different set of skills which most people have never had the opportunity to learn. The game of chess offers a useful analogy. No one in their right mind thinks that you can show up to the chessboard one day and start making moves that will stump your opponent. Even if you know the game well, every move requires a considerable amount of deliberation. What you are doing as you are lost in deep concentration is absorbing the current position of the entire board to develop a big picture context of how the game is set up. You take note of the relative strength of your pieces and those of your opponent and then you consider each move and play it out a few steps ahead— thinking about what will happen if you move one piece, how your opponent will react, how you will then respond to their move and so on. In other words, you are simulating a few moves ahead of the game to evaluate the likely outcome, and then you will select the move to put yourself in a stronger position in the future. This is the strategy that Deep Blue, the most powerful supercomputer in 1998, used to beat the then world champion Gary Kasparov. Deep Blue was able to evaluate moves tens of steps ahead, using its formidable computing power to select the best move which, in the end, proved too much for even the greatest player of all time.

Let's break this down. First and foremost, you need to be able to zoom out and see the big picture of your business. You can do this if you are well versed with the details of your business, the strengths and weaknesses as well as what's going well and where the struggles lie. You also need to have a comprehensive understanding of your market context. We discussed the critical importance of knowing your customers, as that's how you can generate deep insights, which is an important ingredient for good strategy. You need to know what's happening in the overall category—what the rate of growth is, which areas are seeing growth, what is the profitability for various segments and what's happening with other players in the space. You must pay attention to who is winning the market share, who is losing market share and why. In many companies, there is a tendency to dismiss the competition and massively underplay their strengths, but this creates a blind spot.

Knowing what your competition is doing well is a good source of information that you can factor in when you make choices. Lastly, being aware of what the technology trends are is very important as it can help you get ahead of other players, creating a significant competitive advantage. In my Myntra days, I realized by 2012, that mobile phones were where the bulk of traffic in India was going to be and hence we invested ahead of time to be a truly mobile-first company. We created a vastly superior mobile shopping experience to the extent that by 2015, 85 per cent of the revenue was coming from mobile phones. We even experimented with being a mobile-only platform (borrowing from Alexander's burning-the-bridge strategy). While it helped boost mobile market share significantly, it didn't work overall as we had ignored a critical consumer insight. The more affluent consumers had a desktop or laptop at home and preferred to use a large screen for their shopping. These users were not going to shift to mobile phones and hence Myntra was missing out on them. Eventually we had to bring back the desktop site. Sometimes it is good to acknowledge the bad move and completely reverse it.

With all the above context, you need to build long-term scenarios about what possible moves you can make. At any given point of time, many paths are available. Should you go for aggressive growth or bide your time to fix the underlying unit economics? Should you launch in new cities and countries or focus on consolidating your share in current markets? Should you build a parallel new business line or focus on building a sustainable differentiation in the current business line? Should you continue operating an unprofitable product or shut it down? You need to frame these choices and overlay them with what the world will look like one to three years from now. What choices are likely to give you better odds and make you a more formidable business? At CULT, we face the choice of whether to further consolidate our market share in the top six cities or go after smaller towns more aggressively. Our assessment continues to be that there is a huge depth in the top cities and by deep focus here, we can gun for 50 per cent market share in these cities.

It is important to frame the choices clearly and watch out for the tendency to rationalize and try to pursue all possible avenues. Ambitious entrepreneurs are most likely to fall into this trap as they back themselves to be able to do the impossible—stretching themselves across too many projects will give them the least possible shot at success. What helps in these situations is to have an environment that fosters a high quality of debate within the leadership team. This does not just happen suddenly—you need to prepare the ground for it by engaging the team in building a deeper context about the entire business. If people only know about what's happening in their business, they will just argue for more resources for their area as opposed to being able to engage in what's right for the greater good. Similarly, engaging your board and advisers for strategic dialogue can bring in external perspectives and help remove any blind spots that might be colouring your judgement. Good strategy discussions are likely to be contentious and hard choices are meant to be painful, but this is a sign that you are thinking through things deeply and making clear choices.

Changing the Rules of the Game

The film *Moneyball* tells the story of Billy Beane's revolutionary approach as the general manager of the Oakland As, and is a striking example of game-changing strategy in the world of sports. By employing predictive analytics, Beane challenged the traditional metrics of the game, most notably the long-standing reverence for batting averages. His pivotal insight was recognizing the superior importance of on-base percentage—a metric previously undervalued and overlooked in the professional realm. This paradigm shift in baseball analytics exemplifies how questioning and overturning conventional wisdom can lead to groundbreaking success. Time and again we see that when an outsider comes in, they can look at the situation from a completely different vantage point and change the rules of the game to create a significant new strategic advantage that other people didn't see coming. Zoho is a great example of a company choosing to change the rules of the game. While most companies lament about the cost of tech talent and rapidly rising costs, Zoho adopted a completely different approach in which they would hire people with unconventional backgrounds at a very nominal cost and then train them rigorously to get them to the same level of productivity as other candidates from reputed colleges. This has resulted in dramatic long-term cost advantages as well as deep loyalty and very low churn.

In the 1980s, the Swiss watch industry faced a challenge. Renowned for its premium craftsmanship, it was increasingly cornered into a high-end niche by Japanese manufacturers who dominated the broader market with their technologically advanced, cost-efficient quartz watches. Breaking away from the conventions of traditional, manual Swiss watchmaking, Swatch introduced a line of watches targeting the younger, style-conscious demographic. This strategic pivot was not just about product innovation; it was a radical overhaul of market perception. Swatch's watches were not just timekeeping devices; they became symbols of fashion and youth culture. This transformation was bolstered by an aggressive marketing campaign that resonated deeply with the public, elevating the brand to iconic status. This strategy was a stark departure from the industry norms, showcasing Swatch's willingness to discard the traditional playbook and lead the market through a keen understanding of its new target audience: youthful consumers seeking a blend of style and functionality.[10]

When you think of business as a game, one of the ways in which you can change the rules is by actually changing the players. This means that you can either acquire or eliminate your competition in order to change the players in your market. For example, after the 2008 financial crisis in the US, various acquisitions, such as that of US Air by American Airlines or that of Continental by United Airlines, transformed the industry by changing the key players in the game. As a result of this, when the demand for air travel rose again, the surviving airlines could reduce excess capacity while increasing profits. When Flipkart acquired Letsbuy.com in 2012 or when Myntra acquired Jabong in 2017, it changed the competitive landscape and game, giving Flipkart and Myntra decisive advantages in their respective categories.[11]

Good Strategy Is Simple, Bad Strategy Is Complex and Confusing

Occam's Razor is a principle that states that, if all things are equal, the most simple and direct solution with the fewest number of steps is probably the right solution. In the case of strategy, I believe this is true—the best ones are the simplest. A simple strategy can prevent miscommunication and encourage better buy-in within the company, as well as better resource allocation and faster decision-making. Tesla, in order to bring to life its vision 'to create the most compelling car company of the twenty-first century by driving the world's transition to electric vehicles', has followed a strategy of playing the long game. So, Tesla never focused on economies of scale, or creating cheaper cars for a mass market to increase volume. Conversely, their first car was actually a luxurious, high-end model that would never be a product with mass appeal. Part of Tesla's strategy was to lobby governments for subsidies, while another was to take control of the supply chain—all towards achieving its long-term vision.

Whenever you are involved in any kind of strategy discussion, it's important to use a mental filter to determine whether you are on the path towards crafting a good strategy or if you have a bad strategy masquerading as a reasonable one. The book *Good Strategy, Bad Strategy* is one of the clearest articulations of what differentiates a good strategy from a bad one. Author Richard Rumelt outlines the following as the key hallmarks of a bad strategy:

1. **Confusing Strategy with Ambitious Goal Setting**: Merely having a vision or a goal does not constitute a strategy. A strategy should involve a clear plan of how these goals will be achieved.

2. **Lack of Coherent Actions**: Strategies fail when they do not establish coherent actions. For instance, a guiding policy that lacks clear, actionable steps or contains contradictory actions can lead to ineffective strategy.

3. **Failure to Make Tough Choices**: Good strategy often requires prioritizing certain areas and focusing resources there. Trying to achieve everything at once or avoiding tough decisions can weaken a strategy.

4. **Lack of Competitive Advantage**: Strategies that do not offer leverage over competitors or fail to anticipate opportunities before rivals can act are often ineffective.

5. **Inability to Learn from Past Failures**: A bad strategy often comes from not learning from others' past failures or not viewing one's own situation from an external perspective.

A good strategy, on the other hand, is very simple to articulate. Everyone can understand the choices being made, the rationale behind them and the guiding policy that the whole organization can rally behind. If I have to summarize the strategy for CULT in three bullet points, it would be the following:

1. Keep expanding the density of gyms in each micro market
2. Standardize operations to elevate quality while reducing costs
3. Leverage density to acquire customers at almost no cost[12]

There is a test I implement in the company I work as well as with others that I might be involved in as an investor or board member. I ask my teams to articulate their strategy in three bullet points. If they launch into elaborate explanations about market dynamics, business plans and goals, product road maps and other aspects, interspersed with bold proclamations about how they will achieve a certain market share or valuation, I immediately understand that while the company may have big ambitions, they just don't have a clear strategy about how they are going to achieve them.

Another good question to ask is, what are the things that absolutely make sense, but you are choosing to ignore? Steve Jobs famously said, 'I'm as proud of many of the things we haven't done as the things we have done. Innovation is saying no to a thousand things.' If the people involved are not able to come up with many really good ideas that they have chosen to not pursue, you know that the strategy is on a soft wicket.

You can also ask the company to take the entire proposed investment (including all fixed costs) and allocate this in clear categories in descending order of investment. You then look at the top three or five categories and ask if these map with the strategic priorities of the company. Often, these don't match, which implies that the investment is driven more by the inertia of the past and, despite having some articulation for the strategy, the company is not willing to make tough choices.

Disrupting Yourself

Be a Columbus to whole new continents and worlds within you, opening new channels, not of trade, but of thoughts.

—Henry David Thoreau

Kodak has now become a massive cautionary tale in the study of business strategy. The company was the undisputed leader in the camera space. Life's most precious moments were known as 'Kodak moments', as unless you captured the moment on a Kodak camera, it wasn't complete. Given their dominance and massive profit pools, Kodak would also invest heavily in R&D. One such effort led to the invention of the world's first digital camera. Given the state of technology at the time, it was very primitive and a mere glimpse of what might someday be. Kodak's executives dismissed it, seeing nothing more than a cute prototype. But other companies kept at it and powered by Moore's Law, the capacities of digital cameras eventually far surpassed anything that was possible with analogue cameras. In the process, Kodak completely went out of business.

A similar example with a different outcome is Intel, which had the dominant market share in the memory card business. But more nimble Japanese companies were steadily taking away the market share, bolstered by huge government subsidies and low labour costs. Intel also had a very early microprocessor business, but it was a smaller part of the overall revenue pool. Andy Grove, who was the CEO at the time, discussed this with some of the other members of the leadership team and asked the question, 'If the board were to hire a new management team today, what would they do?' The answer was clear—that the new management team would get out of the memory business. That's what they did, literally burning one bridge to pave the way for becoming the world's most dominant microprocessor company for many decades, until they missed seeing the coming GPU revolution where Nvidia now dominates.

Business history is littered with both types of stories. On the one hand, there are companies that were so deeply entrenched in their leadership position in an industry that they wrote off new innovations as a mere novelty, while there are others who grabbed at technological shifts with both hands and completely changed their business models to reinvent themselves. IBM was very slow in accepting the computing revolution brought about by the personal computer, while Microsoft embraced the cloud computing revolution aggressively, positioning themselves as a formidable player in that space. A lot of technology companies today have learnt their lesson from business history and are willing to take major bets to completely reinvent themselves. Recently, when Zuckerberg decided to rename Facebook as Meta and bet billions of dollars on the Metaverse, it was a powerful example of reimagining what the future of the company could be. Many of the big tech companies today are betting heavily on AI and are not afraid to completely disrupt existing business lines.

While it is easy to pay lip service to the idea of disrupting yourself, it is not easy in practice, especially for start-ups in growth stages. Growth itself is so hard to achieve. You have gone past the product–market fit stage, figured out the right channels and established a growth machinery that is beginning to pay dividends. You also know the power of focus and can't afford to invest in every new technology trend. If you indeed try to take a big bet on something new, you will have to divert resources away from the existing business which may curtail growth or may even result in degrowth.

There are many factors a growing start-up should consider while figuring out how to navigate a possible disruption scenario. First and foremost, the defensibility of the current business model. If there are upstarts with totally different product lines or business models who are steadily encroaching upon your market share, you cannot afford to ignore the trend. Most media companies were very slow to acknowledge the disruption that digital media would bring to their business and, as a result, all the new-age media companies are the ones that started in recent years. Second, you should evaluate your financial ability to invest in something new which will be at par with new emerging players. We have seen many traditional Indian business houses trying to build e-commerce businesses, but their funding is way less than that of the purely digital players and, as a result, almost no one has built any meaningful online commerce business.

If you do choose to build a new disruptor business, you must move your best people out and give them sufficient independence and leeway to act like a start-up. Tencent did this brilliantly with WeChat. When they realized that they could potentially build an entirely new platform on top of social media, they carved out a team, moved them to a different building and gave them ample freedom to create a unique culture, move fast and break things—which would not have been possible within Tencent. I have seen this play out repeatedly at the companies I have worked at. Flipkart tried its hand at building payment solutions multiple times but failed repeatedly. It was only when some of the leaders moved out, started PhonePe as a new start-up, achieved strong PMF and then got reacquired, that Flipkart was finally able to have a formidable share of the payments space. Similarly, at CureFit, once we spun out eat. fit and sugar.fit as separate companies, both have thrived, which wouldn't have been possible within CureFit, which has hardcore fitness in its DNA.

Anticipating What Will Go Wrong; Building Ahead of Time

Andy Grove titled his highly insightful business book *Only the Paranoid Survive*. As the title suggests, he believed that being paranoid was a critical leadership skill that enabled leaders to anticipate what might go wrong and then plan for it in a proactive manner. He argues that most businesses will face 'strategic inflection points' at which everything about how they do business will change and their moats stop being moats. The literal ditch around the fort, for example, stopped being much of a defence the moment the long-range cannon was invented. Most businesses are facing perhaps the most transformational inflection point of all time with the advent of AI. As leaders think about their strategy, it is critical to anticipate what might be the new strategic inflection points and build a game plan around those before the change is in sight. The classic fable about the ant and the grasshopper reminds us that summer is the time to gather food, not winter.

You need to anticipate unpredictable events long before they happen. Basing your knowledge solely on past observations will land you in trouble. Think about what E.J. Smith, the captain of the Titanic, said: 'But in all my experience, I have never been in any accident . . . of any sort worth speaking about. I have seen but one vessel in distress in all my years at sea. I never saw a wreck and never have been wrecked nor was I ever in any predicament that threatened to end in disaster of any sort.' Well, we all know what ended up happening to the Titanic. I keep reminding teams that once there is a crisis on hand, the options are quite limited. While crises can be used to make massive changes for the future, current plans cannot be salvaged.

The best time to plan for and avert disaster is when there is peace, and everything is going smooth and steady. Jeff Bezos articulated the importance of planning ahead very eloquently when he said, 'Friends congratulate me after a quarterly-earnings announcement and say, "Good job, great quarter." And I'll say, "Thank you, but that quarter was baked three years ago." We don't focus on the optics of the next quarter; we focus on what is going to be good for customers.' Being the great business oracle of our times, Bezos also popularized the idea of 'It is always Day One', meaning that companies always need to operate with a beginner's mindset and retain the ability to hustle, innovate, and stay nimble and hungry. When an employee asked, 'Jeff, so what comes after Day One?' Jeff had a classic answer ready: 'Day Two is stasis. Followed by irrelevance. Followed by excruciating, painful decline. Followed by death. And that is why it is always Day One.'

The ability to anticipate potential issues and develop effective strategies in business often relies on the capacity to analyse trends, interpret data and project future scenarios. A compelling example of this approach is detailed in Michael Lewis's book *The Big Short: Inside the Doomsday Machine*. This book narrates the true story of Michael Burry, a hedge fund manager who, through meticulous analysis and strategic foresight, predicted the 2008 housing market crash and the subsequent banking crisis. He recognized early signs of the impending crisis, which many in the industry had overlooked due to short-term successes and a lack of willingness to consider long-term consequences. His strategic use of 'credit default swaps' to bet against the industry, which initially seemed counter-intuitive and risky, ultimately yielded significant returns. This move was a result of his deep understanding of the market and his confidence in his analysis.

One of the techniques that astute leaders who manage large projects deploy is called 'pre-mortem'. Unlike the post-mortem that is carried out when something has gone horribly wrong, a pre-mortem refers to the practice of sitting down with a team and articulating everything that could possibly go wrong with a project. You write down technology risks, budget risks, regulatory risks, personnel risks and so on. Then, for each risk, you articulate what is the correct preventive or countermeasure you can deploy so that the risk doesn't play out. By anticipating problems long before they have occurred, you will give yourself plenty of opportunity to problem-solve and insure yourself against risk.

Metrics to Guide Strategy

Every strategy requires a guiding policy—the ability to translate that strategy into practice through coherent action. For example, at CULT, while we want to have a very high density of gyms in every city, it is very important that we have a healthy return-on-capital for every gym that we open. We have defined a three-year capex payback as the guard rail, and hence every business plan for a new gym must prove that it can achieve this payback or else it will not get approved. As you translate strategic choices into guiding policies, it is important to also translate that into a set of metrics that you can track on a regular basis. Leaders often use what's known as 'input metrics'. An input metric is something that goes in at the beginning of the process and is a lead indicator of what the output will be. As an example, at CULT we can look at current revenue and analyse it, but if we were to look at the number of gyms in development, we can forecast future revenue. If we are not opening enough gyms today, we will certainly have revenue problems tomorrow. Similarly, by tracking the number of qualified leads and the rate of growth, you can project your future revenues.

Merely articulating a good strategy is not enough. You should be able to also articulate what the guiding policy and coherent actions are as well as the lead metrics that you can watch on a regular basis. Most leaders know their numbers by heart. Once you know what the critical input and output metrics are, it is a good idea to translate those into a report that is either automated or sent to the leadership team on a regular basis. As you develop this habit of looking at the numbers, you start to gain an intuitive sense of the larger story behind the numbers, and you will be able to spot things that are not in line or a potential predictor of a larger problem at a future date.

While metrics can be an excellent way of seeing strategy in action, companies and their leaders need to be wary of metrics becoming the sole focus and taking precedence *over* strategy. Wells Fargo experienced the nasty consequences of 'surrogation'—or the replacement of strategy with metrics. In 2016, the company's employees opened 3.5 million deposit and credit card accounts without customer consent, as part of its 'cross-selling' strategy. One of the bank's stated strategies was to *'best align our cross-sell metric with our strategic focus of long-term retail banking relationships'*. Unfortunately, employees lost sight of the larger strategy of building long-term relationships with customers in favour of the short-term metric of cross-selling. This turned out to be disastrous for the bank and it took years to recover from it.

Long-Term Strategic Map

Way back in the 1970s, Shell developed 'Shell Scenarios' as a way for senior leadership—in collaboration with experts from the fields of economics, international affairs, energy and others—to think about long-term challenges that the business could potentially face. The system involved envisioning different futures and analysing how the world could evolve under different sets of assumptions. This is not an expression of strategy, but a way to take a long-term outlook and imagine how the world might change, so that the company can adapt to different futures. For example, in one Scenario, Shell considered ideas of energy security and climate change, keeping in mind recent events like the Russian War on Ukraine. By doing this, Shell is preparing itself for different outcomes, for things that could go wrong while anticipating how it could reshape its own strategies for alternate business futures and possibilities.[13]

The ability to think about long-term priorities is going to be crucial to any organization's success. You need to be very clear about what your North Star is. Dorie Clark in her book *The Long Game* talks about the 'shiny object syndrome', where we often fall prey to the desire to chase the next big thing, only thinking about the short-term rewards. Jumping from one thing to another and not having a long-term goal in place will ultimately hamper your progress.[14]

Simon Sinek in his book *The Infinite Game* talks about how, during employee town hall meetings at GE, concerns were raised by employees who felt that the company was too focused on the short-term. When employees raise these questions, it's an obvious sign that they really want to know about the higher cause they are working towards. Jack Welch, the CEO of the company, was known for saying that 'Long-term is just a series of short terms' in response to these concerns. This approach can really affect the morale of the employees and the potential success of your company. This didn't play out well for GE, as while there were many short-term wins and Welch was lauded as the CEO of the century, the entire business started unravelling soon after he left as there was no foundation built for long-term growth.

While setting goals, adopting a long-term strategic approach is akin to preparing for a marathon. Just as marathon runners don't sprint at the start but pace themselves, understanding the terrain and conserving energy for the journey ahead, a successful entrepreneur doesn't chase immediate gains at the expense of future stability. You must map out a strategic plan that anticipates challenges, allocates resources wisely and sets a sustainable pace. This long-term thinking ensures that you're not just reacting to the market's immediate demands but are prepared for the evolving landscape of your industry. It is a good practice for companies to have at least a three-year strategy that should be refreshed every year as well as a five- to ten-year strategic map that chalks out the possible evolution of the business.

When Alan Mulally transitioned from Boeing Commercial to the CEO role at Ford Motor Company in 2006, he embarked on a path that would ultimately lead to a historic revival in the automotive sector.[15] Upon his arrival at Ford, Mulally demonstrated his commitment to authenticity, famously admitting to driving a Lexus, a Toyota make, for its superior quality. This admission was more than a personal preference; it reflected the need for honest self-assessment in corporate strategy.

Prior to Mulally's leadership, Ford had witnessed a significant decline, lost 25 per cent of its market share and was teetering on the brink of bankruptcy. Recognizing the need for a comprehensive turnaround strategy, Mulally delved into understanding Ford's overall condition, extending his analysis beyond mere financials. He identified a critical issue: consumer disenchantment with Ford's offerings. In a departure from the Detroit auto industry's traditional focus on market share, Mulally recognized that profitability and size don't always correlate. He understood that sustainable success for Ford would not come from merely expanding market share through short-term tactics like sales promotions and cost-cutting. Instead, he emphasized the importance of long-term strategic planning, stating, 'We're not going to chase market share.' This approach required a fundamental shift in Ford's operational strategy, particularly in terms of product development and market alignment.

One of Mulally's initial steps was a hands-on evaluation of Ford's product line, personally test-driving different models. Mulally implemented a policy where Ford's executives would regularly drive vehicles from other manufacturers, fostering a deeper understanding of the competitive landscape. Mulally's tenure at Ford underscores the critical importance of a long-term strategic map in business. His approach illustrates how a clear, honest assessment of a company's position, understanding of consumer needs, and a shift from short-term gains to long-term strategic alignment are essential for a company's revival and sustained success. His leadership journey at Ford serves as a prime example of how embracing change, challenging conventional metrics, and fostering a culture of continuous learning and adaptation can transform a company's trajectory.[16]

Strategy is one of the most critical aspects of running a business and, if done right, can be the most fun thing you get to do as a leader. It is a skill that needs to be cultivated with patience. Doing strategy well requires the ability to disconnect from day-to-day operations to be able to see the forest for the trees and make clear choices to double down on some paths while shutting down others. It is also the hardest thing to do. I have often seen that execution is very enticing. You get to hustle every day, can see some progress daily and feel like you are in the middle of the action, while at times strategy can feel like building castles in the air and, even if you have a good document, watching it play out is like watching paint dry. You might not see anything happen from one month to the next. But getting your strategy right and aligning the guiding policy and coherent action around it is going to be the highest return-on-investment activity that you can engage in. To get strategy right is to set yourself up for a win long before the finishing line.

FROM PAGE TO ACTION

Too often we confuse ambitious goals for strategy. Strategy is the alignment between your current capabilities and the grand vision of what you want to achieve in the future. Here are some ways to think about strategy in your company:

a. **Regret Minimization:** Think about a big decision you have been delaying making. Perhaps it is about what direction your start-up should take, or even whether you should start up or not. Now, envision yourself in your retirement, twenty or thirty years from now, and imagine which decision you might regret more.

b. Try and articulate your strategy in just three bullet points.

11

Funding Games

If you can make one heap of all your winnings
And risk it on one turn of pitch-and-toss,
And lose, and start again at your beginnings.
And never breathe a word about your loss . . .

—from *If* by Rudyard Kipling

For many people, entrepreneurship and fundraising are almost synonymous. The short fifteen-year history of the Indian entrepreneurial ecosystem is filled with eye-popping stories about the ever-increasing quantum of funds raised, followed by jaw-dropping valuations. For a while, it may have seemed that the ultimate success of a company was measured by how much money it could raise and at what valuation. Achieving a Unicorn status seems to be synonymous with having arrived as an entrepreneurial superstar, irrespective of how much money your company was losing. Well, the party never lasts forever. There has been recent news of investors writing down

Byju's valuation from $22 billion down to $1 billion, so clearly valuations can go both ways, unless there is a sound business model, profitability and defensibility in the business.

Whenever an early-stage entrepreneur reaches out to me, after exchanging pleasantries and some high-level questions, the main question they have in mind is how to raise money to get their venture off the ground. Once you manage to secure some kind of seed funding, you are on this treadmill for a long time, a journey that requires you to go out into the market trying to raise money from external or internal investors every twelve to eighteen months. Each time, you believe that profitability is just another eighteen months away, only to have to come back to the same point a year and a half down the line. There are notable exceptions to this, and some entrepreneurs are extremely cash efficient, but the truth is that fund raising is an inevitable part of the journey and good founders are very skilled at raising money when needed. Sometimes, money in the bank is the only difference between the companies that survive and those that don't make it.

Where Does Venture Money Come From?

The modern history of entrepreneurship is intricately interlinked with the rise of venture capital, which we covered briefly in an earlier chapter. The access to risk capital, wherein you are risking only the equity stake in a future venture, has unleashed incredible entrepreneurial potential and we have seen this play out in a big way in India in the last two decades. But where does venture capital come from? Around the world, there are many large pools of capital. Some of the prominent ones are large pension funds, university endowment funds, sovereign funds and large family offices. These funds may range from tens of billions to hundreds of billions of dollars. These funds are managed by professional fund managers whose job it is to generate sustainable returns over a very long period. While a large majority of these funds are deployed in conservative assets like US treasuries and debt funds, most will also allocate a small portion (10–15 per cent) for higher risk, higher return asset classes—of which venture capital ranks among the top options. Historically, good venture firms have been able to generate 20 per cent or more annual returns on a long-term basis which is very attractive to these funds.

When a VC raises a fund, let's say, $100 million, they start by pooling in some partner capital which may be 5–10 per cent of the fund size and then go out and pitch to various large fund managers in a bid to raise the capital. They may be able to convince ten to twenty fund managers to underwrite some portion of the fund each, totalling $100 million, and the budding venture capitalist is on her way to a life of glamour and glory—only if she can find the right entrepreneurs to back! A typical fund will have a life cycle of eight to twelve years, which means that this is the window in which the fund has to find the right entrepreneur, deploy the capital to work with the entrepreneur to build a meaningful business and then help find an exit so that capital can be returned to the limited partners (LPs).

A quick dive into the economics of the venture business might be useful at this point. The typical venture business model is commonly known as two and twenty per cent. What this means is that a fund will charge an annual fee of 2 per cent for the duration of the fund's life cycle and will keep 20 per cent of the profits generated, which is known as 'carry'. Let's see what this means in terms of the returns that a fund needs to generate. Even though a fund cycle is around ten years, this doesn't mean that all the money is called on up front. Funds will wait for the right opportunity and only then call for the capital, to reduce the overall holding time. Let's assume the typical holding period is eight years, which tends to be on the longer side in India.

The expectation with LPs is that the fund should return 20 per cent of the IRR (internal rate of return) and, given that 20 per cent of the profits will go to the fund manager, the total return generated needs to be 25 per cent (5 per cent for the managers, 20 per cent for the LPs). Now 25 per cent IRR over eight years for $100 million is about six times that amount. Add another $20 million of fees for the 2 per cent every year over ten years, so the VC will have to generate approximately $620 million for the original investment. This breaks down as follows:

$100 million: Original capital
$400 million: Profit to the LPs
$100 million: Profit to the VCs (20 per cent Carry)
$20 million: Fund Management Fees

A typical venture fund will have three to five General Partners (GPs) who make the final call on investments. Most of the carry is distributed among the GPs. There will be an extended team of investment professionals who help with scouting deals, doing the research and due diligence on the sector as well as the company and working with the company post-investment. Most VC firms are sector-agnostic and will go after a good opportunity, but some are sector- or geography-specific, believing that they have a unique insight or an advantage in that area. There is a lot of segmentation among funds, based on whether they are early- or late stage. Early-stage funds are okay to start with a company in its very early days. This stage comes with the highest possible risk and requires a lot of patience, but when it works, the rewards can be significant. It is not uncommon for investors to make even 100X of the original capital if they get the seed investment in just the right company. Much larger pools of capital are available in what's known as growth stage, where the business model is proven, the company is well past product–market fit and is on a sustained growth trajectory. These funds can deploy large amounts of capital and turbocharge the growth of a company. And then there are crossover or public funds that will invest only if there is a clear IPO window or after the company has gone public.

Another source of funding for early-stage companies are angel investors who are wealthy individuals, typically entrepreneurs who have had large exits, who understand the process of building companies as well as the risks involved.

You Need Chips to Play!

So, you have decided that you are going to start a business. It takes most people many months or even years to get to this point. Deciding to leave your well-paying job is not an easy choice. Suddenly that regular pay cheque disappears. You not only need money for your fledgling business but might have other financial commitments to plan for. It is probably a good idea to get your finances in order so that you have enough savings to pay for your personal expenses for two to three years, unless you have a working spouse or generous parents who can take care of you during this time. Most first-time founders don't have their own capital to invest, but if you are able to deploy some starting capital, that's always a strong signal of your commitment.

In my own journey with Myntra, nearly every investor that we talked to turned us down in the beginning. Some even suggested that we go back to our well-paying jobs instead of wasting time on an online venture! It was only after two years of effort that we were able to find professional funds to invest in the company.

Before you start the fundraising process, you need to work on your venture full-time. Often, people are still in their full-time jobs, just dabbling with an idea on the side, and they still approach VCs with the pitch that they will quit their job once they get funding. This doesn't always work as VCs may not take you seriously. It is much better to take your time, build conviction in an idea, find a strong co-founder, do your homework about the market and opportunity, and only then approach investors. You will only get a limited number of meetings with investors and the better prepared you are, the better the impression you will make.

Getting the Story Right

It is a business of a thousand soap operas.

—Sir Michael Moritz of Sequoia Capital,
on the business of venture capital

The process of fundraising starts with a good story. Good stories are captivating and memorable. But early-stage ventures can be very vague, and ideas are likely to evolve over time. You might be bubbling with ideas and filled with the ambition to build many extensions and adjacencies in the future, and, in your excitement, you might be tempted to talk about every single thing that the business could possibly be. Well, this will leave your audience thoroughly confused. The art of good storytelling is to say as few things as possible and be crystal clear about what you want to say. It's important to recognize the fact that you might have spent months thinking about the concept, but the person on the other end has almost no context and has only the next thirty minutes to process what you're saying—and only if the first few minutes are interesting enough. No pressure!

Good stories don't happen by accident. It takes work, many edits and revisions until you finally have a sharp, inspiring and engaging story to tell. The high-level story of CULT in the early days was as follows:

- Health awareness in India is rising rapidly as can be seen in people adopting things like avocados, quinoa, egg whites, atta Maggi and more.
- Health is complicated as you need to manage everything from fitness and food to mental health and sleep.
- We will build a complete health platform that will make the journey very easy.
- Our starting point is fitness as that is often the first thing people do and we don't have easy, high-quality fitness infrastructure in India.
- Health and fitness are set to keep growing for the next twenty years and, by being an early mover, we will benefit from long-term compounding.

This story can be articulated in less than a minute and anyone listening will get a clear idea of what we are intending to build and why. A good start-up story should have sharp clarity about the following:

- What is the market you are going to serve? Who is the customer?
- What pain point or need will you serve? What is your value proposition to customers?
- What unique capabilities or differentiators will you build?
- What is your starting point? What is the first thing you will win?
- What is the larger vision? If you are successful, what can be built eventually?

Another very important factor to keep in mind is whether you are telling a 'copy of x' story or a 'pioneer' story. Both stories can be compelling but have a different burden of proof. In the 'copy of x' version, your story is going to be that you are building something in India that has already been done elsewhere. For example, Flipkart was a copy of Amazon, Ola was a copy of Uber, Swiggy was a copy of Meituan and so on. Now there is absolutely nothing wrong with building a 'copy of x' story, but you need to be aware of a few things. Typically, these ideas will be crowded as once something starts succeeding in one part of the world, enterprising entrepreneurs everywhere start adopting that business model. But it is very easy to communicate this kind of story. Investors will understand it instantly and there is much lower perceived risk as the idea has already been proven successfully. At the same time, you still need to have a lot more clarity about why this will work in India specifically and what unique adaptations need to be made.

On the other hand, if you are not able to explain your idea as a 'copy of x', it means that you are on a totally new wicket and in a pioneer zone. The climb is much steeper for pioneers. To be able to tell this story well, you need to be very clear about what is going to be your unique advantage as a pioneer. Is there a new emerging technological breakthrough that you can leverage to create a first mover advantage? We saw that play out with ChatGPT in 2023 and early 2024. Or do you have a unique market or consumer insight? For example, if the government has created massive production-linked incentives (PLIs) for electric vehicles, can you take advantage of that? Or have you uncovered a new consumer insight? For example, more and more seniors are now living alone in India, giving rise to age-tech start-ups, while there is a rising and large affluent upper middle class that is looking for premium products and services, giving rise to products catering to them.

Designing a Compelling Pitch Deck

Never forget that underneath all the math and the MBA bullshit talk, we are all still emotionally driven human beings. We want to attach ourselves to narratives. We don't act because of equations. We follow our beliefs. We get behind leaders who stir our feelings. If you find someone diving too deep into the numbers, that means they are struggling to find a reason to deeply care about you.

—Chris Sacca, investor

In his book *Fall in Love with the Problem, Not the Solution*, Uri Levine, co-founder of Waze, reflects on what it takes to successfully raise funds for your company, and the key, he says, is telling an extraordinary story.[1] His theory is that investors say 'no' to investing in companies for only two reasons: they don't like the founder or they don't like the story. First impressions are usually formed in a matter of minutes, and investors don't have much time on their hands. That's why a pitch must begin with a compelling story, not filled with facts but one based on real, emotional engagement. The investor must experience the frustrations you experienced; they must want the solution as much as you do.

In 2007, Levine and his team had a third meeting with a big Israeli venture capital firm, Vertex Ventures. Their main contact at the fund, Ehud Levy, seemed enthusiastic, but Levine knew that the real decision-maker, the one he needed to convince, was Yoram Oron, the fund manager. Before the pitch, Levine got all the partners' home addresses so he could add them into the Waze demo. He knew that the first thing most people search for on a map is their home or office address, and he also knew that investors need to have a 'user's perspective' and believe that they could use the product. Sure enough, Oron's first question was, 'So, you're telling me that my house may be on the map?' And when Levine put in the address and located the fund manager's map, he could see Oron's lips turn up at the corners. This was a moment of connection, the 'wow' effect that Levine was going for. A week later, Waze received a term sheet from Vertex for $2 million.

ENTREPRENEURIAL WISDOM

On Setting Investor Expectations

Founders are often tempted to oversell to investors because of the pressures of the industry. As a result, they fall into a trap of chasing the wrong metrics. The best thing you can do as a start-up founder is to set the right expectations with your investors. If you believe that this is a fifteen- or twenty-year gameplay, be transparent so that your investors can enter the deal with a long-term mindset.

When Should You Raise Funds?

So, when is it the right time to raise funds? If you are starting with some initial capital of your own, you can create a twelve-to-eighteen-month runway to bootstrap your product. The AI company August.ai is an example of founders who have not raised any money but built a good initial product with traction. But if you have no initial capital to start with, you will have to raise money in the first six to nine months to be able to have a small team and build a compelling product. If you are a first-time entrepreneur, you have many avenues, ranging from angel investors and start-up incubators to accelerator programmes and seed fund VCs. There is really no dearth of capital in India, but you need to have a great story to get the right attention. If you can put together a compelling technology demo, it makes a huge difference in the initial pitch.

Once the company is up and running, you will feel the need to raise funds constantly. The general rule of thumb is that whatever money you anticipate your business will need, the chances are you will need two to three times more as there are a lot of uncertainties. It is also impossible to time the markets. When things are going well, as we saw in 2021, just about anyone can raise any amount of money. But when the markets tighten, as we saw in 2023, it becomes very difficult for even good companies to raise capital.

It is seldom the case that the money will be available whenever you need it. It is a good idea to plan to have a twenty-four-month runway at any given point so that you are not at the mercy of the vagaries of the financial markets. If the markets are good and easy money is available, you should raise it—provided it doesn't lead to excessive burn. More companies die of excess capital raise rather than paucity of capital as we discussed in the chapter on start-up failure. It's good to keep in mind that the fundraising process easily takes six to nine months, from the moment you start reaching out to people to finally getting the money in the bank. This is par for the course so you need to plan accordingly. Second-time entrepreneurs might be able to get their seed check immediately but after that, each round will also take the same amount of time. For a company in the hyper-growth stage, there will always be the need for more capital and hence the founders need to always have one eye on the fundraising process.

One way of planning this is to first think about your next big funding milestone, and how much time you'll take to get there. Then add six months more for your next fundraising round, and another six months of buffer—and that's how much funding you need, according to Uri Levine.[2] He also recommends that as founder or CEO, you should focus wholly on fundraising, and only shift into execution mode when the money has landed in your bank. At the same time, though, investors want to keep seeing progress. So, it's a good idea to keep your management team out of the fundraising process and fully involved in execution and day-to-day functioning.

One of the core rules of fundraising is that it is not done until it is done! What that means is that while you may have gotten a term sheet or signed the definitive documents and pretty much taken the round for granted, things can change right up until the last second before the money is in your account. I have seen many situations, right from my early days in Silicon Valley to the pandemic-induced panic, which had investors backing out at the very last minute, and there is nothing you can do about it. Just remember that the world is an uncertain place. Black swan events happen with alarming frequency, and you will do well to stay paranoid and expect the unexpected. The core team that's working on fundraising should remain completely focused and problem-solve actively, as a lot of time is often wasted when there are many parties involved and the round may drag on. If the closing drags on too long, the probability of closing keeps reducing.

Friends and Family . . . with Caution

One of the first ports of call for early-stage founders is the friends and family round, in which you reach out to people you have known for a long time to be your first set of investors. When Jeff Bezos left his job to start Amazon, he got most of his initial $300,000 seed capital from his parents and some friends. Soon thereafter, he reached out to many individuals and eventually secured about $1 million with $50,000 each from twenty wealthy individuals, and thus Amazon was born.

Now, raising money from family and friends can be tricky. The moment you reach out to people in your close circles and ask for investment, it is going to put them in a bind as they will feel a sense of obligation to help you. You should go out of your way to explain that at an early stage the risk of losing the money is very high and they should only put in an amount that they can afford to lose, if at all. Many people might have heard about the phenomenal returns that start-ups bring, and they start believing that they will also reap these returns, without factoring in the immense odds of failure.

When involving friends and family in your venture, clear communication is key. It's essential to set realistic expectations, telling them to treat their investment as high-risk, akin to a lottery ticket rather than a guaranteed return. Additionally, maintain the personal nature of your relationships outside of business. Family gatherings and social events should remain just that, rather than turning into impromptu business meetings or investor updates. By setting these boundaries and structures early on, you can maintain healthy relationships while professionally managing your angel investments.

Many founders are fortunate to have well-meaning friends and family members who want to help them out and it is great to be able to count on their support. But remember that the journey ahead is going to be very difficult, and you will need their emotional support as well, as you navigate the ups and downs of the journey. If they are also going to be worried about losing a significant amount of money, it can create a permanent fissure in the relationship or cause significant financial hardship for the people around you—leaving you with a sense of guilt. While it is a very good option to start out of the door, you should approach raising money from your close circles with caution as there is a lot more at stake in such situations than just the success of the venture.

All Angels Are Not Angelic

The term 'angel investors' is believed to have originated in the theatre industry when producers would reach out to wealthy patrons to secure financing for Broadway productions in return for a certain share of profits if the play did well financially. Over a period of time, the term has come to represent a wealthy individual who is willing to invest in an individual capacity at a very early stage and who is comfortable with the very high risk–reward equation that an early-stage venture entails. In the start-up world, most angel investors are entrepreneurs or venture capitalists who have been through this journey many times. As a result, they have a deeper understanding of trends, an ability to judge entrepreneurial calibre as well as some unique skill sets that they can bring to the table to help the entrepreneur navigate the early stages.

Angel investors come in all shades, and you should take your time to understand the ones you ultimately choose to work with. Many ex-founders choose to become angel investors as they want to be in touch with emerging trends and build relationships with dynamic young entrepreneurs who they can collaborate with. In other words, their motivations mostly stem from wanting to learn, get exposure to new ideas early and help the next generation of entrepreneurs who could benefit from their experience. These kinds of angels are great to work with as you are not likely to face much financial pressure from them. Snapdeal founders Kunal Bahl and Rohit Bansal have invested in more than 100 start-ups with some noticeable success. Similarly, people like Kunal Shah, Binny Bansal and Rajan Anandan are quite prolific in their investments and one of their key motivations is to pay it forward.

Sometimes angel investors will also ask for sweat equity which means additional equity for the time that they will invest in helping the company. This can be helpful sometimes, when the angel involved really does have the time and relevant expertise, but most often angels overestimate how much they can help a company. In most cases, they will not have the time, or even when they are willing to commit the time, they may not have the context of your specific product or business. In general, sweat equity for angel investors' time doesn't always work out very well and you should sign up for it only after thinking it through. If you do go ahead with sweat equity, structure this for a two-to-four-year vesting period and take a call every six months on whether it is really working or not. If you don't see tangible value, you should walk away after a year and explain your position to the angel involved. The sweat equity should not be treated as a discount but rather as equity earned against the time invested and the value generated for the company.

Angels also tend to demand non-standardized terms for the companies they invest in. One survey found that 78 per cent of venture capitalists avoided angel-backed companies because of overly high and unrealistic valuations. Navigating the realm of angel investing, especially when it involves friends and family, requires a careful balance. It's crucial not to let angel investors, valuable as they may be, influence your company's direction too much. While you may be eager to get some funding through any means in the early days, don't give in to very unrealistic terms that some angels may demand as these will come back to haunt you in later years. A general rule of thumb is to study what the standard terms are across many deals that have happened in the last few years and then ask for similar terms.

The Nuts and Bolts of the Fundraising Process

So, you are ready to reach out to investors for funding. The process varies significantly depending on whether you're at a very early stage of the venture or at later stages. Let's look at the key considerations relevant for both scenarios.

If you are looking to raise Series A funding, there is very little business traction for the investors to go by and hence they will focus on two things: the overall market opportunity and the calibre of the founding team. While the former can be objective, the latter is a decidedly subjective but important consideration. Investors have learnt not to take market risks. What this means is that if the market size is small and there is no reason to believe it will become massive, then it doesn't matter who the founders are. Let's take the example of Skyroot, a company building rockets to launch satellites into space. Most investors believe that the market size for satellites is going to be limited and so most funds have passed on Skyroot multiple times, despite the company having an outstanding team and making steady progress—including a successful launch.

So, before you pitch to investors, you need to be very clear about your market size or TAM (total addressable market). Sometimes it makes sense to further distil this down to SAM (serviceable addressable market) as many portions of the market may not be available due to things like being in a grey market, the unorganized nature of a market or small ticket sizes, among other things. You also need to look at compound annual growth rate (CAGR). A market growing at 40 per cent versus one growing at 10 per cent will have 12X more absolute growth in ten years (29X vs 2.5X). This was the case for the e-commerce market between 2011 and 2020. So, despite the market being very small in 2010, the expected growth rates made the opportunity very compelling. One filter I like to use is to ask, 'Is it a given that someone will build a large business here in the next ten years?' If I am convinced, then it is just a matter of finding the right team to execute the idea.

It is very difficult to evaluate early-stage founders, so investors look at proxy signals such as academic background and the roles that founders have played in previous organizations. I think it is helpful to learn the ropes by working at high-growth early-stage companies. Investors will notice if you have that experience. In addition, investors like founders who are committed to their venture full-time and who have done their homework by speaking to many customers, analysing who the other players in the market are, understanding the emerging players in international markets and gaining some unique market and customer insights. Investors find it very compelling if an entrepreneur has also built an initial prototype and can demo the technology or show some early traction. They also look at soft factors such as the conviction of the entrepreneur, a compelling story, the ability to attract good talent and so on. Most investors realize that ultimately, the early stage is a bet on people—as ideas may change but the people will remain the same.

When you are looking for anything between Series A to C (typically in years two to five), two things start to become very important. Is there compelling evidence of a strong product–market fit (PMF) and is there PMF with positive unit economics? Series A still may be doable on the back of a promising product (without PMF yet) but Series B and C are nearly impossible unless you can demonstrate credible PMF. Post-PMF, if the market size is large, companies typically enter a few years of hyper-growth (50–100 per cent YoY) and if you can hit such growth rates consistently, it will make for a very convincing pitch to investors. One of the most compelling pitches you can ever make is to show a slide depicting consistent high growth over the last six to eight quarters while steadily improving your unit economics. Investors will line up in droves behind such growth rates!

As you get to Series D or later, founder charisma and growth rates take a back seat and business fundamentals start to become a lot more important. At this stage, investors will look at what the competitive advantages are, whether there is a significant moat that makes the business defensible, whether you are executing better than your competition, and whether the underlying business metrics (such as CAC, unit economics, retention and others) are steadily improving to demonstrate economies of scale. Investors can deploy large capital at this stage and are happy with any growth rate above 25 per cent, but they want very high predictability, a clear path to profitability and a very long runway.

In the initial days, storytelling is going to be your most important asset, but as the business grows, it will start to shift from storytelling to business fundamentals. By the time you plan to go public, the financial statement and audit reports will do all the talking while storytelling will come down to painting the long-term vision and strategy of the company. Another key thing to keep in mind is that your fundraising process never happens in isolation. In bull markets, you are better off having a hyper-growth strategy. You should capitalize on this, even if you don't need the capital now. On the other hand, if it is a market winter, your pitch will be more compelling if you show superior unit economics, the resilience to survive difficult times and the grind to play it out in the long run. In the final analysis, there is always funding available for good companies if you are able to show in your story and in your numbers that you are among the best companies in your field. Valuations are very much a function of the larger funding environment and not a very important factor if you are on a trajectory to grow the value over the long run.

Understanding the Deal Terms and Process

Once you've got your pitch right, you will start to capture the attention of some funds, and after a few nerve-wracking pitches, you will finally get your first term sheet. As you get ready to celebrate, you glance at the term sheet and suddenly you realize that it seems to be in a foreign language. It is filled with terms such as pro-rate, ROFR, drag along, tag along, preference shares and what not and you are left scratching your head. Well, the VC world has figured out, over a period, what kinds of situations tend to arise as a company grows and how they can protect their interests in the company all the way to exit. The language of the term sheet and subsequently the shareholder agreement (SHA) and share-purchase agreement (SPA) is used to clearly specify all the terms so that the rights and interests of all parties are adequately negotiated and documented.

As a first-time entrepreneur, it will do you a world of good to take a week to just go through books such as *Venture Capital Deal Terms* by Harm F. de Vries, Menno J. van Loon and Sjoerd Mol, or a few of the numerous online tutorials and courses now available to apprise yourself of the lingo that's commonly used. This will help you make informed choices about where to negotiate and where to yield. At the end of the day, your job is to get the deal done—but it should be a deal that you can live with, so the process will require some tightrope walking. The more you prepare yourself, the better off you will be. Now there is an even faster route to learn—you can just sit with ChatGPT and ask questions, getting precedents and examples of all the deal terms and even getting feedback on how best to negotiate. You will get some reasonable answers. Who needs lawyers any more?

The deal terms take some time to get used to, but with a little effort, you will develop a sufficient depth of understanding. Let's take liquidation preferences as an example. In short, liquidation preferences simply refer to the order in which proceeds will get distributed when the company has an exit or is being liquidated. Companies have good and bad outcomes, and the VCs want to ensure that if there is any liquidity in the future, their capital will first be returned and only then will the remaining proceeds be distributed to other shareholders. The most standard form of liquidation preferences is what is known as 1X non-participative. What this means is that in a liquidation event, investors will get the amount they have invested first and the remainder will be distributed among other shareholders. In the case of 1X participative liquidation preferences, investors will first get their invested amount back and will also be able to participate in the distribution in proportion to their shareholding—in what is also known as 'double dipping'. Sometimes it gets crazy, and investors might even ask for something like 2X participative liquidation preferences. If you know what these terms mean and what the overall contours of the deal negotiations are, you can find a solution that works best for your specific situation.

It is at this point that lawyers enter the picture. Most VC firms have reputed (and well-paid!) law firms to represent them and, as a result, most entrepreneurs will also end up having to engage lawyers to represent them during negotiations. While lawyers are very helpful and necessary to get the documents in order, they also take pride in negotiating even the smallest points and notching wins for totally esoteric aspects, mostly for their professional pride—notwithstanding the time it takes. I have seen too many deals being indefinitely delayed as lawyers are not able to find common ground. You must remember that a VC firm will not go out of business if a deal falls through, but you might! As an entrepreneur, you must take control of the deal process to some extent and ultimately you need to take the important calls. Not long ago, I was going to lead a seed round for a small firm, and I thought it was going to be a straightforward deal. Unfortunately, the founders engaged a law firm that kept pushing back on what I thought were irrelevant points, and after many months of back and forth, I ended up walking away from the deal. I am not sure, in this case, if the founders even understood what was worth negotiating as against what was a purely superficial point that wouldn't have mattered in the long run.

One rule of thumb that I use in any negotiation is to ask, 'What are the standard terms in this situation?' There are so many deals that happen all the time and if most people are going in a certain direction for a deal term—say, liquidation preferences, that we discussed earlier—then that's probably the right way to go. You should look at various online resources, speak with other founders or employees of early-stage companies, and even ask the funds that you are working with to share their standard terms. If some terms, let's say, 1X participative, work for most companies, then it should work for your company as well. If someone is asking for differential terms, either in favour of the investors or the founders, you must really think about the rationale for the same. In some cases, you may not have any negotiation leverage as you only have the one term sheet and if you don't close the round, the company may go under. On the other hand, if you have plenty of interest, then you can negotiate harder for the terms that may be more favourable for the company in the long run.

One area that gets negotiated a lot is the valuation. Valuation boils down to how much the investors are willing to value the company at before investments. Let's say, the valuation is $100 million and they offer to add $25 million in funding. This will give the investors a 20 per cent shareholding, and the post-money valuation becomes $125 million. In very early stages, there is no way to arrive at an accurate valuation. In any market, there is a general baseline for typical seed and Series A deals and that's good enough. If you manage to get multiple term sheets, you can negotiate to improve the valuation. Most second-time founders tend to get much higher valuations as the risks are a lot lower and investors are willing to pay a premium to be able to participate. Sometimes, if the initial product or the technology breakthrough is very promising or the start-up is getting very strong customer traction, valuations can go up as well. As companies go from Series A to Series C, people will typically value the companies on revenue multiples basis other companies in a similar space. At a later stage, the profitability profile also starts to become very important as eventually the multiples are going to be a function of the profit potential or the long-term cash generation potential of the company.

Valuations also vary dramatically in bull markets and bear markets. In 2021, when we had the liquidity-fuelled bull market, valuations went through the roof. In India, Mensa went from raising their seed round to becoming a Unicorn in just six months! Cred increased its valuation from $1 billion to over $7 billion in a span of twelve months. Times like these are heady, but never last. When the markets correct themselves, which they almost always do, valuations can come down by a factor of two or even three. Now there is nothing wrong with raising money at high valuations when things are going well, but it is a double-edged sword. With a lot of money in the bank, there is a very high temptation to start many new initiatives, leading to a significant increase in burn and wastage. When the music stops, suddenly you find yourself with unsustainable burn rates and then you must course correct in a big way. Smart entrepreneurs take advantage of the bull markets to raise a sizable capital at attractive valuations without increasing the burn. They are also well aware that the valuations are way ahead of the mark, and they will take the next two to three years to actually grow into them.

Valuation is not a vanity metric that an entrepreneur needs to optimize too much. As long as you are able to raise the capital that you need to build the business and maintain a twenty-four-month runway, anything reasonable is fine. Working with high-quality investors and building a sustainable business will eventually lead to healthy and sustainable valuation. Some companies like Peloton and Klarna, for example, have lost up to 80 per cent of their peak 2021 valuation, but they have good products and so they will eventually bounce back.

Exits and IPOs

In mid-2020, Zomato was on the brink of bankruptcy. With the pandemic sending markets into a frenzy and investors hunkering down, the company was left with barely a few months of runway. The mantra then was to preserve cash at all costs. Zomato founder Deepinder Goyal and the leadership team were knocking on every door and when they couldn't find any promising leads, out of desperation, they decided to go public in record time in a bid to raise money from public markets. This was a gamble that could have backfired, but what Zomato didn't know was that the US Fed was about to unleash the most aggressive monetary easing policy of all time, infusing trillions of dollars of liquidity to boost the economy. Most of this money ended up in public markets, leading to all-time record markets. A narrative also emerged that the pandemic had accelerated the adoption of digital platforms by up to five years and companies would see record growth for many years ahead. With this backdrop, Zomato not only had a phenomenal IPO, but were also able to beef up their balance sheet significantly and used the boost to dramatically outperform the competition in the coming years. The IPO also created the much needed liquidity for Zomato's shareholders and employees.

Flipkart, on the other hand, is yet to go public. The company is seventeen years old now and made history for online retailing in India. Flipkart's exit happened via acquisition by Walmart. Walmart bought out most of the shareholders in the initial transaction and the company has been doing buyback at a regular frequency since then to create liquidity for employees and shareholders. Flipkart has created by far the largest amount of liquidity in the Indian ecosystem and set a high benchmark for what good liquidity looks like.

According to Bain and Company's *India Venture Capital Report 2022*, 2021 was a record-breaking year for tech start-ups in India, with a staggering $14 billion made in exits.[3] Of this total amount, VC and private equity investors earned $5.3 billion from start-ups that went public, and $8.7 billion from over sixty deals across strategic sales or secondary transactions. This means that about 40 per cent of overall exit value came from IPOs. Three key deals in 2021 counted for most of this value—the acquisition of BillDesk by PayU, the Zomato IPO and Paytm's IPO. A relaxation in public listing norms is one of the reasons for the dramatic increase in momentum for IPOs in the country.

Entrepreneurs have to spend a considerable time thinking about exits. When you are raising money from institutional investors, you must remember that funds have to return money to their LPs within the lifetime of the fund and hence, one way or another, they need to be able to exit their investments. There are three possible exit scenarios, but in reality, only two are prominent, IPOs and acquisitions. The third, where the firm itself buys back the shares of shareholders, is seldom exercised by highly profitable firms. In the early years of venture capital, exits were almost evenly distributed between acquisitions and

IPOs, but since the late 1990s, a majority have gone in the direction of acquisitions.[4] For a long time, venture backed companies sought IPOs more than anything else, given that it was extremely difficult to raise more than about $100 million in capital—something we take for granted now. In addition, start-ups were not as much a part of public discourse and popular culture as they are now, so an IPO was a way for a company to develop its public brand.

Myntra was acquired in 2014, in the largest private acquisition in the digital space at the time. Acquisition by a well-capitalized or public firm can create immediate liquidity. At times, acquisitions are also equity-only transactions, but if the acquiring company is going to go public soon, it can create liquidity a lot faster. Acquisitions are a function of how the entire ecosystem is evolving, what kind of cash runway you have and what will give you a larger chance of success overall. When we were considering the acquisition offer from Flipkart, the biggest consideration was whether the combined business would be a lot stronger as a competitor to Amazon and, in retrospect, that's how it panned out. Flipkart and Amazon continue to dominate the e-commerce landscape till date.

Executing an IPO follows a fairly standard process. After creating a prospectus—a comprehensive legal document with all information and risks about the IPO—the underwriter on your company's exit deal will begin the marketing process, called a 'roadshow'. This means travelling the entire country and taking meeting after meeting to pitch the IPO to institutional investors to gauge interest in the offering at different price points to 'build the book', which is basically compiling the list of investors who are committing to buy the company shares. Based on the book, the underwriter will eventually price the IPO, which is never an easy process. If too high, there is a risk that the stock will trade at below this price on the open day in what is known as 'breaking issue price' leading to a negative self-fulfilling prophecy. When Facebook went public in 2012, at a price of $38 per share, it eventually fell to $14. Fortunately, it recovered soon enough, eventually trading at four times its original price. On the other hand, if the underwriter prices the stock too low and it trades much higher, investors might be happy, but the company might feel they suffered unnecessary dilution.

Venture Debt—When It Works and When It Doesn't

Before there was venture capital, the biggest source of financing for all businesses was standard debt from banks and other non-banking financial corporations (NBFCs). But the rise of venture capital enabled entrepreneurs to raise money without any collateral, in exchange for equity in the company. Unfortunately, equity financing is also very expensive as you end up sharing a lot of the upside with investors. In high-growth companies that raise a lot of venture capital, dilution tends to be very high, and founders are left with very little equity. Venture debt is a product that has evolved in the last few decades as a hybrid instrument. It is a lot like debt but with much higher interests and very little equity participation to help balance the risk–reward equation. In venture debt, a firm will loan you the amount, say, $5 million, that you are supposed to pay back with interest in three to four years. In a growth company with positive unit economics, this can work out well as the venture debt amount can be used to accelerate growth and, in the process, generate surplus. Accelerated growth can also help grow the valuation and the debt can be predictably repaid. However, if the firm is only losing money and more growth means losing even more money, then venture debt can be quite detrimental as it does come with very aggressive terms. In any debt situation, including venture debt, the primary concern of the provider is to recover capital in any situation. While venture debt can give a lot of flexibility and is often available where conventional debt might not be available, one does need to approach this with caution. Venture debt enables start-ups to extend their runway and financial growth without having to dilute ownership stakes. But one must be careful about raising venture debt too early. If you don't have a strong PMF, a predictable growth engine or the unit economics are not working, venture debt can end up becoming very onerous. There is nothing more painful than seeing debt collectors start seizing the assets of the company, if you start missing your EMIs. While venture debt opens new non-dilutive capital sources for a company that were not available otherwise, things can go wrong very quickly. In 2021, PharmEasy was on a roll with rapid growth fuelled by the pandemic.[5] A glut of money available meant that the company was able to raise several rounds of funding at rapidly escalating valuations in quick succession. They raised so much money that they decided to make an aggressive bid for Thyrocare, a leading publicly listed diagnostic firm, and they raised structured debt (similar to venture debt) to finance the acquisition. PharmEasy was confident of an IPO in a few quarters and was planning to pay off the debt from the IPO proceeds. But, soon after, the sentiment started to change as consumers flocked back to offline experiences and the IPO plans went on the back-burner. The debt terms were quite onerous and the company was unable to service it. In the end, the company was sold at less than 10 per cent of its last valuation, underscoring the perils of leverage if the underlying business model can't support it.

Mergers and Acquisitions

As a start-up journey unfolds, various merger and acquisition (M&A) situations start to become relevant from an early stage.

As you make progress with your initial product, you will develop a deeper understanding of the domain, develop new skill sets as well as unique capabilities that are going to be valuable even if you don't have a clear PMF in sight. If this is a promising area, many companies will be building solutions in the space—some of which may be very well-funded, while others might even be large, established companies. It is not uncommon for early-stage start-ups to start getting acquisition offers even during the first one or two years of their journey. These can be tricky to navigate as you have just started building your company and someone already wants to acquire you. I think it is a good idea to engage in any credible offer and weigh the situation from a neutral vantage point. Sometimes, the PMF journey might not be going well, but you might have assembled a good team, and someone may be more interested in the team, including the founders, than in the product. This is generally called 'acquihire', a situation in which you get some valuations and even some cash for the team, but the valuations are not meaningful. This still allows you to return the capital back to seed investors, have a psychological win and the chance to continue to build a better product in a well-funded environment.

Sometimes, you might have built a strong product, but the markets might have turned very weak, as it happened in 2023, and you are not able to raise money. In this situation, the progress you have made can be a great starting point for a larger company, and you can get a better valuation after factoring in the product IP and potential acceleration for the acquiring company. Again, it is much better to have a healthy acquisition rather than going down the path of shutting down the company. WiFiStudy was acquired by Unacademy in 2018, giving Unacademy a strong head start in the education content space while being a good win for the WiFiStudy team, who went on to build other businesses later. There are many companies that turn down attractive acquisition offers when they are at their peak only to discover, down the line, that all the offers have disappeared, leaving them struggling for survival. All first-time entrepreneurs should consider potential acquisition offers seriously and turn them down only when they have very high confidence as well as a long runway.

As your company starts to grow, you will continue to find opportunities to acquire other companies while also getting offers to be acquired yourself. In the growth stages, you should keep an open mind about any potential acquisition opportunities. It makes sense to be in touch with other good companies in your space that are building similar or complementary offerings. If you are making steady progress and can raise capital consistently, you can significantly bolster your product portfolio and, at times, also take out a competitor with well-timed acquisitions. One tip to keep in mind is to never assume that a start-up might not be available for acquisition. You just cannot know what's going on in a company until you speak to them—sometimes it will take multiple conversations to build trust to find out. Start-ups face all kinds of challenges. Sometimes founders are fatigued, sometimes the cash runway may be running low, some start-ups have good products but don't know how to make the growth engine work and so on. If the start-up founders see that they have a much better chance of scaling their product through acquisition, they will certainly engage in the conversation. A deal doesn't just fall into your lap. You need to actively nurture it and sometimes it can take years to materialize.

Most growth-stage acquisitions are structured as cash and equity combinations. A relevant valuation benchmark is the last valuation at which the company might have raised funds. If the company has grown significantly since then, they may argue for better valuations. Sometimes they are under severe distress and will be willing to take any face-saving deal that enables them to avoid going under. I believe that if you are acquiring a company at which the founders have spent three years or more, it is important to take care of the founders' and employees' interests first. For those who have worked very hard at a company, this is the only portfolio they have. Most likely, they also worked at much lower salaries than their market salaries would have been. It is common to offer the founders and employees some meaningful cash (say, up to 25 per cent of their equity value) and convert the rest to the acquiring company's equity. Investors are typically only given the convert option to get equity in the acquiring company as they can easily hold till the end of the fund life cycle. At CureFit, we made eight acquisitions during the pandemic period that allowed us to completely transform our business and build an entirely new business line in just two years.

You must also remember that acquiring a company can inject a very strong entrepreneurial energy into your own organization. When Zomato acquired Grofers, they also got someone like Albinder Dhindsa, who is an outstanding entrepreneur and has gone through the wringer in building one of the toughest categories in retail, withstanding many ups and downs. With the acquisition, Zomato was able to make fast inroads in the grocery category, rising to leadership position, with Dhindsa leading the charge, while using the resources of a much larger company judiciously.

Now, if you are on the receiving end of an acquisition offer, there are a few things that you must factor in—some emotional and some psychological. First, try to objectively gauge what the prospects of the company going forward are. Do you feel that you are gaining market share, have adequate runway and some strong moats emerging that will allow you to defend the business in the long run? There are way too many companies that see a lot of initial traction and even very healthy valuations, but they start to stagnate at a certain scale and eventually a lot of value gets eroded. Sometimes cashing in your chips while on a high is a good idea. There are many founders who sold their companies during the 2021 boom who would have otherwise struggled to survive. A successful exit does many things to your career. First, you can get meaningful cash that can free you up from all your financial obligations for a long time, maybe even for life! Second, you have now generated returns for your investors with a successful exit so you will have investor confidence for your next start-up. Third, you can take a few months off, or even longer, to recharge your batteries, with the freedom to pursue a new project or start another venture. Additionally, if you are passionate about the space, you can continue building the company within the larger enterprise with access to more resources and the ability to contribute at larger scale. When Myntra was acquired by Flipkart, I was very excited about working along with the Flipkart leadership team to think about a different level of scale. It ended up being an incredible learning opportunity for me.

On the other hand, if you feel that the company is your true calling in life and you see yourself building an incredible institution over a very long period, then the acquisition may not be the right thing for you. At various stages of their respective journeys, both Paytm and Zomato have received various solicitations, but the founders were committed to building long-term organizations. Both companies are now fifteen years old. Both are all set to continue to innovate and grow in the coming decades.

If you have the staying power, it may not make sense to immediately jump at the first offer that comes your way, but instead to wait for the right offer and the right company. When you sell out of desperation, you will get undervalued. Sometimes you may not have a choice. But if you build a good product and manage your runway well, you can engage with the potential acquirers over a long period of time and wait for the right offer as well as a strong cultural fit. Uri Levine, in his book, recalls the Waze exit story.[6] For months, there were rumours circulating about Apple offering a $400 million deal, and perhaps encouraged by this false news, Google came to Waze with an offer of the same amount. At the time, the Waze management team was disappointed with the offer—they believed that they had good traction and had raised a significant amount in their last round. Levine felt that they should focus on raising another $50–100 million to increase their valuation, so they said no to Google. Not long after this, Facebook approached Waze with a much better offer—$1 billion, to be exact. As negotiations went on, they suddenly said that they would want the entire Waze team to relocate to the US, which was not going to be possible, and the deal soon came to a standstill. Just then, Google came back to Waze with a deal for $1.15 billion, a deal that eventually went through. This is just one example of the complexities and drama that come along with an exit, and the importance of having patience during the process.

Post-acquisition, most entrepreneurs will leave within one or two years, and you should assume that to be the default scenario. The acquiring company has a different culture, different strategic priorities, with things changing every year, and it can be very difficult to get deeply integrated into the new company for the long run. Most entrepreneurs also like their autonomy which is not possible to exercise within a larger company, as the overall strategic priorities take precedence over any specific parts. If you really like the new role, get along well with the leadership team and see a strong long-term prospect in the acquiring company, you can certainly consider this, but assume that it is going to be a much less likely scenario.

M&As are part and parcel of a start-up life. The vibrant cauldron of a fast-growing start-up ecosystem is like a giant melting pot of ideas and teams that are continually being optimized to manoeuvre into a better state, overcoming obstacles and making the most of lucky breaks. Timely acquisitions can significantly bolster your odds and, similarly, a timely acquisition by a much bigger company could secure your win, setting the stage for a next innings, which can be a lot bigger and better.

FROM PAGE TO ACTION

Raising funds is often considered synonymous with entrepreneurship, and it is a big part of the journey. From getting your story right to understanding the vocabulary of the term sheet, an entrepreneur has no choice but to get familiar with the funding process.

a. **Tell Your Story:** Practise telling your story in just one minute. It should be compelling enough to make a VC part with their money, while covering important things like who your customer is, the problem you're solving, your value proposition, your unique capabilities, what your first win will be as well as your bigger vision.

b. Terms to familiarize yourself with:

   i. Series A, B, C, etc.
   ii. Compound Annual Growth Rate (CAGR)
   iii. Moats (what is the moat that gives you an advantage over your competition?)
   iv. Liquidation Preferences
   v. Valuation

12

Financials for Dummies

When we think about start-ups, we think about building products that can change the world. We imagine founders driven by an irresistible desire to solve a problem, discovering an opportunity whose time has come. While these stories of inspiration and that initial spark are true, the fact is that once you start up, the thing you spend most of your time on are the unromantic, practical matters of finance. And, unfortunately, most of us are not quite prepared to take on the mammoth tasks of managing finances. For most of us, finances boil down to our monthly pay cheques, managing expenses at home and making a few investments. Managing finances for a company is a lot more complicated, and in many cases, how well you do it could be the difference between life and death for a start-up. Most entrepreneurs don't get a formal introduction to start-up finance and end up making a lot of mistakes as things get more and more complicated. This final chapter of the book is a crash course on finance, by no means comprehensive, but covering those aspects that every entrepreneur should know.

Understanding these key concepts will help you build a robust foundation from day one.

Understanding and Managing Cash Burn

There was a time in 2013 when things were going well for Flipkart. The growth rate was skyrocketing, consumers loved the product and the brand, valuation was rising every six months and it seemed there was no stopping the juggernaut. The icing on the cake was the company receiving an offer for $200 million investment by a highly reputed VC firm, General Atlantic, at a whopping $1 billion valuation, which was unheard of at that time for an Indian start-up. The investment process typically involves due diligence during which the appointed auditor goes through the books of the company to understand its financial health. As the auditors analysed Flipkart's books, however, they felt that the health of the business in reality was very different from what they had assumed during the high-level pitch, and they backed out of the deal, leaving the company in crisis.

The truth was that the management team had been very transparent about the numbers as they understood them. The difference lay in how they understood the unit economics calculations as against the norms that the VC firm, General Atlantic, applied in calculating the same. Around the same time, the company also learnt that they had only a few months of cash left, whereas their internal reports showed that they had a year of runway. Again, the difference came from EBITDA (an accounting term for representing profits; it stands for earnings before interest, taxes, depreciation and amortization) burn versus cash flows. While the company indeed had the runway on paper, most of the cash was locked away in working capital, leaving very little to pay for other expenses. This led to major panic but, in due course, Naspers and Tiger Global came through with an even larger round of $360 million and the rest is history. Since then, Flipkart has also set very high standards in accounting practices and despite raising billions of dollars, investors continue to trust the numbers and processes.

ENTREPRENEURIAL WISDOM

On Cash Flows

Never forget that cash is the oxygen early-stage ventures need in order to breathe. Running out of cash is not an option if you want to play the long game, so be meticulous in your financial planning; always keeping an eye on your runway.

Most businesses eventually come to realize that cash flow is king. At a very high level, cash flow means the net change in your cash situation at the end of the month. There are many accounting terms that businesses use like EBIT, EBITDA and so on, and some of these terms may project a rosy profitability picture while your cash is still depleting. So, your paper profit or loss may be drastically different from changes in cash flows. In subscription businesses, in which the customer pays for long-term services upfront, cash flows are typically a lot better than what the EBITDA may imply. This is the case for CULT since our primary revenue comes from twelve-month subscriptions. It took us many years to wrap our heads around 'operating cash flow' (OCF) versus accrual EBITDA, which I will explain later.

Since most start-ups must watch their runway—because if you run out of runway you have to face the prospects of shutting down the company—the most important metric to pay attention to is free cash flow (FCF). FCF is calculated very simply as the net of the money outflow and money received. Let's say, you have made a sale and also raised an invoice to the customer, but the customer hasn't paid yet—while you will show revenue growth for the month, your cash flows will not change at all as so far no cash has actually changed hands. If you take the money that you have in the bank and divide it by the total cash burn for the month, you have a good estimate for the actual runway left in the bank. If you want to be safe, you can reduce all liabilities, like payables, and then divide that sum by the cash burn to have an even more realistic sense of runway. While you may not like the answer, you will know exactly what the situation is and you can do something to plan for mitigation and avoid major last-minute surprises.

Another area that causes major confusion for cash burn calculations and overall understanding of the financial health of the business is understanding how working capital works. Working capital can massively dent your cash flows without any major movement in the actual sales. Working capital is the total capital invested across your inventory, money that you owe to your vendors and the money that is owed to you by customers. Here is a very high-level primer on how to think about working capital.

If yours is a business that requires inventory to be procured, this will have a significant bearing on your working capital. Let's say, you are an e-commerce business, like Myntra was, and your business model is to purchase inventory from brands ahead of time and keep stock in your warehouse so that when the customer places an order, you can pick the item and immediately ship it out. If you purchased inventory worth one crore and immediately paid for it, you are down one crore in terms of your FCF, your inventory goes up by one crore, but no sale has yet happened.

So, now your working capital is Rs 1 crore, which means that you have converted Rs 1 crore of cash into Rs 1 crore of apparel inventory and hence the money is locked until you are able to make the sale. Now, let's say, you were able to negotiate a deal where you got thirty days' credit which means that you will have to pay thirty days after receiving the goods from the vendor. In this case, even though you received the goods, you haven't paid anything on day one, and hence your FCF hasn't changed, and your working capital is still zero, while your payables (i.e., the money you owe to the vendor) has gone up. In this case, the inventory effectively becomes the loan that the vendor has given you until you pay it back.

Now, let's say that after receiving the inventory, you were able to sell 25 per cent of it at double the procurement price before the thirty-day credit period was up. So you sold Rs 25 lakh worth of inventory at Rs 50 lakh. If this was done through online orders from various customers, you will receive the money from customers immediately, leaving you with an amount of positive Rs 50 lakh of FCF and you haven't paid anything to the vendor yet. This will amount to an excess working capital (also known as negative working capital or float) that you have generated from the business. All businesses where revenue from customers come first, while the payment to back-end vendors or fulfilment of service happens later, have negative working capital and it effectively becomes its own source of capital for the business. Now, assume that the above sale wasn't to the end consumer but rather to an institutional buyer who bought the goods for Rs 40 lakh (thanks to a bulk sale discount) but negotiated a sixty-day payment period (i.e., they will pay sixty days after they receive the goods). Now you have Rs 40 lakh worth of receivables (money that the customer owes you), but you don't have the money yet. You will be able to account for this sale and show it in your monthly revenue, but your FCF will not change until you get the money from the customer. While you are waiting for this money to come back, the thirty days are over and you must pay the vendor for the inventory and you are back to Rs 1 crore of working capital, as the inventory is now fully paid for.

So, working capital primarily boils down to the following three factors:

1. **Inventory:** What is the size of the inventory that you carry? The larger the inventory, the larger is the working capital and a lot of money gets locked in the inventory, some of which may never sell. Thus, good businesses try to work with very low inventory (lean, just-in-time, etc.) or even no inventory (marketplaces). The most common way of specifying inventory size is 'days-on-hand' (DOH). You take your full inventory and divide it by the daily rate of sales to arrive at how many days of inventory you have on hand. Good businesses will have less than thirty DOH, while inefficient businesses may have up to six months of inventory, leading to large working capitals.

2. **Payables:** This is the amount that you owe your vendors. If you can negotiate a large credit period, your payables (liabilities) will grow, but your working capital will keep going down as you are not actually paying for the goods until much later, by which time you would have recovered some amount. Similarly, if your customers pay you upfront (like they do at CULT gyms), the money received upfront improves your FCF, but your liability goes up (until you deliver the service) and the payables go up proportionately.

3. **Receivables:** Receivables are the amounts that other parties owe you—like in the example of having made the sale and delivered goods or services but without yet having the money from customers. The higher the receivables, the

worse the working capital is, as the money that you should have is with other people until you are able to collect it.

So, the working capital formula is:

Working Capital = Inventory + Receivables – Payables

Some businesses have too much money locked in working capital, leading to a cash crunch. Many in the apparel business face this when they build up inventory, but the sale doesn't happen as planned and they are left with many months of inventory on hand—not an ideal situation. Managing working capital proactively will ensure that you don't have valuable resources locked away in a form that you can't use it in. One should understand working capital dynamics in detail from day one and work towards making it as lean as possible right from the start.

Thinking about Unit Economics

Unit economics ultimately determines the long-term success of a business. No amount of funding can save a company with fundamentally flawed unit economics.

—Marc Andreessen, co-founder,
Andreessen Horowitz

It may seem surprising, but I learnt the importance of unit economics much later in my entrepreneurial journey than you would imagine. In 2011, Indian e-commerce hit an inflection point. The category was growing at breakneck speed and hence a lot of investment dollars were chasing the good companies in the field. The only metric that seemed to matter was the growth rate. If the company was growing at a double-digit rate every month or quarter and there was some money in the bank, everything was fine. If the runway was shorter, you looked for capital and if you closed the round at a higher valuation than the last round, all was well with the world—until it wasn't! In 2013, investment sentiments changed significantly and suddenly investors wanted to know more about unit economics. Suddenly, everyone had to learn what unit economics was. While we might have known it intuitively, it was still a shock to see how much money per unit these companies were losing. It also took a long while for people to compute unit economics accurately—for example, people weren't looking at returns while computing unit economics, which can erode the unit profits by as much as 20 per cent.

Let's look at the fundamentals of unit economics and how to manage this aspect of finance proactively. This is not to say that unit economics must be positive from day one. All nascent businesses are likely to lose money per unit initially, but knowing exactly how much money you are losing and in what areas will help you design your experiments and growth path accurately. We will also cover different business models as unit economics varies quite significantly from one to the other, as do the investments required to fulfil customer orders.

First, what is the spirit of unit economics? Unit economics refers to the fundamental profitability for each unit of product shipped. Every time a customer places an order with you, you will incur certain costs to fulfil that order. If you take all the direct costs and subtract them from the amount that the customer paid, that is going to be your unit profitability. You must factor in both the costs involved in acquiring the order and the costs involved in fulfilling it. Sometimes, the cost of acquisitions is quite high and cannot be recovered in the first order, but if the customer truly buys into the value proposition, they will keep coming back and you will make an incremental profit per order to eventually be profitable on a per customer basis. Thus, you can look at unit economics of a new customer differently than the unit economics of a repeat customer. At some point, the weighted average unit economics across both has to be positive for the business to be viable long-term.

You must keep in mind that if the unit economics is negative, that means you are losing money per unit of goods shipped and if you happen to be growing without robust unit economics, your burn will continue to increase. As I've said before, if you multiply a negative number with a large number, you will get a much larger negative number.

Let's look into how to compute unit economics for a products business, like e-commerce. If it is a buy–sell business, your revenue per unit is the price that the customer is paying you. Remember to use the price minus taxes, as tax is not revenue. Tax is just something that you collect on behalf of the government, and you have to deposit with the authorities each month. People use gross merchandise value (GMV) to denote the total money collected from customers while net revenue is your revenue after subtracting taxes and any returned orders. If you are a marketplace business, then the transaction happens between the seller of the product and the buyer, while you collect the platform commission, say, 30 per cent, which is typical for most e-commerce platforms.

So, you take the net revenue per unit and subtract all the costs involved in fulfilling the order. First is the cost of goods sold (COGS). This is the cost you would have incurred in acquiring the product, which is zero for marketplaces, but then the net revenue is also proportionately lower. This is typically known as gross margin (GM). Then you subtract all direct costs in fulfilling the order, such as warehouse, logistics, returns, packaging, payment gateway and other costs. This will help you arrive at the gross profit (GP). The very first order of business is to get your business to start selling with a positive GP. Someone told me a long time ago that a negative-GP business is like sticking a Rs 500 note on each packet that you ship! Once your GP is positive and growing, you have proven that your customers see enough value in your offering to pay a bit more than it costs you to fulfil the order. But you have not yet accounted for marketing costs. Now you take all your direct marketing costs (like performance marketing, promotions, referrals, activation on the ground, etc.) and divide that number by the net orders shipped in a month (after adjusting for returned orders). This will give you the marketing cost per order. GP minus marketing cost will give you contribution margin (CM). CM is one of the most important unit economics metrics. Positive CM implies a healthy business in which you can recover both the fulfilment and marketing costs. In many ways, a business doesn't achieve true product–market fit (PMF) until CM is consistently positive.

Getting to positive CM is of course only the first of the profitability milestones. Your CM needs to continue to grow so that it can eventually start paying for centralized brand marketing costs that you might not be taking into CM calculations. It will need to grow further to pay for all central fixed costs such as the tech team, general and administrative (G&A) costs, office rentals and various other costs. And you are not done yet! Some companies require capital expenditure, or capex, to operate, such as in the case of CULT fitness centres. At some point, you need to generate enough CM to also pay for depreciation, which is the portion of capex that's attributed to each month depending on the total depreciation period. In the case of CULT fitness centres, we believe that the gym life cycle is seven years, i.e., eighty-four months. If we have spent Rs 2 crore to build the gym and capitalized this expense over seven years, this implies that the capital will be eroded (or depreciated) to the tune of Rs 2 crore divided by eighty-four, or Rs 2.4 lakh per month. For us to be EBIT (earnings before interest and taxes) positive, we need to generate enough CM to also cover for the monthly depreciation that might be coming from earlier capital expenditures that have enabled this revenue in the first place.

Great businesses have very high GM and CM. As a business leader, you should actively watch the trajectory of CM growth, quarter over quarter. You should also be aware of what the industry benchmarks are and what level you need to get to in order to be able to achieve your long-term business plan. Let's say, you believe you can generate 15 per cent EBITDA in a stable state. What is the CM required to be able to get to 15 per cent EBITDA? Maybe you will need to be at 40 per cent CM and at present you are at 10 per cent CM. Now the walk from 10 per cent CM to 40 per cent CM is not going to be easy at all. It will require continuous business optimization and a lot of efficiencies to be able to make that journey and this might take many years. If you face strong competitive intensity or need to invest in building products for the future, it may get even harder. Unit economics optimization is one of the most important activities that you will drive as a leader of your business. The only way to be fully in control of your destiny is to get to a point where you are consistently delivering very healthy unit economics.

Uber, a leading player in the ride-sharing industry, is often cited as a prime example to illustrate the critical role that unit economics plays in business success. In its initial stages, Uber encountered substantial hurdles while attempting to revolutionize the conventional taxi service sector. The company initially faced significant financial losses, driven by rapid expansion and substantial incentives for drivers. The key turning point in Uber's journey was the realization by its leadership of the paramount importance of unit economics. Shifting their strategy, they concentrated not just on expanding their market presence but on ensuring that each individual ride was profitable. This strategic pivot resulted in the development of a more effective pricing strategy, enhanced incentive structures for drivers and advancements in route-optimization techniques. Dara Khosrowshahi, the CEO of Uber, has stressed the criticality of unit economics in the company's revival. He stated that, 'If I could go back in time, I would start focusing on unit economics earlier. That saves you from a lot of distractions.'[1]

One of the categories that struggled for a while with positive unit economics in India is food delivery. Many apps ended up burning cash to fulfil their deliveries at the best available price. While they make money through ad revenue, commissions from restaurants and delivery fees paid by users, their costs include paying delivery executives, offering discounts–something almost all the apps do—and other marketing spends. Let's look at the case of Zomato, which managed to turn things around to achieve positive unit economics before its IPO. In the financial year 2020, their average commission from restaurants per order was Rs 43.6 and the average delivery fee paid by customers per order was Rs 15.3. On the other hand, the average delivery fee per order that Zomato paid its delivery partners was Rs 52, while discounts offered to users averaged Rs 21.7. By the third quarter of 2021— as per the prospectus it filed with SEBI before its IPO—average restaurant commissions per order had risen to Rs 62.8 and delivery fees from customers rose to Rs 26.8, while payments to delivery executives had reduced to Rs 44.6 and discounts went down to Rs 14.8. Thus, on average, per order, Zomato achieved a contribution margin of Rs 22.9, a huge improvement from its negative margin of Rs 30.5 per order. Zomato managed to achieve positive unit economics by cutting spending on discounts and payouts to delivery executives, while increasing restaurant commissions. At the same time, gross order value on the platform increased and they onboarded new partners to increase customer orders as well. This is a good example of how unit economics works and how it can be turned around. Turning around the unit economics not only saved Zomato but the entire food delivery category. It required the rewiring of many different aspects of the business, many tough calls that the company had to take and the relentless focus on optimizing every rupee in the unit economics model.[2]

In the financial year 2022–23, Dunzo—the speedy hyperlocal delivery start-up—reported losses that were four times that of the previous year. When you look at their unit economics for that year, it is evident that something about their financials was just not working. They were spending Rs 9 for every single rupee they earned in that period. Their costs had gone up for various reasons, with increased spending on procurement, advertising, employee benefits and delivery executive fees and incentives. They also lost a significant amount on order cancellations, resulting in the extreme cash crunch they ended up facing in early 2023. This is an example of a player continuing to push growth despite having negative unit economics and, as a result, seeing the absolute burn continuing to rise to levels that became completely unsustainable. Now the company is going through significant restructuring to stay afloat. Dunzo had become a cult brand for those last-minute late-night needs and users still love the brand and its service. Let's hope the company can reinvent itself with a much better unit economics model and stage a comeback in the coming years.[3]

Capex for Long-Term Capability Building

Some businesses need hard assets that require upfront investments such as building stores for retail businesses, building warehouses for an e-commerce company, building factories for the electric vehicle business and so on. This concept can be extended to other types of long-term capability building such as technology platforms that require a lot of upfront investment but will achieve returns only in the long run.

Since capex means upfront expenditure, the accounting standards allow you to treat this differently. If this was treated as a normal expense, the current profit and loss (P&L) statement would show huge losses as the entire capex amount would be shown as a current expense. Instead, what you are allowed to do is to capitalize the amount spent, which means that instead of showing it as an expense, you show the expenditure as a capital asset. In other words, you have converted your cash asset into a retail store asset or factory asset, but they are treated as equivalent assets which is not an expense yet, but an asset in a different format. While cash is a liquid asset that can be used for any purpose, the new asset might be fixed and can only be used for the purpose it is built. Any capitalized asset will have a fixed utility cycle that typically ranges from five to ten years but can sometimes be longer as well. This is the capitalization period. You are supposed to expense off your capitalized amount gradually over this period. So, a tiny fraction of this amount becomes part of your expense statement each month. Over time, this will also coincide with the revenue that the asset might be generating and this paints a more accurate picture of the P&L.

Managing your finances requires that you think deeply about capex. First, you need to be sure that whatever business you start with the capex will generate enough positive CM over a five-year period to completely recover the capex costs. For example, if your capex is Rs 1 crore, to be able to recover the full amount in five years, you need to generate approximately Rs 20 lakh of CM each year which, over five years, amounts to about 15 per cent annual return on capital. The mental model here is that the return on capital should be significantly higher than the cost of borrowing capital. For start-ups, the cost of borrowing will be in the 12–13 per cent range, if you are not a profitable company. In fact, in retail, most people look at a capex return period of three to four years for the returns to be considered healthy and to account for the fact that each retail store may not work out.

As much as possible, you are better off with debt financing or even venture debt financing for the capex, instead of equity capital, which is always the most expensive in the long run. But if the planned capex carries a major risk, the business model is not proven and you are not sure about being able to generate sufficient returns to pay off the debt, then you are better off with equity as unpaid debt liability can cause major problems for the company.

Whether to capitalize technology expenses or not depends on the nature of tech spends. If you can easily show that the cost being incurred is building capability that will be used for many years in the future, you can capitalize this. This will make today's P&L look better, but also remember that it will continue to affect your future P&L for the entire duration of the capitalization.

Making the Business Model Work

To figure out how best to make your business model work for you, it might be good to first delve into some of the many options available to you as a start-up. A business model is simply a way to define how you're going to make money. In all businesses you are going to sell something, either to an individual customer or to an enterprise. The product or service you intend to provide will have a unit cost, that is, the cost incurred in making that product or delivering that service. You will incur costs in building your brand and acquiring the customer. You will also have other fixed costs in building the tech platform, and other central costs. For a business to be viable, the margin you have on each transaction should be more than the costs you are going to incur. As you think about your business model, you should think deeply about what your business model will look like at maturity and how long it will take for you to get there. No business is going to make money from day one, but understanding what the path might look like will help you make better decisions about your business model.

There are other nuances to keep in mind, like what the working capital requirements look like. In an enterprise sales type of business, customers may pay you two to three months after the billing cycle which will result in your working capital requirements to keep increasing over a period of time. If your business requires capex, you will have to understand what the capex payback period will look like. It is very difficult to make unit economics work on day one as many costs can only be amortized over many transactions, so until you hit the critical mass, you will continue to bleed cash. You will have to model what it will take to hit positive unit economics and how long it will take for you to get there.

All of the above are not easy to model. No one has a crystal ball to be able to plot out the next five or ten years accurately and most estimates are going to be irrelevant within the first six to twelve months in early-stage ventures. But you must start somewhere. A good place to start is to study the industry and other players in the space and understand what their business model looks like, drawing relevant inferences from that. Second, try to articulate all the assumptions clearly and build your business model based on these assumptions. You can have these assumptions validated by other experts in the field and do a sensitivity analysis on the impact if these assumptions were to vary.

Most early-stage investors follow a simple rule of thumb. Whatever money the entrepreneur thinks she might need, the investor just doubles that requirement in their minds, as that's how almost all previous journeys have panned out. You might have the best intentions, but you don't know what you don't know—the so-called unknown unknowns!

There are many different business model choices available. You can charge money per transaction or you can have a subscription business. You can sell one item at a time or you can sell in bulk. Selling to consumers is very different from selling to enterprises. Being a completely digital business has very different characteristics compared to being a physical business or a hybrid set-up. All these choices will present different challenges.

In the digital business, many consumer companies start out with what's known as a freemium model. If you've used Spotify, then you know what this means—you can use one version with some basic features for free, but to upgrade to a plan with more features and options, you will have to pay a subscription. Many social media platforms, including Facebook and Instagram, use an advertisement-based model, placing ads within the product so that the actual product is offered to users for free. This works when there are sufficient customers for advertisers to choose your space, as well as when users feel that the value being added by your product makes it worth using in spite of the presence of the ads. Intermediation models are right for you if your product acts as a sort of bridge between a vendor and a user—think about travel or hotel aggregators such as Expedia and Booking.com.

In his book *Fall in Love with the Problem, Not the Solution*, Uri Levine recalls being approached by a start-up founder. The young man said he had figured out his business model and plan by calculating his COGS and doubling that, to reach the amount he would aim to sell in the market. Levine said he had it backwards. The starting point should be how much a customer is willing to pay for your product—the constraint to every business model, in fact, is the willingness of a customer to pay a certain amount. If the amount a user pays for your offering allows you to be profitable, then you have a good idea on your hands, but if not, then you might need to rethink your idea altogether. A good formula to think about this is: LTV (lifetime value) minus COGS, divided by CAC (customer acquisition cost). The number you end up with should be significant enough—at least three or greater—for you to become profitable.[4]

At its heart, running a business is about creating value for your customer, which is why a central question is what you are getting paid for by your customer and how much are they paying. The rule of thumb in B2B business models is to get between 10 per cent and 25 per cent of the value you create. The question on the customer's mind is whether the price is reasonable given the value they are receiving—or whether the ratio between value and price seems fair. In the B2B space, the ways in which you create value for customers could be either by making them money, saving them money or reducing their time to market. Levine offers an example of a B2B software known as Fairly (now Oversee), which helps travel departments of companies to closely monitor travel expenses and save up to 10 per cent of their travel budget. For a big business, this could mean a significant amount of money saved, and this is the value that Fairly creates.

In fact, Levine's company, Waze, went through a struggle to figure out its business model. At first, the founders gauged that map-makers in the market were earning about $1 billion per year, also selling traffic information as demand grew. Waze, on the other hand, being a community-driven navigation platform, had a map-making cost of nearly zero. So, Levine decided that the data would be sold at 25 per cent of the current market. This is the business model he spoke of to his investors. But this sales cycle was too long for the company and just wasn't working. At the same time, they didn't want to start charging users, losing out to other free models like Google Maps. That's why Waze eventually chose an advertising business model. The company, by this time, had a significant number of users, and both the frequency of use of the app as well as the duration spent on it (for entire journeys through a city) made it the perfect platform for ads.[5]

Oftentimes, it becomes necessary to change your business model for your company to generate more revenue and drive growth. So many companies that we know and love today have undergone this transformation. For example, Tesla transformed itself from a car manufacturing company to a clean energy company, offering a range of products from solar panels to electric vehicle charging stations. Zomato transformed itself from a platform that was being used as a restaurant review and discovery platform to a food delivery platform.

You can think of the business model as the heart of your business. Getting this right is the most important thing you will do in building your business. Many businesses do not pay enough attention to this or get to it much later in the game, by which time they have already burnt too much capital and goodwill, and they may find it very difficult to salvage the situation from that point.

Good Start-Ups Refuse to Die

Most start-ups are born to die. Many of the publicly available stats indicate that up to 90 per cent of all start-ups will eventually fold. Most of those closures happen in the first two years. While there are many reasons why companies fail, it ultimately boils down to running out of runway. Most founders are optimistic by nature. After spending some time on the business and going through a few ups and downs, they feel that they can make the next iteration work, having learnt from their mistakes and gained deeper insights about their market and customers. But by the time realization dawns, the company might be completely out of money to continue. In 2013, there was a time when Myntra's runway came down to only a month and we were staring at certain death. We were desperate, trying every avenue for funding, and if it wasn't for a massive stroke of luck, Myntra might have been consigned to the dustbin of history.

In the last decade, I have received numerous panicky calls from one frenetic entrepreneur or the other who is running out of cash and has started looking for any possible bailout. For companies that have good products and decent customer validation, current investors are often willing to create bridge funding. I am an investor in the EdTech company NextLeap, which has built a highly differentiated product, although the market size seems to be small. Recently, the other investors in the company and I decided to extend bridge funding which would extend their runway by another twelve months and give NextLeap a fighting chance to improve their scale and find their Series A funding. But insiders are often not excited about extending bridge financing as it seems like throwing good money after bad. If things have not worked out so far, the chances of them working out with a small bridge amount is small and the investors will lose further amounts beyond their initial investment.

Many companies also seek acquihire or acquisition opportunities, but these conversations only have legs if the company has a talent base that stands out or a product that seems promising and is loved by early adopter customers.

There may be other well-funded companies in this space that might value the talent that you have or see potential in your company to accelerate their own road map by a few months. In 2014, at Myntra, we evaluated the acquisition of the company, Yebhi.com, quite seriously. Yebhi was once a competitor doing good quality work, but they eventually ran out of money and talked to all the players in the space. Myntra made an offer which was not very attractive but could have enabled us to acquire their assets. But the company kept waiting for better offers and eventually ran out of money. We ended up doing a similar acquisition for Jabong.com which was closed in record time.

The reality of running a start-up is that if you don't have sufficient runway, you are at the mercy of external factors and can't be in control of what happens to your company. You might have to cut down costs dramatically, fire a lot of people, cut down product lines and engage in all kinds of face-saving conversations. Entrepreneurship looks anything but glamorous when you go through this phase. Most companies have this near-death experience at some stage or another but very few survive. You are much better off avoiding this situation in the first place. The best way to do that is to try to keep an eighteen to twenty-four-month runway at any given point of time—never letting it drop below twelve months, no matter the situation. Having survived a few near-death experiences myself, I am now very paranoid about this and very actively try to maintain a twenty-four-month runway for all companies that I am involved in.

If you are a very early-stage company that has just raised seed funding, try to arrive at a monthly burn that will give you at least eighteen to twenty-four months. It takes at least that long to learn about the true market reality, build a decent product and iterate with real world customer feedback. If you raise $500,000 seed capital, keep your monthly burn below $25,000. In the

early days, the team must be very lean, most people should work
for much less than market salaries but with generous ESOPs
for the potential upside, and all energies should be focused
on solving just one problem. Building multiple products at an
early-stage company will reduce runway significantly and is
generally not a good idea. Once you have raised a few million
dollars in Series A or beyond, there is absolutely no excuse to
let the runway drop below twenty-four months. You take the
total money in the bank, divide it by twenty-four and make
that amount the cap on your expenses. As this runway drops to
eighteen months, start reducing costs and initiatives so that the
runway remains close to eighteen months, month after month.

Most start-ups that eventually make it can find a way of
surviving each crisis and emerging as a better and stronger
company. But what enables this is the runway which lets you
weather the storm and course correct while laying low. One
should watch the cash balance and cash runway like a hawk and
not take any liberties, or else you will face the real possibility
of being completely wiped out. One should also raise money
when it is available and not wait for the perfect valuation. Many
start-ups that received amazing offers in 2021 saw those offers
vanish by 2022, even if business was in better shape. Things like
venture debt can also extend your runway if you are also seeing
your unit economics improve with time.

In a 2014 essay, Paul Graham, co-founder of Y Combinator,
coined the term 'the fatal pinch'. According to Graham, this
happens at a specific stage of a company—when, despite having
a significant amount of money in the bank, it has only six months
left to survive because it is losing too much money every month
while revenue growth is too low (or nil). With six months of
runway left, founders often believe they can stay in business by
raising more funds—and this, Graham says, is 'the fatal pinch'.
The term refers to a self-reinforcing situation in which founders,

having raised money before, are overconfident about their ability to raise more, and thus become complacent about reaching profitability. Unfortunately, this complacency makes it less likely that they will be able to raise more money! Graham's advice— which is what Y Combinator tells founders—is to approach every round of funding as if it is the last, you'll ever get. Just as the fatal pinch is self-reinforcing, this is too, because it is when you don't need investment that people will want to invest in you.[6]

Understanding and Managing Financials

Building a start-up is about many things. You need to be able to build a good team. You need to build a good product. You need to be good at fundraising. And, you must know your numbers! The story of a start-up, and especially a growing business, can be truly understood in terms of its numbers. A good CEO must have a very strong grasp of numbers. Most of us don't get any formal education in accounting practices and standards, so we end up learning on the job over many years. Unfortunately, that sometimes translates into being reactive instead of being proactive about managing your finances.

A company's financials comprises three key statements: a profit and loss (P&L) statement, a cash flow statement (CF) and the balance sheet. The first two are very important in the day-to-day management of the business while the balance sheet is more relevant for a late-stage mature company. It's a good idea to get into the habit of looking at your P&L and CF statements regularly and at the balance sheet every six months or so. Many start-ups don't have proper financial statements in the early years and hence they miss out on developing a true picture of where their business is. It's important to have a competent finance person in your team right from the start so that you can get timely and accurate financial statements.

The P&L statement reflects all your revenues and costs, calculating the resulting profit or loss for the month. You're likely to be at a loss for the first few years, as you are in the process of building the product and figuring out your business model. A P&L statement starts with your top line or revenue. Many start-ups account for their revenue incorrectly until more rigorous audits help them understand what revenue really is—the adjustment is often a shock. If you are a product business, and you sell something for Rs 10,000, that's your gross merchandise value. But the customer is also paying sales tax, which is not part of your revenue but just something that you are collecting on behalf of the government which you'll pay as part of your monthly GST filing. So, you subtract GST from the amount that the customer paid you (say, 18 per cent), and your revenue is Rs 8200. But not so fast. If you are in an e-commerce business and have a 20 per cent return rate—while you may initially ship ten units, two units will come back to you, and therefore your net revenue will be a further 20 per cent short, leaving you at about Rs 6600. Now you are getting close to your actual revenue, but you need to ask one final question. Are you a first-party business (i.e., do you buy or manufacture the products that you sell) or a marketplace business (where other sellers have listed products on your platform)? If you are a marketplace business, you will have a platform commission (typically 30 per cent), so, in this case, your actual revenue will be 30 per cent of Rs 6600, or about Rs 2000. This is where a lot of early-stage e-commerce companies get into trouble. They say that their revenue is Rs 10,000, while in reality it is only Rs 2000, or about 20 per cent of what they claim!

If you are a subscription business, there is a different level of complexity to manage. Let's say, you are selling a twelve-month subscription for Rs 15,000. Now you acquire a customer who dutifully buys a twelve-month subscription, pays you

Rs 15,000, and you proudly proclaim this amount as your revenue. Well, in truth you have to remove the tax component first (assume it was 20 per cent) so your actual subscription amount is Rs 12,000 (I am using approximations here to keep the numbers simple; ideally you will use the base amount, say, Rs 12,000 and calculate tax on this, which will be Rs 2400 for the selling price to be Rs 14,400). Now, since the customer has paid you upfront for twelve months but is going to use the service one month at a time for the next year, you can only account for services that you have delivered in your revenue. So, in this case what has happened is that at the end of the first month, you have delivered services worth Rs 1000 and that's your revenue, while the remaining Rs 11,000 is the advance that the customer has paid you (which is great for cash flows) which is technically a liability that customers can demand back based on terms and conditions (T&Cs). When the pandemic hit, CULT had advances amounting to almost Rs 100 crore for all the unutilized subscription amounts that we had collected from customers, and this ended up being quite a nightmare for us. This is also known as accrual revenue—when you account for the revenue evenly throughout the subscription duration. While this is painful in the beginning, it catches up eventually as, by the time you hit your twelfth month, you will have one-twelfth of the contribution from month one, one-twelfth the contribution from month two and so on, so your accrual revenue will be Rs 12,000! If you are growing rapidly, accrual will continue to lag, but you will be building a nice float— something we discussed in the section on cash flow.

Costs are relatively easy to account for but can be logically organized into three components. Direct costs which go into fulfilling the order, sales and marketing costs that go into generating the sale, and platform and other central costs that are required to build and run the platform that is enabling the transactions. If you add all these costs and subtract them from your top line—that's your profit or loss amount. It is not likely to look pretty in the initial years.

There are two exceptions of expenses that need not be accounted as costs in your P&L statements. If you are buying inventory in anticipation of future sales, you are effectively converting your cash into, say, mobile phones or apparel that are worth the same amount. You still have the same quantum of assets but in a different form. This is not considered an expense until you sell the inventory. Let's assume you bought inventory worth Rs 1 crore and sold Rs 20 lakh worth in the same month. This means your actual COGS expenses is only Rs 20 lakh, but your total inventory has increased by Rs 80 lakh. This sounds great, but there is a catch. In most inventory businesses, inventory continues to grow, and all inventory never sells out. At some point you realize that some portion of the inventory is as good as junk and at that point, you will have to expense out the bad inventory. Let's say, you have Rs 2 crore worth of inventory that is one year old, and you realize that it isn't going to sell, so you have to write it off and account for it as expenses for that month. This will cause the P&L to look bad, but it is something that needs to be done. Most companies will arrive at the write-off policy in consultation with the auditors and in line with the established practices of that industry.

Why Should You Get Audited?

I don't think I have ever met anyone who likes the word 'audit'. It sounds very boring, reserved for dour accountants and serving to distract business people from the work that they would like to do. Nothing can be farther from the truth. As illustrated by the film *The Accountant*,[7] a rigorous analysis of the books of a company can paint a colourful story, full of twists, drama, overreach and even downright fraud. The healthy functioning of the entire capitalistic system depends on the veracity of the books, something that was recognized a long time ago, as all investment decisions are made based on the numbers in standardized format that the company reports. Now, unfortunately, there is a major conflict of interest involved for a company's management and even its board members, because the better the numbers are, the higher the reward for everyone inside the company, in terms of rapidly appreciating stock prices or ever higher valuations from private investors. This is where auditors come in, to act as an external third-party conscience keeper for the management team. Auditors are appointed by the board, report directly to the board, and conduct independent analyses of the books of the company to rigorously assess if the reported numbers reflect reality. Auditors have developed numerous tools and analytical methods to cross-check the reported numbers from multiple angles. For example, if there is a fictitious invoice, it will not lead to an actual cash transfer to the company.

Of course, there are situations in which the company and the auditor are in cahoots, with a mutual understanding to turn a blind eye to any signs of fudging the numbers, and to certify them. But these arrangements often end very badly, leading not only to the financial but also the reputational ruin of everyone involved. Enron is one of the most well-known cases, in which a mighty company came crashing down, erasing tens of billions of dollars of value from the market once it came to light that the company had been systematically fudging its books. In India, the same story played out for Satyam Infotech when it was found that the company's reported numbers were systematically doctored for several years with the full knowledge of the audit partner, which led to the winding down of the company with a fire sale and the loss of face for the auditor involved.

Byju's, India's largest EdTech company that has been mired in controversy, was recently in the news when Deloitte resigned mid-term as the company's auditor in June 2023. Deloitte said that it was unable to complete its audit process in accordance with accounting standards as it had not received the company's financial statements for the financial year 2022, despite reminders, nor had it received communication regarding the audit report modifications for the previous year. In 2021, Byju's had reported a huge jump in their losses—from Rs 231.69 crore to Rs 4588.75 crore. The company attempted to justify this dramatic increase by citing changes in its accounting standards, a statement that drew a great deal of criticism. Despite all its various existing problems—relating to a post-pandemic fall in users and a funding winter—the resignation of Deloitte came as a particularly hard blow to the company as it was seen as evidence of accounting irregularities, leading to a complete loss of face and credibility.[8]

The midterm resignation reflects a lack of transparency and points to issues with corporate governance, something we will delve into shortly. Having a robust and accurate financial reporting system is essential for a start-up, and audits lend the system credibility, especially when it comes to reassuring investors. Auditors resigning could signal problems relating to integrity or governance. External auditing companies might also step down due to a loss of confidence in management, ethical or other disagreements, and legal or regulatory concerns. Whatever the case, the resignation of an auditor is a huge red flag.

A start-up should engage with an audit firm from its early days. It is not only about the verification of numbers; auditors can also help create deeper numbers-backed insights about the health of the business. It is a good idea for the management team to sit down with the auditors and go over their findings to see how some of the assumptions and the choices in internal MIS (management information systems) reports might be significantly different from what the auditors recognize as revenue. This will help build a shared understanding and healthy practices from the early days that will come in handy as the company grows and matures. Most people start with smaller local firms initially as that is more cost effective, but as you start to raise Series B/C, the investors will insist that you hire one of the Big-Four accounting firms, as they have deep expertise across a variety of industries and among their partners—they have just about seen every possible scenario.

Another good practice for a slightly more mature firm is to have two sets of auditors: internal auditors as well as the board-appointed statutory auditors. The difference is that you can consider the internal auditor as part of your working team who will do the same audit as an external investor, only more frequently—typically every quarter. They share their observations about the weak points and then work with respective teams to strengthen processes so that there will not be any surprises in the formal audit reports. Internal auditors also help design controls which can be thought of as additional checks and balances that prevent unwanted practices in the first place—for example, recognizing revenue on receiving the purchase order instead of when the invoice is raised on delivery of goods, or extending loans to people in the management without formal board approval and other such situations. The management team should meet with the internal auditors once a quarter, go over the findings and make choices about the areas of improvements so that when the time comes for annual audits, things will go smoothly and you can have audit reports without any qualifications. A qualification is when auditors adjust the reported revenue or bottom line based on what they observe, and it can often dilute the numbers and even raise questions about the authenticity of the business practices. In business, reputation can be everything, and if there are obvious question marks around the numbers, investor confidence can be significantly dented, taking years to repair. In fact, some companies never recover.

High-quality audits and audit firms are integral to building a robust business and it is a good idea to take this function seriously. You should work closely with auditors to ensure that you have the best practices baked into the foundation of your company, controls are embedded in all your processes, and you develop a sterling reputation so that all audits and due diligence processes go smoothly. This will prevent any unwanted surprises and shocks in the future, and you can focus on the real job of building a great product and competing in the market to gain market share, building a company that can last for decades.

Corporate Governance Best Practices

The Indian start-up ecosystem has seen a great deal of turmoil in the last few years. The funding scene reached a fever pitch in 2021, triggering a lot of excess in both ambition and the bending of the truth to keep the show going. As growth fuelled by the pandemic came to a grinding halt, once high-flying companies had no significant growth to boast of anymore but still desperately needed to raise money to stay afloat. And so, they resorted to telling stories they thought would fly—notwithstanding the actual ground reality. In my last two years of travelling to the US and engaging in discussions with investors, the name Byju's never failed to come up. When a company goes from a $20 billion valuation to a $2 billion valuation in the span of one year, it creates a lot of pain for the investors who bought into the story. This can lead people to wonder if these problems are systematic and widespread throughout the start-up community. To make matters worse, similar stories come to light almost every month, leaving us wondering if there is in fact something structurally wrong with the entire ecosystem.

First, let me set the record straight as I see it. The Indian start-up ecosystem now has tens of thousands of companies, over a hundred unicorns, many that have gone public or are on track to do so soon. To the best of my knowledge, most of these start-ups are run by ethical founders who are deeply committed to building a good business and staying on the right side of the law. In any large set-up involving people, there are bound to be a few bad apples and, while it may be sensational to extrapolate these few to the whole ecosystem, I do believe that these problems are limited to only a few companies. I also think that these companies could have avoided such scenarios with better oversight, mentoring and governance. A fast-growing start-up is like nine-ball juggling where, if you are not properly trained, you are bound to drop a ball at the slightest distraction.

I also believe that while founders always have to take full accountability for things going wrong—and when the board chooses to remove founders who are potentially involved in fudging the numbers they are fully justified in doing so—it doesn't absolve the board from their responsibility. A board should be more proactive so that problems are structurally avoided or come to light at a much earlier stage. One of my investor friends believes that if the founder is hell-bent on cheating, then no oversight can help. While this may be true for outlier cases where there is a very deliberate and systematic intent to cheat, I feel that most founders who make such mistakes are people who get carried away in a moment of weakness or over-the-top eagerness to project a very compelling story. This could have been avoided with the right support, mentoring and high-quality controls in which the board members can and should play a very active role.

Start-ups can adopt some straightforward policies and best practices to make it nearly impossible for any deliberate fraud to take place. The first antidote to this is a culture of transparency. When everyone knows everything, it becomes nearly impossible to fudge a story. Some founders like to keep information very close to their chests, which is a telltale sign of things not being completely kosher. A start-up that I have worked closely with would share a very limited amount of information with its board and investors. Even when I insisted on getting some data to validate the thesis, I was told outright that they would not be able to share any more details. For me, this was a major red flag and I immediately stopped working with the company and wasn't even a little surprised when some irregularities on their part came to light a few years down the line. If you can ensure that your management team, other senior leaders as well as your board have access to all the information at a very granular level, you will build a very strong defence against any temptations to misrepresent the numbers.

When founders are building a company, they need to solicit the help of many people. In the process, many promises are made and then forgotten later, leading to heartburn and sometimes even legal challenges. It is a good idea to document everything, even over email, so that both parties have a common source of truth instead of recalling vague conversations in a self-serving manner. The film *The Social Network*[9] documents the bitter feud between Zuckerberg and the Winklevoss twins in which the contribution and contract for their early-stage collaboration wasn't documented and ultimately led to a multi-billion-dollar settlement. Sometimes founders make a promise but after a year or two realize that the other side hasn't contributed as much as was expected. It is okay to cut your losses at this point and walk out of future collaborations, but some founders decide not to pay for past work which is not right. Every collaboration you may engage in will not work out equally—some will pay off incredibly well and others will be write-offs, but one should honour the commitment to help build trust in the company.

The best way to prevent any serious issues with the books is to have a good internal audit process in which findings are regularly discussed with the management in an open and transparent manner. There should also be a high-quality statutory auditor who will prepare a comprehensive audit report for discussion with the board. Even if there are minor infringements, they will come to light much earlier and adequate course correction can be initiated before it becomes a widespread cultural issue.

If you can design a set of high-quality controls with your finance team and internal auditors, these will become proactive measures that will prevent anything untoward from happening in the first place. Organizations such as the Tata Group, which are the gold standard in governance, have very rigorous controls and a code of conduct that the entire leadership is deeply trained in and hence there are rarely, if ever, mismanagement issues coming to light.

Having strict accounting practices and other organizational policies also help with governance. If everyone knows what the rules of the game are, there is little chance of cheating. Whenever you do feel the temptation to bend the rules, transparency means that enough people are watching out to ensure that that doesn't happen.

Role of the CFO

The chief financial officer (CFO) is a very important role in any company; most early-stage start-ups don't leverage this role well. The CFO doesn't have to be someone very senior, with decades of finance experience. It can be someone with decent knowledge of accounting and financial practices and even five years of experience may be good for an early-stage company. It is more about the mindset, approach and the ability to work closely with the CEO and the leadership team. Prabhakar, whom I mentioned in the Introduction, had less than ten years of experience when he became the CFO at Myntra and he did an outstanding job of helping the company navigate numerous ups and downs.

If you have your systems in place, the company's everyday operations generate lots of data that leaves a financial footprint in terms of POs, invoices, cash flows and more. For most companies, all this data only resides in accounting systems or even in just an Excel sheet. But these numbers contain within them a very colourful story about what's going on with the business. The CFO should first translate these numbers into metrics that are relevant to the business and then ensure that the metrics are automatically sent to all teams regularly. Even when data is available, there is often inertia when it comes to logging into the right system to fetch the data. So, I have found that having this data come directly into the inbox manually or in an automated manner is most helpful. When people look at data daily over a long period of time, they start to build an intuitive understanding of what the trend lines are, spotting the deviations easily and gaining a deeper insight about where the business is headed.

The role of the CFO is primarily strategic. Yes, the CFO needs to define the accounting policies and put a good system and processes in place, but that's a one-time effort which can be refreshed once a year as the size of the business evolves. But on an ongoing basis, this should not take more than 20 per cent of the CFO's time. The main chunk of time needs to go into big-picture thinking and helping the CEO and the leadership team make smart decisions about where the business is headed. This can be broken down into multiple responsibilities.

First, what goals should the company aspire to achieve? For most companies, macro goal setting is done through the annual operating plan (AOP) during which the financial goals for the year are defined. This requires deep thinking about current capabilities, historical growth rates, a profound understanding of growth drivers, what investments can lead to what kind of growth, runway considerations as well as the competitive situation. After factoring in all these variables, the CFO should help the company arrive at the right answer. Depending on where the company currently is, 20 per cent growth is great, while in other situations, 100 per cent growth is better. Determining this is a choice that the CFO can make, putting the company on the best possible footing. Just going for maximum imaginable growth is not always the best strategy and can often backfire.

Just because goals have been set, doesn't mean a company will achieve them. A lot of things can go wrong and, as Murphy's Law implies, they will go wrong—often when you least expect it. The CFO and her team need to do two things well here. First, the CFO needs to anticipate and articulate what could go wrong, identifying potential risks and creating a mitigation strategy. This will require collaboration and problem-solving with other functions and holding them accountable for the implementation of proactive measures. Second, the finance team should work closely with the business teams to understand how the intended goals will be achieved and triangulate this with the current trajectory to provide proactive insights so that business teams can cover their blind spots and solve problems ahead of time.

Another big area that the CFO helps drive is investment choices. A company can work on a variety of projects and initiatives, and each will require some investments. But you don't have to work on all the initiatives that you can think of. There are cost–benefit trade-offs involved in each investment.

Some will be aligned to the current capabilities while others may be a leap of faith. For example, CULT deciding to expand into a new city is aligned with many existing capabilities, but to get into a new category, like smartwatches to track fitness, is going to be highly risky as that requires building all the capabilities from scratch and competing with many large players in the space.

Most start-ups will need to raise multiple rounds of funding until the company achieves profitability. To be able to raise the money from investors, the CFO needs to be able to tell a compelling, numbers-backed story about what the company can achieve over the next five years. All investors want to understand if they will make money on this investment or not, what the risks are and what is the probability that the company will deliver the returns it is promising. If the company has a credible story that is validated by market facts and the current growth trajectory, investors will consider the company seriously. On the other hand, if the company doesn't understand the underlying dynamics very well and doesn't have the answers to insightful questions about the business, it will dent investor confidence. The CFO plays as important a role in fundraising as the CEO does, by telling a good story and inspiring investor confidence. The same also applies to board interactions. In most companies, the CFO reports directly to the board so that they can present the hard facts of the business to the board as well as be held accountable for good governance and high-quality audit processes—which the board is eventually accountable for from a fiduciary duty point of view.

Finance doesn't need to be a dry and dour function. As the book *Factfulness* by Hans Rosling so colourfully demonstrates, numbers always tell a very interesting story. A good organization creates a system to understand this story and then steers it in a way that helps you build a great business. Businesses that can stand the test of time and build many other businesses are the ones that eventually generate a sufficient surplus which can then be reinvested in future growth. This creates a sufficient cushion so that you are not dependent on the vagaries of the market. All CEOs and leadership teams will do well to treat finance as an important function, investing time and effort to learn the basics so that the most ambitious and hyperbolic statements are also filtered through the lens of financial rationale and rigour. While you race towards conquering the world, you must always have one eye on the financial dashboard that keeps you grounded and helps you make rational choices day after day, to be able to march towards your destination without any major mishaps along the way.

FROM PAGE TO ACTION

Most entrepreneurs, unfortunately, don't get a crash course in finance before starting up. A sound understanding of financials, however, is essential to build a business that provides value to both the customer and the company.

a. **Plan Your Business Model:** Spend some time thinking about how your company is going to make money. Look at how similar organizations in the space have set up their businesses. Now identify the business model you want and write out a detailed plan describing the model and how it will work.

b. If you already have a running business, calculate your unit economics. How much does a unit of your product or service cost you and how much profit does it bring you?

Conclusion

My journey of entrepreneurship was the result of pure coincidence. Driven by a temporary disillusionment with academic studies at IIT Kanpur, I found myself spending most of my waking hours in the massive campus library where, as I've mentioned before, I happened to stumble upon a few books about entrepreneurs like Akio Morita and Sam Walton. These completely blew my mind and sowed the seed of entrepreneurial aspirations. Of course, my notions of starting up were quite romantic at the time—I had no inkling that it would take twelve years, from my first attempt at entrepreneurship at the age of twenty-three, to see my first meaningful success at the age of thirty-five! I guess you do need some romantic optimism and the benefit of the rose-tinted glasses of youth to embark on such an adventure, as no one will otherwise willingly sign up for twelve years of exile. And certainly not in your twenties, in a culture that makes us feel as if we've failed unless we have done something amazing and achieved all our dreams by our mid-twenties.

When I first entered the world of entrepreneurship by joining a very early-stage start-up as a software engineer during the height of the dot-com boom, I was giddy with excitement. Here were thousands of start-ups, all dreaming of changing the world in the matter of a few years and amassing unheard of riches along the way. It was impossible not to get carried away and start believing that yes, of course, we were at a pivotal point in history, and the world was going to change for the better, all driven by the geniuses of Silicon Valley. All of this came crashing down in 2000 with the biggest stock market crash since the Great Depression, wiping out thousands of billions of dollars of market value and exposing numerous companies as nothing more than PowerPoint slides and demo-ware. Way too many entrepreneurs turned out to be in the game more for the get-rich-and-famous-quick effects, rather than out of true passion for building something that would add value to the lives of customers.

By this time, though, I was hooked. I realized that it was a very complex game which I didn't understand at all, and that's when I determined that I would discover everything I could about it. And here I am twenty-five years later: I have worked for four start-ups in the Bay Area, built the largest fashion retailer and the largest fitness company in India, been involved in category leaders such as Groww and Skyroot as the first investor, been in the company of several outstanding entrepreneurs, and I'm still trying to figure out how it all works. I wish I could say that I have figured out all the answers, but I have not, as I don't think there ever is any one answer. Just as there are many possible paths to finding enlightenment, there are many ways to build companies—and none of them guarantee success. What I do know is that there are many patterns that are common across a variety of start-up efforts and many principles that most practitioners would readily agree with. In this book, I have tried to distil what I have observed and learnt from my own experiences to help explain how the game of start-ups works and what the commonly practised tools and principles are which you can adopt in your own journey.

A question that has always driven me is, 'How does this work?' I am not satisfied with only knowing the tools. I want to also understand the science and history behind anything that is touted to be applicable in a particular context. Just as I did in my two previous books, I have covered the history of entrepreneurship to articulate how the modern infrastructure of VCs, seed capital, growth capital, IPOs and more evolved, as well as all the facets that building a company involves in its ten–fifteen-year journey. This book has no quick answers for how to raise capital, how to achieve blitz scaling growth or how to build a perfect product. What it does cover is how you can think about these capabilities, how you can build a strong foundation and what you can learn from the examples and choices of many other companies who have walked this path before.

Very few people ever get to build a company from scratch. Even fewer get to see their company prosper to a point where it can live on for a long time, making an impact on the world. It is a grand adventure in which the odds are tilted powerfully against you. The act of building a company is also associated with impressions of grandeur, adventure, glamour and stories of unimaginable success as well as those of horrific deaths of companies that left their founders with shattered dreams and weakened self-esteem. All of these are extreme outlier portrayals of what's involved, ignoring how the effort of building a company actually shapes you. Entrepreneurship is part and parcel of human nature and we have been engaging in some form of enterprise since the days of the Pyramids and the Silk Route which spanned all of Eurasia a few millennia ago. I believe that entrepreneurship is as much about the journey of self-discovery as it is about building a lasting business which may or may not happen.

We should look at entrepreneurship as just another vocation that suits some people well. There is no need to put one vocation

on a pedestal above any others—it is okay for one person to
be a doctor, another to be a mechanic, one to be an artist and
another to be a volunteer in a remote part of the world. These
are all fulfilling professions and so is entrepreneurship. I believe
that there are so many more people who create massive impact
without ever starting a company and thus contribute in moving
the world forward. Sundar Pichai and Satya Nadella are leading
the charge of technology in the twenty-first century without ever
having started a company of their own, and yet their impact on
the world will be far greater than what most entrepreneurs could
ever dream of. But entrepreneurship is different from most other
professions because of its highly skewed risk–reward equation
that partly contributes to the mystery and allure associated
with it. In this book, I have attempted to break down what
entrepreneurship is, what it is not, what the rules of the game are
and how one can prepare to give oneself the best possible odds
of succeeding without ever fully being in control of the outcome.

While entrepreneurship is the journey at the heart of this
book, I believe that many of its lessons can be applied far beyond
the world of business. Starting a company, with all its highs and
lows, will probably teach you more about yourself and about
human nature than you could ever imagine. You will be forced to
wrestle with your inner demons and confront your deepest fears
and weaknesses. But you will also, hopefully, stumble upon the
thing that brings you true joy and purpose—and it might not
be what you expected. You will learn to observe facts and trends
in minute detail, while developing radically new perspectives to
forge your own narrative—and this will help when things are
looking very bleak. Entrepreneurship will teach you about how
people think and behave. You'll discover that people might say
they will do one thing but do the very opposite. You'll learn to
gauge a person's character by how they handle failure and how
they celebrate success.

Starting your own business will also teach you practical skills that will serve you well in everyday life. Whether it's negotiating a better deal when you buy a house (thanks to skills you picked up while discussing your first term sheet with an investor) or planning your family finances better (thanks to those reports your CFO sends you every fortnight), every lesson at work is a lesson for life.

I sincerely believe that the entrepreneurial journey is worth the effort irrespective of the outcome. Most people who can spend five or more years of their career pursuing a start-up idea that they genuinely believe in will have such an accelerated learning curve, both in terms of personal growth and new skill sets, that the learning itself will come in very handy in anything they do after the start-up journey is over. Come to think of it, even if your start-up works out very well, you will end up working for a large company anyway. Today the founder of Zomato, Deepinder Goyal, runs a large public company with all the responsibilities that an externally hired CEO would have. In fact, that's a good benchmark for a founder–CEO: to keep pace and be the best possible CEO who can do the job as well as or better than an external CEO. So, either way you will go back to working for a more stable organization, but the acquired skill set and personal growth that the start-up journey enables will result in a much more fulfilling and rewarding career.

But I don't want to make it sound like a bed of roses either. Start-ups are hard, very hard, and if one doesn't pursue entrepreneurship for the right reasons and with the right preparation, it can end up causing lasting damage. Most of the world's population works for a stable organization. A good company not only provides a stable monthly pay cheque that always comes on time, but also offers work that can be fulfilling, a social environment with a diverse set of colleagues, sufficient holidays to take a break and recharge and many learning opportunities. Most people don't recognize just how much a stable job contributes to attaining a certain quality of life. You don't have to worry about the next pay cheque, health insurance is taken care of, your evenings and weekends are free for personal and family time, and you often end up building a lasting personal connection with colleagues that you work closely with. But then some people want to be their own bosses or are driven by a strong urge to build something new— so much so that the relative safety of a job isn't meaningful anymore. And that's great. In fact, I have written this book for people who feel this calling, but you need to be aware of what you are walking away from and what the journey ahead will be like. While I believe that each entrepreneurial journey is rewarding in its own way, very few journeys are going to be financially rewarding and some factors will always be beyond your control.

We have covered all the facets of the entrepreneurial journey in this book. While this is not meant to be a definitive guidebook for any one aspect, such as product or strategy or fundraising, I have attempted to help offer a bird's-eye view of the entire journey, touching upon various concepts and tools that I have personally found useful or those that I have learnt from various practitioners and experts. Entrepreneurship is far from an exact science, and no one can claim to have found the ten principles that are guaranteed to work. If that was the case, 90 per cent of start-ups would not fail. But there are definitive patterns, ways of looking at things and choices that can eliminate some of the common pitfalls. Hopefully, these guides will ensure that every step makes the probability incrementally better, while also helping you truly enjoy the journey and benefit from it irrespective of how it plays out.

As we conclude the book, let's recap some of the core principles and concepts we have covered.

1. Starting up is a game with the dice loaded against you

It doesn't matter how you look at it, the stats are always going to be against you, even if you are a proven founder with strong success behind you. Travis Kalanick, Uber co-founder, has been building Cloud Kitchen for over five years now with no notable success so far. Marc Lore, who has had two mega-exits in the e-commerce space, started building an ambitious meal company, Wonder Group, and is still going through pivots and searching for a business model, despite having raised a crazy amount of seed capital. Taking a start-up from seed to scale requires numerous things to go well, from market timing to building a product that truly delivers major improvements over existing solutions, to navigating the interpersonal dynamics among the founders and team. It is always going to be a bumpy ride and you cannot predict how it will unfold. The journey is going to challenge you, probably at every turn, and therein lies the rub. If you greet each challenge with the spirit of 'Hello, Problem,' though, seeing it as an opportunity to apply your problem-solving chops, to dig deeper and find that resolve that you didn't know you had, all while maintaining equanimity in the eye of the storm, you will start to notice unmistakable signs of growth right out of the gate.

2. Product is marketing

While there are many ways to build a company, as well as numerous tools and principles to pick from, a start-up, at its core, has to be an outstanding product that you build. This is often an underrated and underappreciated aspect of company-building. Founders are in a hurry to fail-fast and get to product–market fit quickly while doing just enough to cobble together a product. That is never going to wow the early adopters and customers.

Even though early-stage start-ups have limited resources, they can still be highly focused and do a few things really well. If you have a sharp insight into what the core of the problem is and do that one thing 10X better with everything else being maintained as hygiene, you will get noticed for that feature and that becomes the talking point among early customers. We discussed the idea of 1000 true fans, which is well within the reach of almost any start-up, irrespective of the amount of funding available. It does require an obsessive focus on building outstanding products and a lot of patience and iterations. No one gets the product right in the first iteration, but you have to start somewhere and then keep chiselling away until something unique starts to emerge—and more importantly, the product gets noticed by customers. In my opinion, a deep and passionate obsession with building an amazing product is one of the most critical requirements for being an entrepreneur. The journey to craft something unique is deeply fulfilling in and of itself. This is why artists and inventors can toil away for years and even decades in the pursuit of the sublime, which may or may not result in any acknowledgement or worldly rewards. Product creators are no less artists in this sense and if you get it right, the rest of the journey will become a lot easier.

3. Why do something in the first place

If you are a well-qualified person, you will have no dearth of opportunities to build a career in an established organization. But if you are choosing to embark on a career in entrepreneurship, you will be making a massive trade-off for many years. It is very important to understand what's driving you to make this choice. Often, influenced by what we see around us, we get carried away and start to embrace other people's dreams as our own, which may have more to do with FOMO or even a bit of jealousy rather than what we believe is our true calling. Entrepreneurs need to know who they are and what they want in life. As Buddha said, 'Knowing oneself is the hardest thing to do.' It will not be easy to know who you are and what really matters to you, but you can make progress towards finding this through ongoing deep reflection, journaling, speaking with mentors and other contemplative practices. It also helps to look back at the trajectory of your life so far, the major choices that you made, what were the factors involved in making those choices, when you took a major risk, how you dealt with setbacks and failures in the past. The more you analyse how your life has unfolded so far, the more insights you will glean to create a picture of what drives you and what matters to you. Someone who has absolute clarity about who they are will be in a much better position to decide if this is the right path and, if it is, what kind of opportunities may be best suited to their strengths and temperament. Getting carried away with fads can backfire easily as what's a fad today may fizzle out tomorrow or market hype may give in to gloom and a long funding winter as we have seen during the 2021–24 cycle. When you choose this path with much longer-term clarity, then a few years of ups and downs will hardly matter. There is an old saying that if you can make your passion into your vocation, then you will never work for a single day in your life. Entrepreneurship is a definitive way to do that, provided you have enough clarity about what your passions are and the conviction to be able to follow through, despite the inevitable highs and lows.

4. Prepare yourself

I spent ten years in Silicon Valley, bouncing from one start-up to another before I had the know-how and confidence to finally start on my own. That was my decade-long preparation and even then, things didn't fall in place for another four years. I recently met an entrepreneur who is building an AI-powered robotic arm that can replace a lot of the manual work that requires the dexterity of a human hand in factories—for example, packaging in an e-commerce warehouse. While his start-up is eighteen months old, he has been working in the robotics space for over a decade and the depth of his knowledge about the space clearly shows through. To become a doctor, one studies for nearly ten years and even then, you start with a residency under more experienced doctors to develop enough field experience. Entrepreneurship is no different. No one quits their job and becomes a jedi-like entrepreneur in six months. So, if this is the path you wish to pursue, you need to have a game plan to prepare yourself.

Just as you prepare yourself for a trek in the mountains, you must prepare to ensure that by the time you start, you have all the skills as well as the mindset you need for the journey. If you do this, you will meet every challenge as an opportunity to dig deeper and solve problems that you wouldn't have been able to solve before. What does preparation for starting up look like? I think the best way to do this is to work at an early-stage company where you can go through the whole experience from the sidelines and volunteer to solve many problems that you will not get the opportunity to solve otherwise. You can also continue to hone your skill in your functional area so that you are good in that specific function. Curiosity is a dear friend to every entrepreneur, and you can indulge in it by speaking with a lot of your colleagues in other functions, actively collaborating with them so that you know a lot more about other aspects of building and running a company.

There are many outstanding books on entrepreneurship and the journey of various entrepreneurs you can read both for inspiration and useful tools that you may be able to use in your own work. Another key aspect of preparation is to just spend a lot of time on introspection, developing a deeper understanding of who you are, what matters to you, what your strengths and weaknesses are and the mindsets that you currently operate with. You can become a learning machine by continuously learning about new domains, technical skills, business skills and more so that all of these become second nature. By the time you start, then, not only will you have the ability to pick up anything new rapidly, but you'll have a whole set of skills to draw upon as you start the arduous process of building something from scratch.

5. Organization is product

A start-up is always about people. It starts and ends with people and often this aspect is underappreciated when it comes to company building. Put very simply, a start-up is a group of people who come together and sign up to do something very difficult, rising to the occasion to get this done. Nothing about it is easy. First, each individual needs to raise their bar to be able to meet the challenges of building a new company. Then, the group needs to be able to operate like a high-performing team in which mutual trust, collaboration, transparency and helping each other perform at an elevated level are as critical as individual performance. Eventually every organization adopts a certain belief system, a set of cultural practices and ways of doing things that are very unique. Unfortunately, however, this is often not a deliberate choice but rather an accidental by-product of factors such as who joined at an early stage, what various individuals believe or what best practices they bring to the table from their previous organizations. But this may not be the culture that the new organization needs. Ideally you want to engineer the culture very intelligently from an early stage. I believe that the first fifteen to twenty employees have a disproportionate say in how the culture ends up getting built. In good organizations, founders and early employees think deeply about what kind of organization they want to build, what choices will set the organization up for long-term success and then encode all this in the form of purpose, core values, policies and rituals. As Peter Drucker says, 'Culture eats strategy for breakfast'. If it plays such a crucial role, we cannot leave it to chance.

I believe one should approach organizational design the same way one approaches building a product. A product has a variety of features that someone thoughtfully designs and implements, after which the designer looks for signs of PMF. The features of the organization can be thought of in a similar vein. Instead of taking any way of working for granted, one can think from first principles and design the right feature for the organization that you want to build. Something as simple as whether you want reimbursements to be approved by a manager or not is a choice that will have a subtle impact on culture. By designing all the critical features of the culture very deliberately and discarding features that don't deliver the intended outcome, you will be playing the role of the architect, shaping the culture into what your vision requires and not ending up with a hotchpotch of miscellaneous ideas cobbled together.

6. In the end, the customer has the final word

Entrepreneurs tend to have very strong opinions about the products they are building, and rightly so. The only reason to start a company is that you see a unique angle to a problem that no one else can see and you are willing to bet your time, money and reputation to solve it. But you are ultimately going to be serving a customer who must like, or preferably love, your product. Unless you understand your customers very deeply, you will not be able to create something that genuinely makes the lives of the customers dramatically better. This is an area that is very easy to pay lip service to but very difficult to put into practice. Customers are not a single entity. There are many different individuals, age groups, socio-economic profiles, and most people are generally happy with the products and services they are currently using. If you want to create something new and be considered by customers, you need to truly get their attention by building something that is head and shoulders above what they use. When a Zepto delivers an order in ten minutes at a time when customers are used to two-hour deliveries, everyone stops and takes notice. While many in the industry wondered why anyone would need groceries in ten minutes and doubted that the model would work, customers knew better, and they embraced it so much that the face of grocery e-commerce in India had to change to accommodate this ultra-fast supply chain. It is an art and science to truly uncover deep consumer insights and unless you spend a lot of time with customers, you will never understand that insight.

At CULT, we realized over a period that the 'wow moment' for our customers happens at the end of the class when they are dripping with sweat and feel the equivalent of the 'runner's high' with endorphins pumping through their system. Much later we also learnt that CULT has become a meeting place for younger people as a safe, healthy place to do activities together and start a conversation around the shared interest of staying fit. The best way to learn about customers is to put yourself in their shoes. The best consumer insights come from spending time with customers in their environment and paying attention to what they do and not what they say. The customers are the final authority on their lives, and they understand what gives them joy, what they struggle with and what their aspirations are. As a product creator, it is your job to uncover these insights and then translate them into products that consumers will love. If you manage to get 1000 true fans, you have started your journey well and you will end up building a pretty healthy business. Every single large-scale business starts by attracting a small fanatic base that not only validates the offering but also provides a lot of initial feedback to make the product dramatically better in every iteration. If you can become very good at taking care of your customers, they will take care of you by helping you build a great business.

7. Numbers always add up in the end

Business is an act of generating healthy returns on investments. Financial investors invest their capital, and you invest many precious years of your life to create something that you believe must exist in the world. But for your creation to be a successful business and last for many decades, the business model has to work, and you must generate enough return-on-capital for your investors. While every great product and business idea starts (or should start!) in the heart, where you feel this deep calling to create something new and unique, the true story of success will be written in the language of numbers, and you must start understanding these numbers deeply from an early stage. Almost every business sells something. It costs a certain amount of money to build the product or deliver the service. The customer either pays you enough to cover the cost and some premium on top which is your margin, or the customer is paying below what it costs (as in the story of e-commerce in India) and you (or your investors, to be accurate!) are eating the losses. This is your contribution margin that must turn positive at some point. It is okay to have a negative CM while you are figuring out the product–market fit but until your CM is positive, you are not a real business.

Once your CM is positive, you need to figure out how to acquire customers in such a way that you can recover the cost of acquiring them from the margin you make in the first transaction or from many transactions over the customer's lifetime. You need to invest money in capabilities such as technology, brand business, operations and so on which are your fixed costs and eventually the margins need to expand to a point where you can recover all your fixed expenses as well. But you are not done yet! If your business requires upfront capital investments, you need to eventually pay it back as well, including the interest costs for that capital and hence the surplus you generate each month needs to exceed the EMI equivalent for the capital expenditure. If all this works out, you are a company that now has a cash engine and that's a beautiful place to be in. With every crank of the wheel, you have more cash in the bank, and this is almost like the second birth of the company. Businesses like Reliance and TCS generate many billions of dollars of surplus each year and that allows the management teams to think of building newer businesses. Using their cash flows from the oil business, for example, Reliance has built India's largest telecom and retail business.

8. The art of getting investors to part with their money

Almost all entrepreneurs start with starry-eyed dreams and empty pockets! But a start-up cannot be built on a foundation of thrilling ideas, undying passion and the conviction that you're going to change the world. A start-up needs resources from day one. You need to have people on your team. You need money to host your platform on the cloud. If it is a product business, then you also need money for the initial inventory, logistics or the first store, and so on. And that's why you need to be able to pitch to and raise money from different types of investors. The good news is that there is now a whole variety of investors available to invest in a company as it goes through different stages. But raising money requires that you have a good story.

A good story is not just about how well you tell it. It is about what the story is.

If you can clearly articulate who your customer is, what your initial product will look like, what the unique value proposition is and what could be the long-term scale that you can achieve, you will certainly get the attention of the people you pitch to. Investors will also pay a lot of attention to whether you can execute well and that's where your past record, the initial traction with your new product and the calibre of your team come in. What's also equally important is the passion that you exude for what you are building. If you are genuinely excited about what you are building, investors can feel the passion and commitment. A lot of early-stage bets are made based on the founders and the market opportunity, so a big part of pitching is about how you gain the trust of investors. As the company evolves, the track record will matter more and more. If you can consistently demonstrate that you will deliver whatever you commit to, investors will believe in you. Fundraising is also contingent on market sentiments. Most markets run in cycles where the confidence keeps cycling between irrational exuberance to doom and gloom every four to six years. Good founders figure out a way to play these cycles well. The bottom line is that money will always be available for good teams and ideas and hence one should focus on the problem and how you are going to build a differentiated company.

9. Failure and success: two sides of the same coin!

The start-up world tends to celebrate outlier successes with front-page stories, while companies that don't work quietly fade away. Unfortunately, I think this is just the way it is and any talk about 'celebrating failure' is not going to change the media narrative. In fact, if a company that has raised a huge amount of money doesn't do well, the schadenfreude around the story can get nauseating as nothing sells like a fall-from-grace story. The media will gleefully tell the cautionary tale without any consideration for the deeper nuances, external factors beyond one's control, genuine mistakes that the entrepreneurs made and the excesses that investors are prone to indulge in when times are good. When you embark on a start-up journey, it is critical to embrace the fact that failure is going to be a much more likely outcome than success—and you must be okay with either outcome. Having the resolve to make the outcome successful at any cost is also important, but if you act as if success is the only outcome, you will set yourself up for a deeper failure. It is like Virat Kohli saying, 'I will not lose any matches because I am the best player in the world.' That's not going to happen. He has lost nearly as many matches as he has won despite being the best player of his generation. As an entrepreneur, you are putting yourself way outside your comfort zone. This will accelerate your growth as an individual and as a professional and nobody can take that away from you, no matter the outcome.

10. Enjoy the ride!

Start-ups look very glamorous from the outside, but the everyday reality can be very painful. When you make it big, you may feel like you're on top of the world, but that outcome has a very low probability and may take a decade or more. But your mindset and how you approach the journey on a day-to-day basis will make a huge difference to your well-being. The reality is that a lot of things will be outside your control, and you are likely to have more bad days than good ones in the early part of your journey. If you are able to still enjoy the journey every single day irrespective of the outcome, you will get a lot more out of the experience than if you focus only on the outcome. There is a lesson from the Bhagavad Gita that is very relevant to the entrepreneurial journey—if you can have laser sharp focus on what you need to do every day irrespective of the outcome, you will be growing every day and this growth will be useful over the long run. Very few people will ever get the opportunity to build a company from scratch. If you are able to get a few people to join you, get investors to back you with money, build a real product that customers use, you are already breathing very rarefied air. You should breathe this in, take a pause and reflect on how fortunate you are to be in this position, feeling gratitude for all the people and circumstances that have enabled this. If you approach this with the right attitude, you will always look back on this time with immense gratitude as this will be a period of intense growth for you and the learning will spill over into every aspect of your life. We are all very fortunate to live in a time when the entrepreneurial system has become quite democratic. If you have a dream to build something amazing, you can get a shot at it. This wasn't possible for most people even just a generation ago.

This brings us to the end of this book. We have covered a very wide spectrum of topics involved in an entrepreneurial journey. One book is perhaps not enough to do justice to everything that entrepreneurship involves, but hopefully you now have an idea about what to expect from this journey, how to prepare yourself so that you are ready when you take the plunge and are able to enjoy the process every day, irrespective of how the journey unfolds. If approached in the right manner, it is going to be an immensely fulfilling experience.

Happy Building!

Acknowledgements

This book is very close to my heart, and I have immensely enjoyed writing it. It has given me the opportunity to relive my entrepreneurial journey, with all its ups and downs. I'd like to acknowledge all the people I have had the good fortune of meeting and working with over the last two and a half decades—from VCs and mentors to co-founders, colleagues and everyone else who has been a fellow traveller on this adventure. In particular, I have learnt invaluable lessons from the colleagues and investors who I've worked with at Myntra and CureFit; these lessons have made me a better entrepreneur and a better person. In addition, I have interacted with and invested in several early-stage entrepreneurs. These enriching conversations and the relationships we've built have profoundly shaped my thinking and approach to entrepreneurship.

There are many other people who have helped make this book what it is today. Aneesha Bangera and Sakshi Batavia spent countless hours reading, watching and listening to everything they could on the subject of entrepreneurship. Their editorial and research support have made this a better book. I'm grateful to Anantika Jain for her thoughtful insights and constant motivation to ensure that I wrote every single day to finish this book! I'd also like to thank Anu Saraogi and Sunidhi Bhatnagar for their research inputs and support.

The terrific team at Penguin had faith in this book when it was just the seed of an idea and was committed to bringing it to life. A special thanks to my editor, Manasi Subramaniam, for her keen editorial eye and valuable inputs at every step of the way.

I'd also like to acknowledge and thank all the wonderful founders, investors and thought leaders who have been guests on my podcast, Sparx. I have learnt so much about the world of entrepreneurship from the stories and wisdom they have been generous enough to share with me.

A lot of the material in this book was tested in the real world through Entrepreneurship, Leadership and Design (ELD), a sixteen-week programme for aspiring and early-stage entrepreneurs. I'm grateful to Monil Singhal, Rohit Manchanda and Sriram K., who have helped iterate on and refine this content over five cohorts.

Notes

Introduction

1   Reid Hoffman, *Masters of Scale: Surprising Truths from the World's Most Successful Entrepreneurs* (New York: Penguin Random House, 2021).

2   Brad Stone, *The Upstarts: How Uber, Airbnb and the Killer Companies of the New Silicon Valley Are Changing the World* (New York: Little Brown and Company, 2017).

3   Embroker, *106 Must-Know Startup Statistics for 2024*, https://www.embroker.com/blog/startup-statistics/.

Chapter 1: Lessons from History

1   Theodore McDarrah, 'What Socrates' Prison Tells Us About Finding Your Own Meaning', *Forbes*, 26 March 2024.

2   Wilbur C. Martin et al., 'China: The Five Dynasties and the Ten Kingdoms', *Encyclopaedia Britannica*, https://www.britannica.com/place/China.

3   Mark J. Joshua, 'Johannes Gutenberg', *World History Encyclopaedia*, https://www.worldhistory.org/Johannes_Gutenberg/#citation_info.

4   Sebastian Mallaby, *The Power Law: Venture Capital and the Making of the New Future* (New York: Penguin Press, 2022).

5   Arthur Herman, *How the Scots Invented the Modern World: The True Story of How Western Europe's Poorest Nation Created Our World and Everything in It* (New York: Broadway Books, 2001).

6   'Global Startup Ecosystem Report 2019', *Startup Genome with New Life Sciences Ecosystem Ranking*, May 2019, https://url.uk.m.mimecastprotect.com/s/cmM6CL7ZzT7 BRz6SBf8FyU8p0?domain=startupgenome.com"https://startupgenome.com/reports/global-startup-ecosystem-report-2019.

7   Adrian Bridgwater, 'How Israel Became a Technology Startup Nation', *Forbes*, 21 February 2020, https://www.forbes.com/sites/adrianbridgwater/2020/02/21/how-israel-became-a-technology-startup-nation/.

8   Charles R. Morris, *The Tycoons: How Andrew Carnegie, John D. Rockefeller, Jay Gould and J.P Morgan Invented the American Supereconomy* (New York: Owl Books, 2005).

Chapter 2: Foundation Matters

1   Rashmi Menon, 'How Zepto Co-Founders are Disrupting Grocery Delivery', *Mint Lounge*, September 2022, https://lifestyle.livemint.com/news/big-story/how-zepto-co-founders-are-disrupting-grocery-delivery-111662052923972.html.

2   'Jen Hsun-Huang: Stanford Student and Entrepreneur, co-founder and CEO of NVIDIA', Stanford Online, 24 June 2011, https://www.youtube.com/watch?v=Xn1EsFe7snQ

3   Alison Beard, 'Life's Work: An Interview with Vera Wang', *Harvard Business Review* (July–August 2019), https://hbr.org/2019/07/lifes-work-an-interview-with-vera-wang.

4   Beard, 'Life's Work: An Interview with Vera Wang.'

5   Reed Hastings and Erin Meyers, *No Rules Rules: Netflix and the Culture of Reinvention* (New York: Penguin Press, 2020).

6   Emma Hinchcliffe, '35-year-old Canva founder Melanie Perkins got rejected by 100 VCs. Now her $26-billion-dollar startup is ready to take on Microsoft and Google', *Fortune*, 4 October

2022, https://fortune.com/longform/melanie-perkins-canva-founder-ceo-interview/.

Chapter 3: Start with Why

1   Viktor E. Frankl, *Man's Search for Meaning: The Classic Tribute to Hope from the Holocaust* (Boston: Beacon Press).
2   Dorothy Sayers, 'Why Work?', C.S. Lewis Institute, https://www.cslewisinstitute.org/wp-content/uploads/Why_Work_Dorothy_Sayers.pdf.
3   Lalit Keshre, 'How to Master Financial Markets? Founder of Groww Talks Investing, Finance in India, and His Journey', *Sparx by Mukesh Bansal* (March 2024).
4   Sindhu Kashyap, 'Starting out on WhatsApp, how Dunzo became India's go-to hyperlocal delivery startup', YourStory, 12 February 2020, https://yourstory.com/2020/02/product-roadmap-dunzo-whatsapp-hyperlocal-delivery-startup
5   Prerna Lidhoo, 'How Rapido has disrupted the ride-hailing business with its unique business model and offerings', *Business Today*, 21 January 2024, https://www.businesstoday.in/magazine/deep-dive/story/how-rapido-has-disrupted-the-ride-hailing-business-with-its-unique-business-model-and-offerings-412236-2024-01-08.
6   Patagonia: Company History https://www.patagonia.com/company-history/.
7   Afdhel Aziz, 'The Power of Purpose: How Salesforce and the Pledge 1% Model Is Inspiring Silicon Valley to Do Good', *Forbes*, 18 April 2019, https://www.forbes.com/sites/afdhelaziz/2019/04/18/the-power-of-purpose-how-salesforce-and-the-pledge-1-model-is-inspiring-silicon-valley-to-do-good/.

Chapter 4: Why Start-Ups Fail

1   Janet D. Stemwedel, 'The Philosophy of *Star Trek*: The Kobayashi Maru, No-Win Scenarios, And Ethical Leadership',

Forbes, 23 August 2015, https://www.forbes.com/sites/
janetstemwedel/2015/08/23/the-philosophy-of-star-trek-the-
kobayashi-maru-no-win-scenarios-and-ethical-leadership/.

2 Tom Eisenmann, *Why Start-Ups Fail: A New Roadmap for Entrepreneurial Success* (New York: Currency, 2021).

3 Noam Wasserman, *The Founder's Dilemma: Anticipating and Avoiding the Pitfalls That Can Sink a Startup* (Princeton University Press, 2013).

4 Michael Bohanes, 'Seven lessons I learnt from the failure of my first startup, Dinnr', *Medium, Thoughts and Ideas*, https://medium.com/indian-thoughts/seven-lessons-i-learned-from-the-failure-of-my-first-startup-dinnr-c166d1cfb8b8.

5 Sarah Perez, 'What happened to Artifact?', TechCrunch (18 January 2024), https://techcrunch.com/2024/01/18/why-artifact-from-instagrams-founders-failed-shut-down/.

6 Eisenmann, *Why Startups Fail*.

7 Christian Stadler, '3 Lessons Startups Can Learn from Quibi's Failure', *Forbes*, 24 November 2020, https://www.forbes.com/sites/christianstadler/2020/11/24/3-lessons-startups-can-learn-from-quibis-failure/?sh=2834526225aa.

Chapter 5: Everything Starts with Customers

1 Darshan Patel: Entrepreneur of the Year Category Award Winner: Start-Up, *EY India*, 1 March 2017, https://www.youtube.com/watch?v=vUKkY73haeY.

2 'Kudos, Leaderboards, QOMs: How Fitness App Strava Became a Religion', *Guardian*, 14 January 2020.

3 'The Mad Billionaire Behind GoPro: The World's Hottest Camera Company', *Forbes*, 4 March 2013, https://www.forbes.com/sites/ryanmac/2013/03/04/the-mad-billionaire-behind-gopro-the-worlds-hottest-camera-company/.

4 Reid Hoffman, *Masters of Scale: Surprising Truths from the World's Most Successful Entrepreneurs* (New York: Penguin Random House, 2021).

5   'How We Came Up with the Groundbreaking Soundbox: In the Words of Vijay Shekhar Sharma', Paytm Blog, 26 September 2022, https://paytm.com/blog/investor-relations/how-we-came-up-with-the-groundbreaking-soundbox/.

6   Michael I. Norton, Daniel Mochon and Dan Ariely, 'The IKEA Effect: When Labor Leads to Love', *Journal of Consumer Psychology* 22: 3 (2012).

7   Tom Kelley and David Kelley, *Creative Confidence: Unleashing the Creative Potential Within Us All* (New York: Crown Business, 2013).

Chapter 6: Product Is Marketing

1   *Jeff Bezos: A Great Product Matters More Than Marketing*, Startup Archive, https://youtu.be/5kJmgl7fXj4?feature=shared.

2   Sharan Kaur, *How Sriracha Became the World's Favourite Hot Sauce*, ReferralCandy, 2 May 2016. https://www.referralcandy.com/blog/sriracha-word-of-mouth-marketing.

3   The Two Types of Quality', Zeno Rocha, 4 August 2022, https://zenorocha.com/the-two-types-of-quality

4   Sam Altman, *Customer Love Is All You Need,* Masters of Scale, Episode 17, November 2023, https://mastersofscale.com/sam-altman-why-customer-love-is-all-you-need/.

5   Altman, *Customer Love Is All You Need.*

6   Ashee Sharma, *How Pulse Candy Captured the Market: The Full Story*, afaqs!, 27 April 2016, https://www.afaqs.com/news/marketing/47821_How-Pulse-candy-captured-the-market-The-Full-Story.

7   Kevin Kelly, *1,000 True Fans*, Kevin Kelly Blog, 4 March 2008, https://kk.org/thetechnium/1000-true-fans/.

8   Rafayel Mkrtchyan, *Using Sean Ellis Test for Finding Product/Market Fit*, Product Coalition, 15 June 2020, https://review.firstround.com/how-superhuman-built-an-engine-to-find-product-market-fit/.

9   Anonymous, *New Coke: The Most Memorable Marketing Blunder Ever*, The Coca-Cola History, https://www.coca-colacompany.

com/about-us/history/new-coke-the-most-memorable-marketing-blunder-ever.

10 Ellen Merryweather, *Understanding Product–Market Fit: A Product Manager's Guide*, Product School, 10 January 2023, https://productschool.com/blog/product-fundamentals/understanding-product-market-fit.

11 Deepsekhar Choudhury, *Decoding the Product Frameworks That helped BigBasket log $1Bn in GMV*, Inc42, 20 February 2021, https://inc42.com/infocus/indias-product-matrix/decoding-product-frameworks-that-helped-bigbasket-log-1-bn-in-gmv/.

12 Deep Nishar, 'The Art of Product Management & The Science of Building Teams', *Sparx by Mukesh Bansal* (December 2023).

13 Sean Ellis and Morgan Brown, *Hacking Growth* (New York: Crown Currency, 2017), p. 65.

14 Chip Heath and Dan Heath, *Made to Stick* (New York: Random House, 2007), p. 192.

15 Marty Cagan, *Inspired: How to Create Tech Products Customers Love* (New Jersey: Wiler, 2018).

16 Scott D. Anthony, *Kodak's Downfall Wasn't About Technology*, *Harvard Business Review*, 15 July 2016, https://hbr.org/2016/07/kodaks-downfall-wasnt-about-technology.

17 Reid Hoffman and Chris Yeh, *Blitzscaling: The Lightning–Fast Path to Building Massively Valuable Businesses* (New York: Crown Currency, 2018).

18 Walter Isaacson, *Steve Jobs: The Exclusive Biography* (London: Abacus, 2015).

19 Ashlee Vance, *Elon Musk: Tesla, SpaceX, and the Quest for a Fantastic Future*, HarperCollins Publishers, 2021.

20 Leanna Jackson, *Let's talk about Duolingo*, Better Marketing, 17 January 2022, https://bettermarketing.pub/lets-talk-about-duolingo-a-case-study-on-marketing-design-1bd24f5ec33b.

21 Sean Ellis and Morgan Brown, *Hacking Growth* (New York: Crown Currency, 2017), p. 11.

22 James Vincent, *Twitter Taught Microsoft's AI Chatbot to Be a Racist Asshole in Less Than a Day*, The Verge, 24 March 2016, https://www.theverge.com/2016/3/24/11297050/tay-microsoft-chatbot-racist.

23 Chip Heath and Dan Heath, *Made to Stick* (New York: Random House, 2007), p. 38.

24 Jim Collins, *Good to Great: Why Some Companies Make the Leap and Others Don't* (Random House Business Books, 2010).

25 *Bill Bowerman: Nike's Original Innovator*, Nike, 2 July 2024. https://about.nike.com/en-GB/stories/bill-bowerman-nike-s-original-innovator.

Chapter 7: Growth Engine

1 Ruhi Kandhari, 'Firstcry is levelling up. Will its customer acquisition do the same?' *The Ken*, 3 May 2024, https://the-ken.com/incitingincident/firstcry-is-levelling-up-will-its-customer-acquisition-game-do-the-same/.

2 'Luxury cab service Uber launched in B'lore,' *Condé Nast Traveller*, 2 September 2013, https://www.cntraveller.in/story/luxury-cab-service-uber-launches-b-lore-trident-hyderabad-opens/.

3 Aneesha S., 'Decoding Figma's Meteoric Rise Part 5: Figma's Acquisition Strategy', Product Monk, September 2022, https://dfeldman.medium.com/how-did-figma-succeed-a-brief-history-b816492da146.

4 Peter Thiel, *Zero to One: Notes on Startups or How to Build the Future* (New York: Currency, 2014), pp. 133–34.

5 Brian Balfour, 'Product Channel Fit Will Make or Break Your Growth Strategy,' *Brian Balfour*, 12 July 2017, https://brianbalfour.com/essays/product-channel-fit-for-growth.

6 Sean Ellis and Morgan Brown, *Hacking Growth: How Today's Fastest Growing Companies Drive Breakout Success* (New York: Crown Currency, 2017).

7 Reid Hoffman and Chris Yeh, *Blitzscaling: The Lightning-Fast Path to Building Massively Valuable Companies* (New York: Crown Currency, 2018).

8   'Bringing a culture back from the brink,' *Masters of Scale* (Podcast Episode 40), https://mastersofscale.com/dara-khosrowshahi-bringing-a-culture-back-from-the-brink/.

9   Dara Khosrowshahi, 'Uber's new cultural norms,' LinkedIn, 8 November 2017, https://www.linkedin.com/pulse/ubers-new-cultural-norms-dara-khosrowshahi/.

10   Zachary Crockett, 'How One of the World's Fastest Growing Startups Burned Through $300mn', *Hustle*, 17 January 2021, https://thehustle.co/how-one-of-the-worlds-fastest-growing-startups-burned-through-300m.

11   'How Notion Does Marketing: A Deep-Dive Into its Community, Influencers & Growth Playbooks', *First Round Review,* https://review.firstround.com/how-notion-does-marketing-a-deep-dive-into-its-community-influencers-growth-playbooks/.

12   Sean Ellis and Morgan Brown, *Hacking Growth: How Today's Fastest-Growing Companies Drive Breakout Success* (New York: Crown Currency, 2017).

13   Dr Ajay Sethi, 'Swiggy's Growth Formula that Drove 30X in 3 Years', *Product Growth*, 1 May 2020, https://medium.com/product-growth/swiggys-growth-story-how-to-grow-30x-in-3-years-df2b04d540b9.

Chapter 8: Organization Is Product

1   Jack Nicas, 'Apple is Worth $1,000,000,000,000. Two Decades Ago, It Was Almost Bankrupt', *New York Times*, 2 August 2018, https://www.nytimes.com/2018/08/02/technology/apple-stock-1-trillion-market-cap.html.

2   Nick Carbone, 'Girl Launches Her MIT Acceptance Letter Towards Space', *TIME*, 8 February 2012, https://newsfeed.time.com/2012/02/08/girl-launches-her-mit-acceptance-letter-into-space/.

3   C. William Thomas, 'The Rise and Fall of Enron', *Journal of Accountancy*, 1 April 2002, https://www.journalofaccountancy.com/issues/2002/apr/theriseandfallofenron.html.

4   Reed Hastings, 'Why Culture Matters', *Masters of Scale*, February 2020, https://mastersofscale.com/reed-hastings-culture-shock/.

5   Timothy Lee, 'How a Culture of Secrecy Set Theranos up for Failure', *Vox*, 23 October 2015, https://www.vox.com/2015/10/23/9603442/theranos-elizabeth-holmes-secrecy.

6   Meryl Sebastian, 'Byju's: The Unravelling of India's Most Valued Start-up', BBC, 10 July 2023, https://www.bbc.com/news/world-asia-india-66126095.

7   Howard Schultz, *Onward: How Starbucks Fought for Its Life Without Losing Its Soul* (Emmaus, Pennsylvania: Rodale Books, 2012).

8   John Lewis Gaddis, *On Grand Strategy* (Penguin Press, 2018).

9   Sawdah Bhaimiya, 'Billionaire Jeff Bezos Still Uses a Homemade Scrappy Door Desk from Early Days of Launching Amazon', *Business Insider*, 29 January 2024.

10 Laura He, 'Google's Secrets of Innovation: Empowering its Employees', *Forbes*, 1 April 2013, https://www.forbes.com/sites/laurahe/2013/03/29/googles-secrets-of-innovation-empowering-its-employees/.

11 Manav Jain, 'Implementing Amazon's Bar Raiser Process in Hiring: A Quick Guide', *BarRaiser*, 23 March 2023, https://www.barraiser.com/blogs/implementing-amazons-bar-raiser-process-in-hiring.

12 Elizabeth Stone, 'How Netflix Builds a Culture of Excellence', *Lenny's Podcast*, February 2024, https://www.lennyspodcast.com/how-netflix-builds-a-culture-of-excellence-elizabeth-stone-cto/#:~:text=The%20reason%20the%20keeper%20test,order%20to%20encourage%20the%20behavior.

13 Alex Hern, 'The Two-Pizza Rule and the Secret of Amazon's Success', *Guardian*, 24 April 2018, https://www.theguardian.com/technology/2018/apr/24/the-two-pizza-rule-and-the-secret-of-amazons-success.

14 Jesse Freeman, 'The Anatomy of an Amazon 6-Pager', *The Writing Cooperative*, 16 July 2020, https://writingcooperative.com/the-anatomy-of-an-amazon-6-pager-fc79f31a41c9.

15 Hubert Joly, 'Does Your Company's Culture Reinforce Its Strategy and Purpose', *Harvard Business Review*, 10 June 2022, https://hbr.org/2022/06/does-your-companys-culture-reinforce-its-strategy-and-purpose.

16 Masters of Scale Podcast, *How Great Cultures Are Built and Rebuilt*, https://mastersofscale.com/how-great-cultures-are-built-and-rebuilt/.

17 Aneel Bhusri, 'The Elusive Formula for Great Hiring', *Masters of Scale*, November 2018, https://mastersofscale.com/aneel-bhusri-the-elusive-formula-for-great-hiring/

18 Andreas Holmer, 'The Netflix Culture Deck: Great Talent, Minimal Process, and Maximum Freedom', *WorkMatters*, 1 August 2022, https://medium.com/workmatters/the-netflix-culture-deck-great-talent-minimal-process-and-maximum-freedom-bf548e4d505b.

19 Robert I. Sutton, *The No Asshole Rule: Building a Civilized Workplace and Surviving One that Isn't* (Business Plus, 2010).

20 Adam Grant, 'A World Without Bosses', *WorkLife with Adam Grant*, April 2018, https://open.spotify.com/episode/4Bfi6ndSIU0EAey0V5rXjE?si=sxyZ3YK3Ro6f0Wv0EIoB_A&dl_branch=1&nd=1&dlsi=fb3077a7dae946fd.

21 Theron Mohamed, 'Jeff Bezos gave a nod to Warren Buffett in his letter to Amazon employees: I still tap dance into the office', *Business Insider*, 3 February 2021, https://markets.businessinsider.com/news/stocks/amazon-ceo-jeff-bezos-letter-warren-buffett-tap-dances-work-2021-2-1030039039.

22 Judith Stein, *Using the Stages of Team Development*, MIT Edu. https://hr.mit.edu/learning-topics/teams/articles/stages-development.

23 Patrick Lencioni, *The Five Dysfunctions of a Team: A Leadership Fable* (New Delhi: Wiley India Pvt. Ltd, 2006).

24 Louis V. Gerstner Jr, *Who Says Elephants Can't Dance?: Leading a Great Enterprise through Dramatic Change* (HarperCollins, 2003).

25 Reid Hoffman and Chris Yeh, *Blitzscaling: The Lightning-Fast Path to Building Massively Valuable Companies* (New York: Crown Currency, 2018).

Chapter 9: Leaders Lead

1 Steven Bartlett, *The Diary of a CEO: The 33 Laws of Business & Life* (London: Ebury Edge, 2023).

2 Guy Kawasaki, *The Art of the Start 2.0: The Time-tested, Battle-hardened Guide for Anyone Starting Anything* (Penguin, 2015).

3 Jeff Bezos, CEO and Founder, Amazon, *The Economic Club of Washington D.C* (21 September 2018), https://www. .com/watch?v=zN1PyNwjHpc.

4 Dede Henley, 'Your Team Might Like You More After Reading This', *Forbes*, 18 April 2021, https://www.forbes.com/sites/dedehenley/2021/04/18/your-team-might-like-you-more-after-reading-this/.

5 Steven Bartlett, *Diary of a CEO: The 33 Laws of Business and Life* (London: Ebury Edge, 2023).

6 John C. Maxwell, *The 21 Irrefutable Laws of Leadership: Follow Them and People Will Follow You* (Nashville, Tennessee: Thomas Nelson, 2007).

7 Jim Collins and Bill Lazier, *Beyond Entrepreneurship 2.0: Turning Your Business into an Enduring Great Company* (Gurgaon: Penguin Random House India, 2020).

8 Gautam Mukunda, 'Churchill the Failure: The Paradoxical Truth About the Best and Worst Leaders', *Forbes*, 1 July 2020, https://www.forbes.com/sites/gautammukunda/2020/07/01/churchill-the-failure-the-paradoxical-truth-about-the-best-and-worst-leaders/?sh=19b31d85636e.

9 Graymatter Iconversations, 'Uber CEO Dara Khosrowshahi', https://greylock.com/reid-hoffman/uber-dara-khosrowshahi-navigation-systems/.

10 Steven Bartlett, *Diary of a CEO: The 33 Rules of Business and Life* (London: Ebury Edge, 2023).

11 Jim Collins, *Good to Great: Why Some Companies Make the Leap . . . And Others Don't* (Gurgaon: HarperCollins, 2011).

12 Simon Sinek, *Leaders Eat Last: Why Some Teams Pull Together and Others Don't* (New York: Portfolio/Penguin, 2014).

13 Ken Blanchard and Spencer Johnson, *The New One Minute Manager* (HarperCollins India, 2006).

14 Peeyush Ranjan, 'Google Pay VP Decodes Indian Tech Trends', *Sparx by Mukesh Bansal*, December 2023.

15 Jeremy Kourdi, *Business Strategy: A Guide to Effective Decision-Making* (London: Economist Books, 2015).

16 Adam Grant, *Give and Take: Why Helping Others Drives Our Success* (New York: Viking Press, 2013).

17 Doris Kearns Goodwin, *Team of Rivals: The Political Genius of Abraham Lincoln* (Simon & Schuster, 2006).

18 Ajeet Singh, 'Crafting Work Culture, Decoding SaaS and more', *Sparx by Mukesh Bansal* (November 2023).

Chapter 10: Strategy: Where to Play, How to Win

1   Hal Brands, *The New Makers of Modern Strategy: From the Ancient World to the Digital Age* (Princeton, New Jersey: Princeton University Press, 2023).

2   John Gaddis, *On Grand Strategy* (Penguin Random House, 2018).

3   Gaddis, *On Grand Strategy*.

4   A.G. Lafley and Roger L. Martin, *Playing to Win: How Strategy Really Works* (Brilliance Audio, 2014).

5   Richard Rumelt, *Good Strategy, Bad Strategy* (Profile Books Ltd, 2023).

6   Patrick Bet-David, *Your Next Moves: Master the Art of Business Strategy* (New York: Gallery Books, 2020).

7   Chris Miller, *Chip War: The Fight for the World's Most Critical Technology,* (New York: Scribner, 2022).

8   Achyut Mishra, 'Sam Manekshaw, the General Who Told Indira When Indian Army Wasn't Ready for a War', ThePrint, 27 June 2019, https://theprint.in/theprint-profile/sam-manekshaw-the-general-who-told-indira-when-indian-army-wasnt-ready-for-a-war/254796/.

9   Bennett Miller, *Moneyball* (Columbia Pictures, 2012).

10 Young-Mi Lim, 'Lessons Learnt from the Marketing Strategy of Swatch Watch in 1980s', *Core*, https://core.ac.uk/download/pdf/148781218.pdf.

11 Peter Cohan, '5 Ways to Get an Edge by Changing the Game', *Inc*, 14 September 2021, https://www.inc.com/peter-cohan/5-ways-to-get-an-edge-by-changing-game.html.

12 Richard Rumelt, *Good Strategy, Bad Strategy* (Profile Books Ltd, 2023).

13 Shell Scenarios (https://www.shell.com/energy-and-innovation/the-energy-future/scenarios/what-are-scenarios.html).

14 Dorie Clark, *The Long Game: How to be a Long-Term Thinker in a Short-Term World* (Brighton, Massachusetts: Harvard Business Review Press, 2021).

15 Simon Sinek, *The Infinite Game* (New York: Portfolio/ Penguin, 2019).

16 Sinek, *The Infinite Game*.

Chapter 11: Funding Games

1 Uri Levine, *Fall in Love with the Problem, Not the Solution: A Handbook for Entrepreneurs* (Dallas: Matt Holt Books, 2023).

2 Levine, *Fall in Love with the Problem, Not the Solution*.

3 Salman S.H., 'VC and PE Investors Net $5.3bn in exits from Indian start-up IPOs', *Financial Express*, 30 March 2022, https://www.financialexpress.com/market/ipo-news-vc-pe-investors-net-5-3-bn-in-exits-from-indian-start-up-ipos-2475630/.

4 Scott Kupor, *Secrets of Sand Hill Road: Venture Capital and How to Get It* (Penguin Random House, 2019).

5 Nikhil Subramaniam, 'Is PharmEasy's Debt-Laden Bubble About to Burst', Inc42, 5 July 2023.

6 Uri Levine, *Fall in Love with the Problem, Not the Solution* (Dallas: Matt Holt Books, 2023).

Chapter 12: Financials for Dummies

1 Deirdre Bosa and Ryan Browne, 'Uber CEO Tells Staff Company Will Cut Down on Costs, Treat Hiring as a Privilege', CNBC, 9 May 2022, https://www.cnbc.com/2022/05/09/uber-to-cut-down-on-costs-treat-hiring-as-a-privilege-ceo-email.html.

2   Deepsekhar Choudhury, 'Zomato Posts Positive Unit Economics as It Files for An IPO', Inc42, 28 April 2021, https://inc42.com/buzz/zomato-posts-positive-unit-economics-as-it-files-for-an-ipo/.

3   Debarghya Sil, 'Dunzo Spent INR 9 to Earn Every Single Rupee from Operations in FY23', Inc42, 7 November 2023, https://inc42.com/buzz/dunzo-spent-inr-9-to-earn-every-single-rupee-from-operations-in-fy23/#:~:text=Dunzo%20has%20raised%20around%20%24457,Alteria%20Capital%20among%20its%20investors.

4   Uri Levine, *Fall in Love with the Problem, Not the Solution* (Dallas: Matt Holt Books, 2023).

5   Levine, *Fall in Love with the Problem, Not the Solution*.

6   Paul Graham, 'The Fatal Pinch', *Paul Graham Blog*, December 2014, https://paulgraham.com/pinch.html.

7   Gavin O'Connor, *The Accountant* (Warner Bros Pictures, 2016).

8   Rajiv Singh and Nasrin Sultana, 'From alarm to alarming to panic: Byju's and its auditing lessons', *Forbes India*, 23 June 2023, https://www.forbesindia.com/article/news/from-alarm-to-alarming-to-panic-byjus-and-its-auditing-lessons/86059/1.

9   David Fincher, *The Social Network* (Columbia Pictures, 2010).

Scan QR Code to access the
Penguin Random House India website